Lecture Notes in Computer Science

Commenced Publication in 1973
Founding and Former Series Editors:
Gerhard Goos, Juris Hartmanis, and Jan van Leeuwen

Springer
Berlin
Heidelberg
New York
Hong Kong
London
Milan
Paris
Tokyo

Grigori Melnik   Harald Holz (Eds.)

Advances in Learning Software Organizations

6th International Workshop, LSO 2004
Banff, Canada, June 20-21, 2004
Proceedings

 Springer

Volume Editors

Grigori Melnik
University of Calgary, Department of Computer Science
2500 University Dr. N.W., Calgary, Alberta T2N 1N4, Canada
E-mail: melnik@cpsc.ucalgary.ca

Harald Holz
German Research Center for Artificial Intelligence (DFKI) GmbH
Knowledge Management Department
Erwin-Schroedinger-Str. 57, 67663 Kaiserslautern, Germany
E-mail: harald.holz@dfki.de

Library of Congress Control Number: 2004106916

CR Subject Classification (1998): D.2, K.6, H.5.2-3, I.2.4, K.3, K.4.3

ISSN 0302-9743
ISBN 3-540-22192-1 Springer-Verlag Berlin Heidelberg New York

Springer-Verlag is a part of Springer Science+Business Media

springeronline.com

© Springer-Verlag Berlin Heidelberg 2004
Printed in Germany

Typesetting: Camera-ready by author, data conversion by Olgun Computergrafik
Printed on acid-free paper   SPIN: 11013808   06/3142   5 4 3 2 1 0

Preface

Software-intensive organizations cannot help but learn. A software organization that does not learn will not exist for long, because the software market is continuously on the move, because of new customer demands and needs, and because of new competitor products and services. Software organizations must adapt quickly to this ever-changing environment, and the capability to adapt is one of the most important aspects of learning. Smart organizations will attempt to predict future software demands, and develop a corresponding knowledge road map that identifies the capabilities needed over time in order to meet these demands.

Organizational learning typically occurs when experienced organization members share their knowledge with colleagues, such that the organization as a whole can profit from the intellectual capital of its members. While knowledge is typically shared in an ad hoc fashion by means of direct, face-to-face communication, a learning software organization will want to ensure that this knowledge sharing occurs in a systematic way, enabling it whenever and wherever it is needed.

Since 1999, the annual International Workshop on Learning Software Organizations (LSO) has provided a communication forum that brings together academia and industry to discuss the advancements in and to address the questions of continuous learning in software-intensive organizations. Building upon existing work on knowledge management and organizational learning, the workshop series promotes interdisciplinary approaches from computer science and information systems, business, management and organization science as well as cognitive science.

The LSO workshop series differs from other conferences in that it puts a particular focus on organizational (rather than mere technological) questions such as: How to introduce knowledge management approaches in a software organization in minimally intrusive ways? What IT support is successful in fostering a culture of knowledge sharing? What roles are required to effectively disseminate available knowledge? How can information overload be avoided, while ensuring that relevant information is not overlooked? What knowledge management approaches scale up to the needs of large, multisite organizations? Approaches that address these issues often have to integrate a number of diverse techniques, methods, and tools.

This volume contains 13 full papers and 3 short papers selected by the program committee for presentation at the 6th International Workshop on Learning Software Organizations (LSO 2004). The workshop was held in conjunction with the 16th International Conference on Software Engineering and Knowledge Engineering (SEKE 2004) which allowed for further fruitful, inter-disciplinary discussions between both groups of participants. In addition to the oral presentation of the papers contained in this volume, the LSO 2004 program included a keynote talk by Philippe Kruchten.

As the workshop chairs, we would like to thank the authors and presenters for their willingness to share their expertise and report on their latest results. Moreover, our thanks go to the members of the program committee who did a great job reviewing the submitted papers. Last but not least, we would especially like to thank our keynote speaker Philippe Kruchten for sharing his insights with us.

We hope that this volume conveys to its readers at least some of the vital and interesting discussions that were stimulated by the presentation given at the LSO 2004 workshop.

June 2004   Grigori Melnik
                                                             Harald Holz

Workshop Organization

Workshop Chairs

Grigori Melnik, University of Calgary, Calgary (Canada)
Harald Holz, DFKI GmbH, Kaiserslautern (Germany)
Scott Henninger, University of Nebraska-Lincoln, Lincoln (USA)

Program Committee

Klaus-Dieter Althoff, Fraunhofer IESE (Germany)
Ralph Bergmann, University of Hildesheim (Germany)
Andreas Birk, sd&m AG (Germany)
Raimund L. Feldmann, Fraunhofer Center Maryland (USA)
Christiane Gresse von Wangenheim, Universidade do Vale do Itajaí (Brazil)
John C. Grundy, University of Auckland (New Zealand)
Frank Houdek, DaimlerChrysler AG (Germany)
Franz Lehner, University of Regensburg (Germany)
Mikael Lindvall, Fraunhofer Center Maryland (USA)
Makoto Matsushita, Osaka University (Japan)
Frank Maurer, University of Calgary (Canada)
Günther Ruhe, University of Calgary (Canada)
Ioana Rus, Fraunhofer Center Maryland (USA)
Martin Schaaf, University of Hildesheim (Germany)
Markus Strohmaier, The Know-Center, Graz (Austria)
Carsten Tautz, empolis GmbH (Germany)
Rosina Weber, Drexel University (USA)
Yunwen Ye, University of Colorado at Boulder (USA)

Additional Reviewers

Michael M. Richter, University of Kaiserslautern (Germany)
Torsten Willrich, Fraunhofer IESE (Germany)

Steering Committee

Klaus-Dieter Althoff, Fraunhofer IESE (Germany)
Raimund L. Feldmann, Fraunhofer Center Maryland (USA)
Scott Henninger, University of Nebraska-Lincoln (USA)
Frank Maurer, University of Calgary (Canada)
Wolfgang Müller, University of Applied Science, Ludwigshafen (Germany)

Sponsoring Institutions

The organizers of LSO 2004 would like to thank the following institutions for their generous support:

- informatics Circle of Research Excellence (iCORE), Canada
- University of Calgary, Canada
- German Research Center for Artificial Intelligence (DFKI) GmbH, Germany

Furthermore, the organizers thank for administrative support and logistics:

- Camille Sinanan, University of Calgary (Canada)
- The Banff Centre (Canada)

LSO Workshop Series

Materials of past and upcoming workshops in the Learning Software Organizations series are available from:

http://www.iese.fhg.de/Publications/lso

Table of Contents

Introduction

Experience-Based Information Systems

Software Maintenance

Communities of Practice

Planning LSOs

Case Studies and Experience Reports

Research on Learning Software Organizations – Past, Present, and Future

Harald Holz[1] and Grigori Melnik[2]

[1] DFKI GmbH, Knowledge Management Department,
PO Box 2080, 67608 Kaiserslautern, Germany
Harald.Holz@dfki.de
[2] Department of Computer Science, University of Calgary,
Calgary, Canada
melnik@cpsc.ucalgary.ca

> *Knowledge itself is power, not mere argument or ornament.*
> Francis Bacon (Meditations Sacrae, 1597)

1 Introduction

In order for a software organization to stay competitive, its software development needs to be part of organizational change. The organization's ability to change and to adapt quickly to environmental changes provides a foundation for growth and power [7]. For such changes to happen, the learning capabilities of the organization have to be enhanced, being an essential part of producing more effective and efficient work practices. Moreover, continuous learning is essential for surviving – let alone prospering – in dynamic and competitive environments [15]. The Learning Software Organization (LSO) workshop series has been promoting this vision since 1999, addressing the questions of organizational learning from the software development point of view.

Though the workshop series is relatively young, the ideas it is based on have been circulating for decades. As early as in 1971, Weinberg recognized software development as learning: "writing a program is a process of learning – both for the programmer and the person who commissions the program" [23]. This was superseded by the engineering approach, when software development began to be considered as "software engineering", omitting for a long period the humanistic people-centric aspect of it. The history of LSO workshops reflects this development to a certain degree. In 1999, LSO started with the premise that "with continuous technological change, globalization, business reorganizations, e-migration, etc. there is a continuous shortage of the right knowledge at the right place at the right time. To overcome this shortage is the challenge for the Learning Organization." [20]. In other words, the main challenge considered six years ago was the *availability* of knowledge. As a result, many solutions were built to address this. The proliferation of knowledge bases is a clear indication of this. The knowledge is primarily considered to be an object, and, thus, it can be codified, stored, retrieved and distributed. Unfortunately, many such solutions suffered from the "build it and they'll come" syndrome which resulted in a lack of user involvement and enthusiasm. Researchers and practitioners in LSO began to realize that knowledge externalization and storage are not automatically equal to knowledge re-use, that building an experience factory for the sake of experience fac-

G. Melnik and H. Holz (Eds.): LSO 2004, LNCS 3096, pp. 1–6, 2004.
© Springer-Verlag Berlin Heidelberg 2004

tory will not pay off the investment. Thus, new efforts to enhance the utilization of knowledge/experience bases/repositories along with improving the software development process commenced. Years 2000 and 2001 were greatly influenced by the Software Process Improvement (SPI) initiatives. The challenges addressed went beyond the availability of knowledge – but further into its *understandability*, *re-use*, *relevancy* and *applicability*. The LSO 2001 main theme was the enablement of the members of the learning software organizations "to effectively quarrel situational requirements, taking past experience into account. Besides improving internal communication (group learning), this also includes documenting relevant knowledge and storing it (for reuse) in an organizational, corporate memory" [1].

Nowadays, it is commonly recognized that promotion of a learning culture and fostering of the exchange of experiences are imperative. Increasingly, experts agree that approaches to achieve this must be based on interdisciplinary research, taking into account results from economical, organizational, cultural, psychological and technological areas.

The year 2002 was marked by the symbiosis of organizational learning and *agility*, the problems facing both the LSO community and the agile methods community seeming to be complementary [10]. Specifically, for the LSO community, the issue is how to quickly adapt to new technologies and market pressures, while for the agile community the issues are how not to lose institutional knowledge and how to enable inter-team learning. The participants commonly recognized the need for a balance between knowledge capture/dissemination and flexibility that enhances the ability of an organization to quickly adapt. In the meantime, the debate about the epistemology of knowledge – whether knowledge is an object or a relation (a context-bound one) – continues.

In 2003, the workshop progressed into the aspects of the evolution of learning organizations and the resulting evolution of repositories they use. Essentially, the workshop focused on the issues of *maintainability* and *scalability* of externalized knowledge [17].

This year (2004), we continue the advancement of the concepts, approaches and techniques to help learning software organizations succeed. The papers included in this volume clearly build upon the results of the previous five workshops. Though a good portion of research today is still dedicated to the development of knowledge management methods and tools, there is an increasing trend towards knowledge management approaches that are lightweight, i.e., do not introduce a considerable additional burden on developers and end users, while at the same time ensuring that the hoped for experience factories do not become "experience cemeteries" which no employee uses. Consequently, the focus is on practical knowledge management initiatives that:

- allow for an incremental adoption without a large up-front investment;
- are flexible enough to allow quick and easy improvements;
- encompass not only the structure, the strategies and the systems of the learning organization itself, but also of those who develop, follow and utilize these structure, strategies and systems.

The following section briefly summarizes current work reflecting the state-of-art and state-of-practice in learning software organizations as presented at the Sixth International Workshop on Learning Software Organizations (LSO 2004) in Banff, Canada.

2 Current Topics in LSO Research and Practice

The 13 full papers and 3 short papers in this volume are drawn from an international base of authors (53), including Belgium, Brazil, Canada, Germany, Mexico, New Zealand, Norway, Portugal, Spain, Switzerland, and United Arab Emirates. A consistent message across all these diverse contributions is that, in order to be effective and agile, we should consider organizational learning as a holistic process, taking into account the particularities of the organization under consideration. Most concepts, approaches and tools will be applicable only in a certain context. The contributions are organized into the following chapters:

- Experience-Based Information Systems
- Software Maintenance
- Communities of Practice
- Planning LSOs
- Case Studies and Experience Reports

Experience-Based Information Systems

Software development processes consist of various knowledge-intensive tasks during which software engineers need to make informed decisions. The contributions in this chapter describe information systems that support users in their decision-making in diverse tasks such as risk management and COTS selection.

Falbo et al. present an ontology-based to support organizational learning in risk management [5]. Their tool GeRis supports novice project managers in the identification, evaluation, ranking, and contingency planning of risks for a current project by providing the manager with corresponding experience from similar, stored projects.

Santos et al. present an enterprise ontology that provides the basis for various tools as part of an enterprise-oriented software development environment (EOSDE) [21]. They illustrate their approach by describing two tools that make use of this ontology: Sapiens, a corporate 'yellow pages' tool, and RHPlan, a resource allocation planning tool. Their EOSDE is already being used in 18 small and medium-size software companies.

In [9], Gomes et al. describe their tool REBUILDER, a CBR system that supports designers by retrieving former UML designs similar to the current design diagram, and by automatically augmenting the current diagram by missing elements from former designs. Moreover, the system provides functionality to evaluate the resulting diagrams based on various object-oriented metrics.

Mohamed et al. propose a conceptual model to support decision making during COTS selection processes [13]. They outline how this model can be implemented as an agent-based decision-support system that addresses important issues such as changing stakeholder preferences and evaluation process simulation to try out different scenarios.

Ras and Weibelzahl argue that experience packages retrieved from repositories are often inadequate for learning and competence development, e.g., because users might not have sufficient knowledge to understand the package content, or because users might be unsure of the risks involved on applying the packaged experience [16]. Their approach addresses these issues by automatically enriching experience packages with additional learning elements based on didactical considerations.

Software Maintenance

Several studies indicate that the processes needed to correct errors in a software system, or to adapt a system to the ever-changing environment incurs most of the overall expenses during the life-cycle of a software product.

In [22], de Sousa et al. propose to use postmortem analysis (PMA) to help manage the knowledge gained during maintenance projects, both knowledge on the maintenance process itself and on the system maintained. Based on a standardized maintenance process, they detail when to conduct PMA during process execution, what knowledge to look for, and how to perform PMA during maintenance.

Rodríguez et al. outline the architecture of a multi-agent system designed to manage knowledge generated during the software maintenance process [18]. Their web-based system aims at proactively providing maintenance engineers with knowledge sources that could help them in carrying out their current tasks.

In [19], Roth-Berghofer reports on experience gained from setting-up and running an internal CAD/CAM help desk support system for IT-related problems at a large company. He discusses lessons learned from this project, where a systematic maintenance process needed to be established, e.g. in order to enhance the domain model appropriately whenever necessary because of environmental changes.

Communities of Practice

Communities of Practice (CoP) are informal groups of organization members that share common interest, practices, and subjects. Approaches that integrate CoPs into daily work processes by lightweight IT support as well as the advantages of informal knowledge exchange are discussed in this chapter.

Chau and Maurer present the lightweight, Wiki-based knowledge management tools MASE and EB [2]. These tools support agile teams by providing them with a process support systems that enables users to share their experience by a collaborative creation and task-specific retrieval of WIKI pages containing information related to the task type. Moreover, first result from a study on inter-team learning using MASE and EB are reported.

In [14], Montoni et al. present a knowledge management approach for acquiring and preserving knowledge related to specific software processes. Their tool ACKNOWLEDGE supports the capture of different knowledge items such as lessons-learned or ideas, as well as their subsequent evaluation by an evaluation committee, and the packaging by knowledge managers. Knowledge items can be retrieved from a community of practice repository via a web-based system with regard to a given process type, user-specified keywords and knowledge types.

In [12], Melnik and Richter analyze the role of imprecise statements in conversations among software developers. They argue that impreciseness can be very useful in interaction, and describe how finding an optimal level of impreciseness can be interpreted as a learning problem for software organizations.

Planning LSOs

An important characteristic of learning software organizations is that learning processes are systematic – learning should not occur in an ad-hoc, chaotic fashion, but as part of the organization's overall strategy, where continuous learning is identified as an explicit goal and methods are deployed to achieve it.

In order to be agile, integrated and aligned, an organization must be architected accordingly. Therefore, Goethals et al. present their framework FADE for managing the concurrent development of the business and the ICT side of an enterprise [8]. FADE identifies several enterprise life-cycle phases as well as their links to the strategic, tactical, and operational level.

Case Studies and Experience Reports

The contributions in this chapter report on experiences and case studies conducted in an industry context. The discuss successes achieved as well as mistakes made, and outline lessons learned.

In [3], Doran reports on his experience with the implementation of knowledge management techniques in an agile software development department of a start-up company. He outlines the difficulties encountered ant approaches chosen for handling knowledge related to process, problem domain and technology, and discusses the tools introduced into the company to support these approaches.

Based on their experience with an industry partner, Draheim and Weber outline general conditions for an approach to collaborative learning of software organizations and academia [4]. They propose a co-knowledge acquisition and sharing process that is lightweight, peer-to-peer, and demand-driven.

In [6], Folkestad et al. report on a case study on the effect of introducing the Unified Process and object-oriented technologies into a company. The authors demonstrate the application of activity theory in a qualitative approach, and identify the iterative development introduced by the Unified Process to have a large effect on organizational and individual learning, flanked by new roles and more formal communication patterns.

John and Melster report on their experience from building and using a knowledge model for a knowledge network for know-how transfer in the area of software engineering, using a classical approach to model building [11]. Based on this experience, they outline a personal and peer-to-peer knowledge management approach that better takes into account the flexible and social structures of knowledge expert communities.

3 Conclusion

The diversity of topics addressed by the contributions presented at LSO 2004 clearly reflects the interdisciplinary viewpoint required for successful knowledge management approaches for software-intensive organizations. Despite the advances reported on, further effort will need to be spent on a number of outstanding issues and challenges, in particular: Techniques, methods, and tools that allow for a lightweight, incremental phase-in of knowledge management; peer-to-peer knowledge sharing; scalability of proposed knowledge management approaches; measuring the success of these approaches, to name but a few.

Notwithstanding innovations in the domain of learning software organizations, we continue to recognize that human skills, expertise, and relationships will remain the most valuable assets of a software-intensive organization.

References

1. K.D. Althoff, R.L. Feldmann, W. Müller (Eds.): Advances in Learning Software Organizations, Third International Workshop, LSO 2001, Lecture Notes in Computer Science, vol. 2176, Springer Verlag, 2001.
2. T. Chau, F. Maurer: Tool Support for Inter-Team Learning in Agile Software Organizations. LNCS 3096, Springer Verlag, 2004.
3. H.D. Doran: Agile Knowledge Management in Practice. LNCS 3096, Springer Verlag, 2004.
4. D. Draheim, G. Weber: Co-Knowledge Acquisition of Software Organizations and Academia. LNCS 3096, Springer Verlag, 2004.
5. R.A. Falbo, F.B. Ruy, G. Bertollo, D.F. Togneri: Learning How to Manage Risks Using Organizational Knowledge. LNCS 3096, Springer Verlag, 2004.
6. H. Folkestad, E. Pilskog, B. Tessem: Effects of Software Process in Organization Development - A Case Study. LNCS 3096, Springer Verlag, 2004.
7. Gartner UK Ltd.: "The Age of Agility", Report prepared by Gartner for BT, July 2002.
8. F. Goethals, J. Vandenbulcke, W. Lemahieu, M. Snoeck: A framework for managing concurrent business and ICT development. LNCS 3096, Springer Verlag, 2004.
9. P. Gomes, F.C. Pereira, P. Paiva, N. Seco, P. Carreiro, J.L. Ferreira, C. Bento: REBUILDER: A CBR Approach to Knowledge Management in Software Design. LNCS 3096, Springer Verlag, 2004.
10. S. Henninger, F. Maurer (Eds.): Advances in Learning Software Organizations, 4th International Workshop, LSO 2002, Lecture Notes in Computer Science, vol. 2640, Springer Verlag, 2002.
11. M. John, R. Melster: Knowledge networks -- managing collaborative knowledge spaces. LNCS 3096, Springer Verlag, 2004.
12. G. Melnik, M.M. Richter: Impreciseness and Its Value from the Perspective of Software Organizations and Learning. LNCS 3096, Springer Verlag, 2004.
13. A. Mohamed, T. Wanyama, G. Ruhe, A. Eberlein, B. Far: COTS Evaluation Supported By Knowledge Bases. LNCS 3096, Springer Verlag, 2004.
14. M. Montoni, R. Miranda, A.R. Rocha, G.H. Travassos: Knowledge Acquisition and Communities of Practice: an Approach to Convert Individual Knowledge into Multi-Organizational Knowledge. LNCS 3096, Springer Verlag, 2004.
15. M. Popper, R. Lipshitz: Organizational Learning: Mechanisms, Culture, and Feasibility. Management Learning, 31(2), 2000: 181-196.
16. E. Ras, S. Weibelzahl: Embedding Experiences in Micro-Didactical Arrangements. LNCS 3096, Springer Verlag, 2004.
17. U. Reimer, A. Abecker, S. Staab, G. Stumme (Eds.): Proceedings WM 2003: Professionelles Wissensmanagement - Erfahrungen und Visionen. GI-Edition - Lecture Notes in Informatics (LNI), Vol. P-28, Bonner Köllen Verlag (Germany), 2003.
18. O.M. Rodríguez, A. Vizcaíno, A.I. Martínez, M. Piattini, J. Favela: How to Manage Knowledge in the Software Maintenance Process. LNCS 3096, Springer Verlag, 2004.
19. T.R. Roth-Berghofer: Learning from HOMER, a Case-Based Help Desk Support System. LNCS 3096, Springer Verlag, 2004.
20. G. Ruhe, F. Bomarius (Eds.): Learning Software Organizations. Methodology and Applications, Lecture Notes in Computer Science, vol. 1756, Springer Verlag, 1999: 4.
21. G. Santos, K. Villela, L. Schnaider, A.R. Rocha, G.H. Travassos: Building ontology based tools for a software development environment. LNCS 3096, Springer Verlag, 2004.
22. K.D. de Sousa, N. Anquetil, K.M. de Oliveira: Learning Software Maintenance Organizations. LNCS 3096, Springer Verlag, 2004.
23. G.M. Weinberg: The Psychology of Computer Programming, Dorset House Publishing, 1998: 12.

Learning How to Manage Risks
Using Organizational Knowledge

Ricardo A. Falbo, Fabiano B. Ruy, Gleidson Bertollo, and Denise F. Togneri

Computer Science Department, Federal University of Espírito Santo, Vitória - ES - Brazil
{falbo,fruy,gbertollo}@inf.ufes.br, togneri@terra.com.br

Abstract. In spite of being an important software activity, many software organizations present difficulties in managing risks. This happens mainly due to their low maturity level, and because Risk Management is a complex and knowledge intensive task that requires experienced project managers, which many times are not available. In order to overcome this barrier, novice software engineers must learn how to perform this task, and organizational knowledge concerning it can be very useful. In this paper, we present a knowledge management approach to support organizational learning in Risk Management.

1 Introduction

In order to survive, an organization must be committed with learning. Its success depends heavily on its tailoring and flexibility capabilities, and it can only be achieved through learning. But we shall not think learning as an individual process only. Organizations should learn with their own experiences, lessons learned must be registered and shared, and relevant knowledge must be institutionalized and reused, preventing repeating mistakes [1].

This holds for software development, i.e. software organizations must conduct themselves as learning organizations. Software development is a collective, complex, and creative effort, and in order to produce quality software products, software organizations should use their organizational software engineering knowledge. Several software process activities can be improved by offering knowledge management facilities to support their accomplishment, such as resource allocation, quality planning and requirement specification, among others. Risk Management is one of them. Risk Management is a complex and knowledge intensive task that requires experienced project managers, which many times are not available.

In this paper, we present an ontology-based knowledge management approach to support organizational learning in Risk Management. There are some related works (presented in section 5) that aim to offer knowledge management (KM) support for risk management, but none of them is centered on ontologies. For us, as pointed by Steffen Staab and his colleagues [2], ontologies are the glue that binds knowledge subprocesses together, and they open the way to a content-oriented view of KM, where knowledge items are interlinked, combined, and used. Thus, we first developed a risk ontology (presented in section 4). Based on this ontology and on a Risk Management general process (discussed in section 2), we built GeRis, a KM-based tool for supporting Risk Management (presented in section 4). Since GeRis is built based on an ontology, the knowledge items handled by it are annotated with ontological tags

G. Melnik and H. Holz (Eds.): LSO 2004, LNCS 3096, pp. 7–18, 2004.

that guide knowledge retrieve and dissemination. In fact, GeRis was developed in the context of an ontology-based Software Engineering Environment, called ODE [3], and it uses ODE's KM infrastructure (presented in section 3).

2   Risk Management and Knowledge Management

Several issues contribute to increase the complexity in software development. Technological innovations, delivery periods more and more tight, and high demand for quality products are examples of factors that become software development an uncertain task. In this context, risk analysis is an essential activity in software project management. Its main goal is to identify potentials problems before they happen, taking actions to reduce the probability and impact of them.

The need for risk management in software projects is unquestionable. Almost all norms, quality models and standards of project management claim that risk management is essential. As an example, we can mention CMMI [4], which treats risks analysis in the maturity levels 2 (Project Planning, and Project Monitoring and Control Process Areas) and 3 (Risk Management Process Area).

Generally, risk management includes the following activities:

- Risk Identification: attempts to establish threats (risks) to the project. Its goal is to anticipate what can go wrong in the project. The identified risks in previous similar projects can help the software engineer in that task;
- Risk Analysis: concerns analyzing the identified risks, estimating its probability and occurrence impact (exposure degree);
- Risk Assessment: aims to rank the identified risks and to establish priorities. The goal is to allocate resources only for the most important risks, without managing risks with low probability and low impact;
- Action Planning: concerns planning mitigation and contingency actions for the managed risks (those of higher priority). Mitigation actions aim to reduce probability or impact of a risk before it occurs. Contingency actions assume that mitigation efforts have failed, and are to be executed when a risk occurs;
- Risk Monitoring: as the project initiates and proceeds, managed risks should be monitored. Risks' exposure degrees could change, new risks could appear, or anticipated risks could be no more relevant. It is necessary to control managed risks, to identify new risks, and to accomplish the necessary actions and evaluate the effectiveness of them.

Managing software project risks allows avoiding problems. Disregarding risks is dangerous. It can bring several negative consequences, such as delaying the schedule, increasing costs, or even causing the project cancellation. But, in spite of being an important activity, many software organizations present difficulties in managing risks. This happens mainly because Risk Management is a complex and knowledge intensive task. In this context, managing organizational knowledge about risks is important to improve the accomplishment of this activity, and to allow organizational learning about risk management. In this way, inexperienced project managers can learn while they work. Learning can be viewed as an evolutionary process that starts when workers execute a task. Supported by KM, project managers can use the organizational knowledge about risk management together with their own previous knowledge to perform the task. During the job, learning can take place in many ways: through the assimilation of the organizational knowledge by the project managers; by the growth of the organizational memory, when project managers relate their experiences; and by the arising of new knowledge, or improvement of existing knowledge, originated from the practice of the task execution. Thus, there is an integration of the project managers' knowledge with the organization's knowledge, in which both learn.

In sum, project managers and organization learn while the firsts work. Thus, to be effective, a knowledge management system should be integrated to the software process. Since Software Engineering Environments (SEEs) integrate collections of tools supporting software engineering activities across the software lifecycle [5], it is natural to integrate KM facilities into a SEE [6]. In this way, to actually offer KM-based support to risk management, we need to integrate the KM system into a SEE. This is what we did: we built GeRis, a KM-based tool supporting risk management that is integrated into ODE, a SEE that is presented following.

3 ODE: An Ontology-Based Software Development Environment

ODE (Ontology-based software Development Environment) [3] is a Software Engineering Environment (SEE) developed based on some software engineering ontologies. Since the tools in the SEE are built based on ontologies, tool integration is improved, because the tools share a common conceptualization. ODE's architectural style reflects its basis on ontologies. It has two levels, as shown in Figure 1.

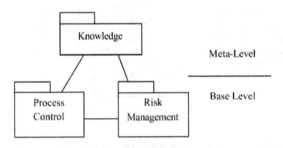

Fig. 1. ODE's Architectural Style.

The base or application level concerns classes that address some software engineering activity. The meta-level (or knowledge level) defines classes that describe knowledge about objects in the base level. The classes in the meta-level are derived directly from the ontologies, using the systematic approach to derive Java object frameworks from ontologies described in [7]. All classes derived directly from the ontology are prefixed by the character "K", indicating that they constitute knowledge in ODE. Meta-level objects can be viewed as instances of ontologies.

The classes in the base level are also built based on ontologies, but since an ontology does not intend to describe all the knowledge involved in a domain, new classes, associations, attributes and operations are defined to deal with specific design decisions made in the application level. Moreover, several classes in the base level have a corresponding Knowledge class in the Knowledge package. In this way, the meta-level can be used to describe base-level objects' characteristics.

Ontologies are also used to deal with knowledge management (KM) in ODE. In ODE's KM approach, ontologies are used to structure the organizational memory (OM), as well as to support the main knowledge services. Figure 2 shows ODE's KM infrastructure [6]. The *organizational memory* (OM) is at the core of the infrastructure, supporting knowledge sharing and reuse. Arranged around it, KM services are available, supporting activities of a general KM process, including knowledge capturing, retrieve, dissemination, use, and maintenance.

It is worthwhile to point that knowledge dissemination is a tool specific service. Knowledge dissemination is proactive in the sense that it is initiated by the system, without requiring the user to explicitly formulate a query. But it is not possible to provide proactive knowledge dissemination without knowing details about the task being done. Thus, knowledge dissemination is not provided by the environment. It is a service that must be implemented in each tool with KM support. In ODE, this service is developed using agents. Each tool with KM support must implement an agent (or a community of agents) that monitors developers using it. When the agent perceives that there are knowledge items that can help the user, it acts showing them. Both ODE's classes and agents are implemented in Java.

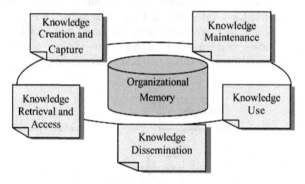

Fig. 2. ODE's KM Infrastructure.

ODE's OM contains four types of knowledge items: artifacts, instances of ontologies, lessons learned and discussion packages. Artifacts created during the software process are submitted to configuration management and become available in ODE's central repository, which is also accessible from the KM infrastructure. Instances of ontologies are used to index other knowledge items. They are also used as suggestions given to developers performing tasks related to the corresponding ontology. Discussion packages are created by packing messages exchanged in ODE's groupware applications. Finally, lessons learned register important findings made during software development.

4   A Knowledge Management Approach for Learning about Risk Management

Managing software project risks is a complex task that requires practitioners with high level of knowledge and experience. Ideally, an experienced project manager should be allocated to this task. But unfortunately, many times organizations do not have practitioners with this profile available for all projects. Attempting to attenuate this problem, we proposed a KM approach to support organizational learning about risk management that consists in providing a risk management tool, called GeRis, integrated to ODE. GeRis uses ODE's KM infrastructure to promote organizational learning for the accomplishment of this task. Using GeRis, inexperienced project managers could accomplish risk management using organizational knowledge and experience about risks accumulated in the software engineering environment.

GeRis was developed grounded on a risk management ontology. Thus, the concepts related to risks are consistently defined and, together to the knowledge items derived from the ontology, they can be used to support learning while the tool is used.

Using the ontology as basis, and capturing experts' knowledge about risk management, an initial knowledge repository (GeRis' meta-level) is built. This repository contains potential software project risks, their categories, and actions that can be taken.

As project managers use GeRis to manage risks, learning occurs, and knowledge share and reuse proceeds by two flows: initially GeRis provides knowledge-based suggestions to the project managers, who uses it to perform the desired task; after that, project managers supply knowledge to GeRis, as lessons learned gather when accomplishing the task, and the generated risk plans. Thus, project managers learn with the tool and with the practice, the organizational knowledge increases, and GeRis could offer a better support next time.

4.1 An Ontology of Software Risks

Before we can devise a strategy for supporting organization learning about Risk Management, we must understand what software risk means. There are several information sources (books, standards, papers, experts, and so on) talking about this subject matter, many times using different terms with no clear semantics established. In order to establish a shared conceptualization about software risks, we developed an ontology of software risks. Several books, standards, and experts were consulted during the ontology development process and a consensus process was conducted.

The method for building ontologies described in [7] was applied. This approach consists of: (i) defining the ontology competence, using competency questions (ontology requirement specification); (ii) capturing concepts, relations, properties and constraints expressed as axioms, using a graphical representation (ontology capture); (iii) formalizing the ontology using a formal language, such as predicate logics (ontology formalization); (iv) evaluating and (v) documenting the ontology.

Following, we present the software risk ontology, using UML as modeling language. It is worthwhile to enhance that we are using the enough subset of UML adequate to represent ontologies, as discussed in [8]. Due to limitations of space, we present only part of this ontology, concerning the following competency questions:

1. What is the nature of a risk?
2. What are the identified risks in a project?
3. What are the manageable risks in a project in a given moment?
4. What is the probability of occurrence of a risk in a project in a given moment?
5. What is the impact of occurrence of a risk in a project in a given moment?
6. How will a given risk in a project be managed?

7. What actions can be taken to try to avoid the occurrence of a risk or to minimize the consequences of its impact?
8. What actions can be taken in the case of a risk occurs?
9. What were the actions effectively taken to manage a risk in a project?

To address these competency questions, the concepts and relations shown in Figure 3 were considered.

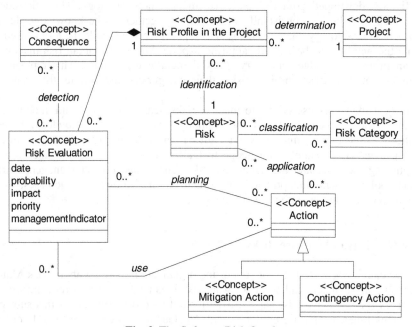

Fig. 3. The Software Risk Ontology.

A *risk* is any condition, event or problem whose occurrence is not certain, but that can affect the *project* negatively if it occurs. A risk can be classified into several *risk categories*, such as risks associated with product size, risks associated with the technology to be used to build the product, risks associated with the people that will do the work, and so on. During the software project planning, risks that can affect the project should be identified and evaluated with the objective of prioritizing and defining what risks will be treated and how they will be treated. Each risk associated to the project defines a *risk profile in the project*. Each project-risk profile is composed of several *risk evaluations*. The first risk evaluation is done during the project planning. Others are done in each one of the project milestones, when the risks of the project should be reevaluated. A risk evaluation determines the state of the risk in a given instant of the project, i.e. it registers when the evaluation was done (*date*), the *probability* of risk occurrence and its *impact* in case the risk occurs in the course of the project, its *priority*, and if the risk is to be managed (*management indicator*).

Several *actions* can be applied for controlling a risk. These actions can be classified into: *mitigation actions*, which are accomplished proactively with the purpose of reducing the probability of a risk, its associated impact or both, and *contingency ac-*

tions, which are planned to be accomplished when an event or condition effectively occurs in the project, making the risk be a reality. During risk evaluation, mitigation and contingency actions can be planned or used. The last refers to actions effectively taken to control a risk.

Finally, if a risk occurs in a project, it has a *consequence* for the project. Therefore, the detection of the occurrence of a risk in a project leads to an analysis of its consequence.

Beyond the model presented in Figure 3, several axioms were defined in the software risk ontology. Those axioms are classified according to [9] as epistemological, consolidation and ontological axioms. The first class of axioms concerns the way concepts and relations are structured. Those axioms are captured by the lightweight extension of UML used to model ontologies [8]. For instance, the following axiom regards the multiplicity of the whole-part relation:

$$\forall (e, p1, p2)\ (compositionProfile(e, p1) \land compositionProfile(e, p2)) \rightarrow (p1 = p2)$$

In this epistemological axiom, the predicate compositionProfile formalizes the whole-part relation between Risk Profiles in Projects (*p1, p2*) and Risk Evaluations (*e*). According to this axiom, a risk evaluation (*e*) is part of only one Risk Profile in the Project (*p*), since it is a composition.

Consolidation axioms define constraints for establishing a relation or for defining an object as an instance of a concept, such as:

$$\forall (a,e,p,r)\ ((planning(a,e) \lor use(a,e)) \land compositionProfile\ (e,p) \land identifica\text{-} \\ tion(p,r) \rightarrow application(a,r)$$

This consolidation axiom states that if an action (*a*) is planned or used in an risk evaluation (*e*) of a risk profile in a project (*p*), then that action (*a*) should be applied to the risk (*r*) identified in that profile (*p*).

Ontological axioms, in turn, concern the meaning of concepts and relations and allow new information to be derived from the previously existing knowledge. For instance, if an evaluation (*e*) has planned or used some action (*a*), then that evaluation (*e*) is considered controlled.

$$\forall (e)\ controlled(e) \leftrightarrow \exists (a)\ planned(a,e) \lor use(a,e)$$

4.2 Managing Software Risk Knowledge

Applying the concepts of Risk Management, KM and Organizational Learning, we built GeRis, a risk management tool. GeRis offers KM-based support to the main activities of the risk management process, using ODE's KM infrastructure.

Like any ODE's integrated tool, GeRis architecture follows the two-layer architecture style of the environment, as discussed in section 3. The classes regarding software risks of *Knowledge Package* were derived from the software risk ontology, and their instances represent part of ODE's knowledge repository about software risk. Figure 4 presents the part of *Knowledge Package* model that addresses software risks. According to this model, GeRis allows registering risks that generally occur in projects, classifying them according to risk categories, and defining actions that can be used to mitigate or to threat a risk. This knowledge is entered in ODE's knowledge repository through a tool for instantiating ODE's software engineering ontologies.

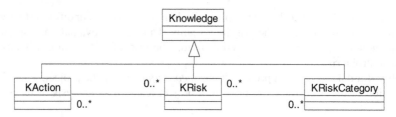

Fig. 4. Knowledge Package's classes regarding software risks.

Figure 5 presents GeRis' class diagram of the Base Level. Those classes are used to support the risk management process described in section 2.

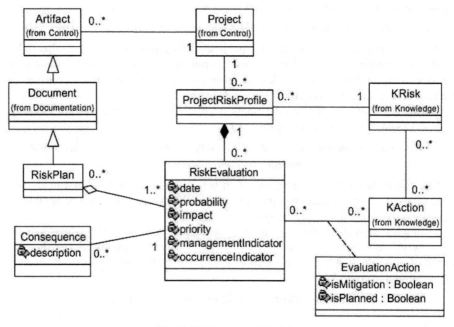

Fig. 5. GeRis Internal Model.

Each project's identified risk holds a risk profile, composed by evaluations. Each risk evaluation determines the probability and impact of the risk, its priority, mitigation and contingency actions planned and used, an indicator pointing if the risk is being managed or not, and an indicator pointing if the risk occurred, or not, in the evaluation date. If the risk occurred, consequences must be indicated. Finally, risk plans can be generated by GeRis, assembling several risk evaluations.

As discussed in section 3, ODE's KM infrastructure provides KM services. Except knowledge dissemination, those services are provided for the environment. Collect and approval of lessons learned, retrieval and maintenance of knowledge items are examples of general services available in ODE that can be used at any time. The dissemination service, however, should be implemented in each tool that uses the infrastructure, through software agents.

Risk planning in GeRis involves the following steps:

1. The project manager has to identify potential risks for the project. In this step, as shown in Figure 6, ontology instances are presented as suggestions, i.e. the risks stored in ODE's knowledge repository (instances of *KRisk*) are presented, so that the project manager does not need to start risk planning from scratch. Also the GeRis' software agent acts in this moment, making risk plans, lessons learned and package discussions available for the project manager (see the icon in right of Geris' menu in Figure 6). This is done based on similarity between projects, using ODE's project characterization that includes: staff features, such as team experience; problem features, such as problem complexity and application domain; and development features, such as development paradigm and software type (Real Time Systems, Information Systems, Web Systems, and so on).

2. Once the risks are identified, they should be evaluated, defining their probability and impact of occurrence. In this step, the project manager can look for similar projects to see what has gone right and wrong in past projects. Also, GeRis' software agent shows relevant knowledge items, such as risk plans for similar projects, and lessons learned.

3. The identified risks should be ranked and prioritized. Again, past experience can be used to support this step.

4. Finally, mitigation and contingency actions for the managed risks (those of higher priority) should be defined. An analogous support to that offered in step 1 is used, that is, ontologies instances are presented as suggestions (instances of *KAction*), and other knowledge items can be retrieved or disseminated by the agent.

In sum, during risk planning, GeRis uses ontology instances as initial suggestions for risk identification and action planning. Also, as a way for favoring learning, a software agent promotes knowledge dissemination. Basically, this service concerns making available other knowledge items from ODE's knowledge repository, including risk plans, lessons learned and discussion packages. From similar projects that had already their risks managed, and from lessons learned in performing risk management, GeRis gives other guidelines for risk planning, presenting identified risks and planned actions defined in previous projects, and reporting risk probabilities, impacts and priorities previously defined in those projects. In this way, project managers are guided by knowledge items of ODE.

We should reinforce that project managers can also use, at any moment, the general KM services, writing his/hers owns learned lessons or searching for knowledge items. These services are available from the *Knowledge Management* menu shown in Figure 6.

Finally, during risk evaluation, the agent acts in a similar way as described early, making available information on: (i) how this risk was evaluated previously, (ii) which were the defined probabilities and impacts for it, (iii) an indication if the risk occurred, and (iv) its consequences. Besides, the learned lessons about evaluations of this risk can be readily made available.

As GeRis is used more and more, the organizational knowledge on risks evolves, being reused and enriched through the experience acquired by the project managers. Thus, along the time and with the amount of managed projects, the organization accumulates its own risk knowledge, generated from the collective learning of its members.

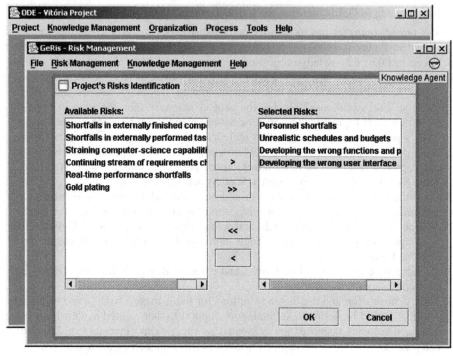

Fig. 6. Identifying Risks in GeRis.

5   Related Works

There are several works in the literature that describe different approaches for supporting risk management, some of them integrated to software engineering environments. Barros et al. [10] presented a software risk management approach for the Odyssey environment. The risk management process is divided into two risk subprocesses: one for domain risk management, other for application risk management. The main goal of the risk management process for domain models is to identify the most common risks that occur in projects developed within a specific application domain, organizing this information and allowing its reuse in risk management processes for specific software projects. Within this process, risks are identified and documented by risk patterns, a standard information structure that describes a potential recurring problem to the software development process or product. A risk pattern includes contextual information upon the forces that enable or inhibit the problem in a software project, presenting standard solutions to solve the problem or to minimize the effects of its occurrence. During the risk management process for application development, risks of a project developed within a specific domain are identified reusing the domain risks.

Comparing the Odyssey's approach with ours, we should observe two main aspects. First, they share some ideas. In both cases, the most common risks that occur in software development projects can be registered, shared and reused. Second, while Odyssey's approach uses risk patterns, ODE uses a KM approach, which allows handling several types of knowledge items, such as lessons learned, ontologies instances, discussion packages, and risk plans. The Odyssey's risk patterns are related to ODE's lessons learned, but none of the others ODE's knowledge items have corresponding ones in Odyssey.

Kontio & Basili [11] proposed a risk knowledge capture framework that was built upon the Riskit Method and the Experience Factory. The Riskit's framework enables the knowledge captured to be stored into an Experience Base. The knowledge in the Experience Base can be in various forms, such as raw and summarized data, experiment reports, and lessons learned. In those aspects, ODE's KM infrastructure is very similar to the Riskit framework approach. In fact, ODE's KM infrastructure is also based on the concept of Experience Factory that underlies the Riskit framework. But ODE's KM infrastructure uses other important technologies for KM, such as ontologies and software agents.

Farias et al. [12] presented a software risk management approach based on KM and developed RiscPlan, a tool to support this approach, which is integrated to TABA Workstation, a SEE. Comparing RiscPlan's approach with ours, we should observe that in both cases, the risk management process is supported by KM. But RiscPlan does not use ontologies to establish a common vocabulary, does not have offer proactive knowledge dissemination, as GeRis does through software agents, and does not support several knowledge item types.

6 Conclusions

KM facilitates access and reuse of knowledge, and consequently organizational learning, typically by using several emerging technologies, such as ontologies and software agents. In this paper we presented an approach for managing risk knowledge. In this approach, knowledge workers constantly create new knowledge as they work. Some benefits of this approach can be pointed out: (i) With KM integrated to the environment, it is easier for developers to create new knowledge. In this way, the organizational memory is always evolving. A major concern for KM in ODE is to capture knowledge during the software process without developers' extra effort. Thus, KM is actively integrated into the work process. (ii) In the case of GeRis, project managers are not passive receivers of knowledge, but are active researchers, constructors, and communicators of knowledge. So that, learning can be improved. (iii) A KM system must provide the information workers need, when they need it. GeRis' agent monitors the project manager actions as he/she works, and inform him/her about potentially relevant knowledge for the task at hand. In this way, GeRis plays an active role in knowledge dissemination.

We are now working to put ODE and its tools, including GeRis, in practice in a software house. Especially concerning GeRis, this effort is being very important, since this software organization does not have a solid culture of accomplishing risk management. But they are looking for an ISO 9000 certification, and then they need to learn more about how to perform this task.

Acknowledgments

The authors acknowledge CAPES and CNPq for the financial support to this work.

References

1. D. A. Garvin, Learning in action: a guide to putting the learning organization to work, USA: Harvard Business School Press, 2000.
2. S. Staab, R. Studer, H.P. Schnurr, Y.Sure, "Knowledge Processes and Ontologies", IEEE Intelligent Systems, vol. 16, No. 1, January/February, 2001.
3. R.A. Falbo, A.C.C. Natali, P.G. Mian, G. Bertollo, F.B. Ruy. "ODE: Ontology-based software Development Environment", Proceedings of the IX Argentine Congress on Computer Science (CACIC'2003), La Plata, Argentina, 2003, pp 1124-1135.
4. *Capability Maturity Model Integration*, Version 1.1, Pittsburgh, PA: Software Engineering Institute, December 2001.
5. W. Harrison, H. Ossher, P. Tarr, "Software Engineering Tools and Environments: A Roadmap", in Proc. of the Future of Software Engineering, ICSE'2000, Ireland, 2000.
6. A.C.C. Natali, R.A. Falbo, "Knowledge Management in Software Engineering Environments", Proc. of the 16th Brazilian Symposium on Software Engineering, Gramado, Brazil, 2002.
7. R.A. Falbo, G. Guizzardi, K.C. Duarte. "An Ontological Approach to Domain Engineering". Proceedings of the 14th International Conference on Software Engineering and Knowledge Engineering, SEKE'2002, pp. 351- 358, Ischia, Italy, 2002.
8. P.G. Mian, R.A.Falbo, "Supporting Ontology Development with ODEd", Proc. of the 2nd JIISIC, Salvador, Brazil, 2002.
9. R.A. Falbo, C.S. Menezes, A.R.C. Rocha. "A Systematic Approach for Building Ontologies". Proceedings of the 6th Ibero-American Conference on Artificial Intelligence, Lisbon, Portugal, Lecture Notes in Computer Science, vol. 1484, 1998.
10. M.O. Barros, C.M.L. Werner, G.H. Travassos. "Risk Analysis: a key success factor for complex system development". Proceedings of the 12th International Conference Software & Systems Engineering and their Applications, Paris, France, 1999.
11. J. Kontio, V.R. Basili, "Risk Knowledge Capture in the Riskit Method", SEW Proceedings, SEL-96-002, University of Maryland, 1996.
12. L.L. Farias, G.H. Travassos, A.R.C. da Rocha, "Managing Organizational Risk Knowledge", Journal of Universal Computer Science, vol. 9, no. 7, 2003.

Building Ontology Based Tools
for a Software Development Environment

Gleison Santos, Karina Villela, Lílian Schnaider,
Ana Regina Rocha, and Guilherme Horta Travassos

COPPE/Federal University of Rio de Janeiro
Caixa Postal 68511 CEP 21945 – 970 Rio de Janeiro – RJ, Brasil
{gleison,darocha,ght}@cos.ufrj.br

Abstract. Knowledge has been thought to be the most important asset in an Organization, having a significant impact on its competitiveness. Software development is knowledge-intensive but software development environments lack from specific support of knowledge management. In this paper, we present an enterprise ontology that supports the development of two case tools: an 'yellow pages' tool that aims to represent the distribution of knowledge, skills and experiences trough the organizational structure and a tool to support human resource allocation planning in software projects based on the reuse of organizational knowledge about human resource skills and allocation. The work is concerned with Knowledge Management and Enterprise-Oriented Software Development Environments concepts.

1 Introduction

Software development is knowledge-intensive. Knowledge has been thought to be the most important asset in an Organization, having a significant impact on its competitiveness. Several knowledge representations and transformations are required throughout the software development process. Different kinds of knowledge are important to software developers into this context, such as: domain knowledge, organizational guidelines, best practices and previous experiences with techniques, methods and the software process. Enterprise-Oriented Software Development Environment (EOSDE) [1] supports the activity of Software Engineering, making possible to manage knowledge that can be useful to software engineers when accomplishing Organization's software projects. The EOSDEs have the following goals: (a) to provide software developers with all relevant knowledge for software development held by the company, and (b) to support organizational learning about software development. EOSDEs are strongly based on ontologies.

This paper describes an enterprise ontology that has been used for the construction of two EOSDE case tools. Section 2 presents brief comments on knowledge management and ontologies use. Section 3 presents the structure of the enterprise ontology and the description of its main concepts. In section 4 Sapiens and RHPlan tools, and their use of the enterprise ontology, are described. Section 5 presents future perspectives and the conclusions of this work.

G. Melnik and H. Holz (Eds.): LSO 2004, LNCS 3096, pp. 19–30, 2004.

2 Knowledge Management and Ontologies

Knowledge management can be defined as an approach that promotes an integrated view, trying to identify, capture, recover, share and evaluate knowledge assets of a company [2]. One of the great restrictions for knowledge sharing is the use of different words and concepts to describe a domain for different systems. The development of ontologies that can be used by multiple systems can facilitate the sharing of a common terminology. The term ontology, sometimes, is used to refer to a knowledge body, typically a common sense on one specific domain, using a vocabulary as representation [3]. In knowledge management systems, ontologies can be used to [4]:

1. provide an appropriate precision level in search mechanisms, making systems based on knowledge able to determine, in a non-ambiguous way, which topic can be found in each knowledge base;
2. supply keywords or concepts that capture the nature of the desired knowledge for information filtering systems, and;
3. establish a common language and, thus, to prevent misconceptions in systems that provide means of contribution and use of knowledge withheld by experts.

The use of ontologies in the EOSDE knowledge infrastructure is critical to make easier the communication between multiple users and the retrieval of knowledge stored in the environment. Considering communication, the defined ontologies have the purpose of reducing terminological and conceptual mismatch in a company. When retrieving knowledge items, the ontologies' purpose is to supply vocabularies whose terms are used as links among multiple knowledge/data bases contents. Besides, when defining synonyms and acronyms for the concepts, ontologies provide linguistic equivalents which may occur in text documents and can be used to classify and access non formal knowledge.

The Software Engineering Ontology defines a common vocabulary to guide the registration/distribution of a company's knowledge map and software engineering knowledge in an EOSDE. A company's knowledge map defines for each employee its level of skills, knowledge and experiences. The Enterprise Ontology provides concepts and attributes related to the structure, behavior and knowledge owned by companies, defining a common vocabulary to guide the description of any company. This ontology is better explained in the following section.

3 Enterprise Ontology

The enterprise ontology aims to supply a common vocabulary that can be used to represent useful knowledge for the software developers on the involved organizations in a software project. Among other factors, it can be useful for:

- supplying a structure that assists knowledge organization and guides knowledge acquisition on one or more organizations;
- easing the development of generic tools based on the ontology structure, reducing the effort in the construction of software development environments for different organizations;

- facilitating the tools integration that manipulate knowledge related to the ontology, allowing the creation and sharing of databases generated based on the common structure defined;
- facilitating the development of systems that manipulate knowledge on the organization (for example, systems that support processes or management information of the company), for example, facilitating requirements elicitation by providing a common vocabulary to be used by developers;
- allowing the reuse of organization's available knowledge to compose a first version of the requirements;
- allowing the identification of whom can give information about the system, and;
- providing knowledge on the Organization that can assist the identification of the professionals with the abilities adjusted for composing a team in accordance with the project characteristics or to argue or guide the execution of a task.

Due the ontology capture, terms and phrases potentially useful had been identified, had had its semantics defined and had originated sub-ontologies (as shown in Figure 1) describing concepts that allow understanding, for example:

- how the organization is perceived in its environment;
- how the organization is structured, which are their objectives and how it behaves;
- how Organization's projects have been lead and how the desired and possessed abilities have been distributed into the organization;
- who are the available resources on the organization and how the distribution of authority and responsibility in the organization are accomplished.

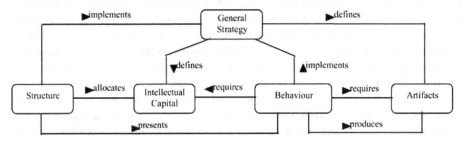

Fig. 1. Sub-ontologies of enterprise ontology

This paper aims to discuss just the ontology usage not its structure, thus only the most important concepts used by the tools that will be presented in section 4 will be defined as following. The EOSDE Enterprise Ontology was developed combining new concepts with others defined by Fox et al. [5] and TOVE's (TOronto Virtual Enterprise) ontology [6].

The **sub-ontology of Intellectual Capital** establishes the vocabulary to describe the intellectual capital of an Organization. It deals with aspects as: taxonomy of competence, interaction between experience and knowledge, availability of competences and decomposition of knowledge domain. **People** are the basic components of an Organization's workflow, acting in the execution of necessary activities to the organization mission fulfillment. The competences owned by a professional have great importance to others organization's professionals, because these competences are used to establish his/her role and value inside the Organization. These competences are also part of the organization value, representing its intellectual capital. **Competences** are characteristics that turn people capable to execute activities that involve some degree of difficulty. They can be classified according to its nature in *knowledge, skill and experience*. **Knowledge** are the information, understanding and skills that are gained through education or experience, for example: knowledge on object-oriented analysis, knowledge on air traffic policies etc. **Skills** are personal characteristics or acquired abilities non-associated to an activity or specific knowledge domain, for example: leadership, negotiation ability etc. **Experiences** are acquired through practice or through the execution of activities, for example, experience defining client-server architectures, experience in airports administration etc.

The **sub-ontology of Structure** establishes the vocabulary needed to describe how the Organization is structured. It deals with the decomposition of organization, distribution of authority and responsibility between Organizational Units, decomposition of Organizational Units, distribution of authority and responsibilities among positions, specification of jobs and positions, vacant fulfilling, staff allocation and definition of objectives. An **Organization** can be defined as being an organized group of people working together for the fulfillment of a mission. People are distributed in several Organizational Units that compose the structure of the Organization. An **Organizational Unit** is a grouping of Organization's components (activities, people etc.) so that the Organization can be economic and efficient. Each Organizational Unit has some positions and becomes related through cooperation or subordination relations. **Agent** represents a profile that allows the Organization to accomplish its mission throughout the execution of activities and it could represent a job or a position. Fulfilling a vacancy in an Organization is represented by allocating available resources to existing positions. The consequent occupation of these positions, takes into consideration the competences of the available resources and the competences required by the jobs and positions. A **Job** specifies the set of activities to be executed by the person who occupies a certain position, its responsibilities, and desired abilities beyond the offered conditions of work. A **Position** defines a structure, necessary to allow the Organizational Unit to be efficient and economic, specifying activities, responsibilities and competences in compliance with the purpose of the specific Organizational Unit. A position also determines the location of a person in the organizational structure, establishing whom s/he must report and command, taking in consideration the occupied position. Each position relates itself with other positions through subordination relationships.

The **sub-ontology of Artifacts** groups the concepts and relationships that define the devices in terms of its nature and composition. Artifact is anything produced by the man and not by natural causes, being able to exert different roles in an Organization, such as the product of an activity.

The aspects mentioned on the **sub-ontology of Behavior** are: activity as action of transformation, taxonomy of activity, decomposition of process and activity, adoption of procedures, taxonomy of procedures, method as systematic procedure, automation of procedures, processes defined in the Organization and related rules beyond organizational projects.

The **sub-ontology of General Strategy** establishes the vocabulary to describe the general aspects that define how the Organization interacts with the environment. It deals with aspects like general characteristics, domain performance, available artifacts/services and relationship with the customers.

4 Building Enterprise Ontology Based Tools

Skill Management (or Capability Management) is a sub-area of knowledge management whose goal is to understand the abilities that an organization needs to accomplish its business objectives. It consists in identifying which individual abilities exist in an Organization and comparing the required knowledge with the available knowledge to allow filling gaps in accordance with the strategic goals of the organization [7]. With the identification of "who" is making "what", it is possible, in the long term, to identify the basic or really important values of software development for the Organization as well as a correct identification of people involved in the quality management of products, software processes and the Organization itself [8].

The management of human resources allocation can be enriched through the use of the concept of "corporative yellow pages", in which is kept information about the competence profile for each professional of the Organization [9]. Due to it, each professional profile should be captured, mapped in accordance with some previous established criteria, stored and continuously brought up to date. It is also necessary to perform searches over these databases because, without an infrastructure capable to deploy these "corporative yellow pages", to manage this knowledge distribution may become very difficult.

In the following subsections we describe the two tools and their use of the Enterprise Ontology.

4.1 Sapiens

The analysis of corporative yellow pages has a great importance to human resources selection. Because usually most of time the desired competence exists somewhere inside the Organization, being, however, necessary to expend much time to identify, find and have access to who possess it [10]. The yellow pages support and optimize these tasks, stating a way not to only organize and keep control of the competences, but also to search for the human resources that possess them [11]. The corporative yellow pages are also important for stating a set of competences previously mapped, supplying a guide to the project manager, and sets the terms to be used [12].

Sapiens is a software tool for the representation of the organizational structure with the competences required along it. Besides supporting staff allocation, including the competences of each professional, it also contains search and navigation mechanisms. This way, it is possible the creation of a culture of identification, acquisition and dissemination of the existing knowledge that can be used by the organization to know itself better and take off greater advantage of its potential. Sapiens has the intention of being generic, it means, independent of a specific organization or domain. It is based on the infrastructure defined for EOSDE, making usage of the enterprise ontology to describe the organizations that develop and maintain software for other companies or for its own use. Software developers can use it to find the most appropriate person to help in the solution of a problem inside the organization. The tool promotes the sharing of the organizational knowledge and also promotes the communication among the employees in a way to speed problems solution during the initial staff allocation phase of a software project. Moreover, it can be useful to support the activities of the Human Resources Department.

For each position in the organizational structure it is possible to indicate which competences are necessary or relevant for its performance, and it is also possible to indicate which of these competences are obligatory or not. In a similar way it is possible to indicate which competences are owned by a person. The association between people and competence, as well as between position and competence, is not always equal and must take in consideration a certain level of variation. This leveling of the competences allows the standardization of the different degrees of "expertise" existing for a specific ability [9]. For each competence it is associated a specific scale of values. For example, a scale for a specific skill could be constituted of the following items:

1. "Do not possess the skill nor took part at training";
2. "Took part at training";
3. "Capable with ability";
4. "Capable with great ability".

The organizational structure can be viewed through an organizational chart that shows the subordination relationships between Organizational Units and allows the visualization of each item details. A hyperbolic tree structure [13] (as shown in Figure 2), which is indicated to the visualization of great amounts of organized data in a hierarchic form, is used to browse through the contents of the organizational database by exploring the relations between the items that compose this database.

The initial root node is the Organization itself. From this point of view the user can browse on its relations with the others items of the database. When the user clicks on some item its data are shown and the focused item and its relationships with the others items become more evident. For example, when the user clicks on an Organizational Unit, the existing positions inside of this unit appear in the center and, then, the user can see who are allocated to the positions and which competences are related to each one of the items.

It is possible to make searches on the organization's database. There are some searches previously registered and the user can create a totally new one if desired. Examples of available registered searches are:

− Who has a specific competence?
− Who occupies a specific position?
− Which are the competences for a person?
− In which positions a certain competence is required?

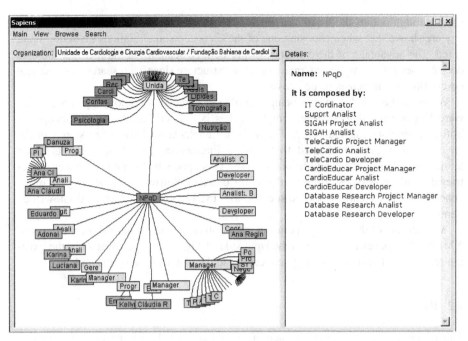

Fig. 2. Visualization of the organizational structure through the hyperbolic tree

The enterprise ontology described in section 2 provides the knowledge on the structure of a generic organization. The concepts and relations described by the ontology have been used during the construction of the class model used by all tool modules. Each class of this class model keeps a reference to the ontological concepts that originated it. This fact is extremely explored in the search module, considering that ontologies are particularly useful for recovery and access knowledge [4]. The ontology defines relationships between the concepts, however, sometimes due to some implementation reasons, not all the relationships are mapped into the class model. When doing searches the original relations described in the ontology become important to allow the identification of the related concepts to the class of the class model. Thus, the ontology becomes helpful, showing the relationships between the concepts and, also, showing each concept structure.

The use of ontology allows the derivation of relations between items of the organizational memory and allows the derivation of additional descriptions. By doing that, the search for information becomes independent of the physical model, meaning that, even if two classes do not have direct references one for the other, the relationships can be inferred if they exist, directly or not, between the concepts of the ontology.

The search form shows some previously defined consults created on the basis of the existing relations between the concepts that compose the enterprise ontology, thus the user is capable to carry through searches even without knowing the ontology structure or making a very specific question. Each pre-defined search contains a description, an item to be looked (generally an ontology concept) and a related item to this (possibly another ontology concept related with the first one). In case the user does not desire to carry through one of the listed searches, the existing concepts in the enterprise ontology are shown. So, when choosing one of these concepts, the relations involving it are listed. The advantage of the existence of pre-defined searches is the fact that the user does not need to know the enterprise ontology structure since each search has a textual description that indicates its objective.

When the knowledge map is being recorded or updated, the knowledge about Software Engineering that a certain employee has is defined based on the concepts of Software Engineering Ontology. The software engineering knowledge stored in the environment is also associated to Software Engineering Ontology concepts. Each knowledge item is associated to one or more concepts, which enables subsequent retrieval of different types of knowledge items based on Software Engineering Ontology concepts, independently from the specific tool used to obtain or to record knowledge items.

Another use of the ontology is in reports exhibition. The data are shown in form of XML/HTML pages (as shown in the right side of Fig. 2) created using only the existing relations between the ontology concepts and the classes used by the tool.

4.2 RHPlan

The resource allocation planning activity is carried out during the project planning, when the adequate skills to perform the project activities need to be identified so the human resources can be allocated. The knowledge used by the project manager to execute these activities must be shared all over the Organization, so the Organization can learn from its success and failure actions. This knowledge, however, should be properly managed, in ways to support its identification, organization, storage, usage and diffusion. This section describes a software tool to human resource allocation planning in software projects based on organizational knowledge reuse about human resource competences and allocation.

RHPlan goal is to help the human resources allocation in a software development project. It also has mechanisms to help the contract order or qualification of professionals order when the necessary human resources cannot be found inside the Organization. It is based on the definition of the necessary competence profiles to the accomplishment of project activities, and posterior search for organization's professionals who possess similar profiles to the desired one. The project manager can search the knowledge on the existing competence inside the organization and find who possesses them, beyond being able to use lessons learned. The database of professional's capabilities is provided by the Sapiens tool, as described in the previous subsection.

Fig. 3 presents a screenshot of RHPlan tool, showing an example of human resources allocation in project activities. In the right side is possible to see all activities for the staff allocation plan creation: definition of profiles needed in the execution of each process activity, selection of professionals, request of hiring or training for professionals when the available professionals in the organization do not fit the desired profile, and visualization of the human resources allocation plan.

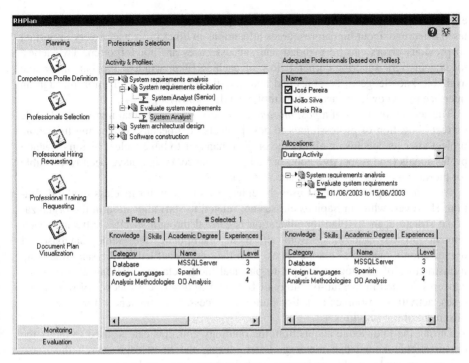

Fig. 3. Professionals Selection in RHPlan tool

The first step while planning the human resources allocation is the identification of the necessary competences to perform each of the activities of the project's development process. During this phase, after comparing the necessities of each activity and the competences of each professional in the Organization, it is necessary to allocate the adequate professionals to all the project's activities. At this phase the professionals whose competences are compatible to the profiles defined for each project activity are shown. It is assumed that a professional have a compatible profile when each competence owned by the professional has a level equal or higher than the desired level for the activity. Thus, after analyzing the competence profiles of the professionals presented by the tool, the project manager should select the most adequate to participate the project.

During the project its manager can monitor the human resources allocation by checking the development of activities and doing the allocation or reallocation of each selected professional who participates in the project. Periodically throughout the software project life cycle and after its conclusion, an evaluation of the human resources can be carried out. This evaluation allows bad performances to be identified and corrective actions adopted, assigning a new resource to the activity or providing training to the currently allocated professional.

Beyond the knowledge on the available competences inside the Organization, the analysis of past experiences has also great importance helping project managers in planning and controlling the human resources allocation. Project experiences are an important source of knowledge in Software Engineering and, therefore, the acquired experiences must be identified and shared [16]. Moreover, the (successful or not) lessons learned about human resources allocations in other projects are very important so previous errors can be avoided and success cases are not forgotten. Two icons, located in right superior corner below of each RHPlan window top bar, allow the available knowledge to be consulted and also the knowledge acquisition through an interface to a knowledge acquisition tool named Acknowledge [14].

The accomplishment of a *post mortem* evaluation is also of great importance for the correct allocation of professionals to new projects [15] because evaluating the whole project after its conclusion allows the project manager to have a clear vision of which professionals (and respective good or bad performances) might have been responsible for the success or failure of some specific task.

As well as Sapiens, RHPlan uses the enterprise ontology for its class model definition. However, while in Sapiens classes are related to staff allocation in the organizational structure, in RHPlan the allocation is carried through specific software development process activities. Both of them manipulate the same database of organization's members' competences; then they are benefited by the same mapping infrastructure of ontology concepts to physical model classes. RHPlan also uses the concepts defined in the sub-ontology of Behavior to describe projects, software processes, activities, resources and distribution of necessary competences for the accomplishment of the activities.

During the knowledge acquisition, the ontology concepts can be used to index the organizational knowledge memory. Later, during the knowledge search this same information can be used to assist the search for a specific knowledge.

4.3 Tools Usage

Since the end of 2003, EOSDE and its case tools have started to be used as support tools to the definition and introduction of software process based development approach in 18 small and medium-size Brazilian software companies. For each software company, a standard software development process is defined and an initial project is chosen. The available case tools in the EOSDE, including Sapiens and RHPlan, are used to support specific activities such as processes' definition, quality evaluation, process planning, and so on. After the software processes are defined, organization employees are trained in software engineering and in the tools that will be used during the project. We have observed that at the end of training session, when Sapiens and RHPlan are presented to the organization's employees, the interest about both tools is proportional to the size of the organization and its projects: the bigger the organization the greater the interest. A possible explanation for this is about cost-benefits: abilities formalization is very laborious for small companies in relation to the possible benefit they can acquire from this. In small companies, the available resources to be allocated to software projects are restricted and, probably, the manager in charge to make this allocation already possesses tacit knowledge about the employees. On the other hand, in bigger companies these information are harder to manage and a competence database about the staff and support services to deal with it becomes clearly necessary.

5 Conclusions

In this paper we presented an enterprise ontology used to assist the construction of an enterprise-oriented software development environment and examples of software tools supported by this ontology. Beyond the tools Sapiens and RHPlan presented here, several case tools in EOSDE are also benefited from its infrastructure and make use of the enterprise ontology. Among these tools there are some for processes' definition, quality evaluation, process planning (involving time, costs, resources, documentation, risks [17], configuration management etc), requirements elicitation, and metrics collecting and planning. Most of these tools are also benefited of the integration with the Acknowledge tool for knowledge acquisition [14].

Since the end of 2003, EOSDE have started to be used in Brazilian software companies. Two big Brazilian public companies of national performance will be initiating its use in 2004. The initial results regarding the use of these tools are promising; however we do not accomplish a complete evaluation yet. The current set of users already makes possible an evaluation of the tools through an experimental study that is being planned and will be executed during this year.

Further information about Enterprise-Oriented Software Development Environment and its case tools can be found at http://www.cos.ufrj.br/~taba.

Acknowledgement

The authors wish to thank CNPq and CAPES for the financial support granted to the project Enterprise Oriented Software Development Environments. We also acknowledge K. Oliveira, R. Falbo, M. Montoni, S. Mafra and S. Figueiredo for their contributions to this project.

References

1. VILLELA, K., OLIVEIRA, K. M., SANTOS, G., ROCHA, A. R. C., TRAVASSOS, G. H. Cordis-FBC: an Enterprise Oriented Software Development Environment In: Workshop Learning Software Organization, Luzern, Switzerland, 2003.
2. MARKKULA, M. The Impact of Intranet-based Knowledge Management on Software Development, Federation of European Software Measurement Associations – FESMA99, Amsterdam, The Netherlands, pp. 151-160, 1999.
3. CHANDRASEKARAN, B., JOSEPHSON, J. R., BENJAMINS, V. R., What Are Ontologies, and Why Do We Need Them?, IEEE Intelligent Systems & their applications, v. 14, n. 1 (Jan/Feb), pp. 20-26, 1999.
4. O'LEARY, D. E., Using AI in Knowledge Management: Knowledge Bases and Ontologies, IEEE Intelligent Systems, v. 13, n. 3 (May/Jun), pp. 34-39, 1998.
5. FOX, M., BARBUCEANU, M., GRUNINGER, M.: An Organization Ontology for Enterprise Modeling: Preliminary Concepts for Linking Structure and Behaviour", Computers in Industry, v. 29, pp. 123-134, 1996.
6. USCHOLD, M. et al.: The Enterprise Ontology, The Knowledge Engineering Review, v.13, 1998; In: www.aiai.ed.ac.uk/project/enterprise/ enterprise/ontology.html.

7. STADER, J. E MACINTOSH, A., Capability modelling and knowledge Management. In: Applications and Innovations in Intelligent Systems VII, Springer-Verlag, pp 33-50, 1999.
8. ACUÑA, S. T., et. al, Software Engineering and Knowledge Engineering Software Process: Formalizing the Who's Who, In: The 12th International Conference on Software Engineering & Knowledge Engineering, Chicago, USA, pp. 221-230, June 2000.
9. DINGSOYR and ROYRVIK Skills Management as Knowledge Technology in a Software Consultancy. Company, K. – D. Althoff, R.L. Feldmann, and W. Müller (Eds): LSO 2001, LNCS 2176, 96-103.
10. BASILI, V., LINDVALL, M., COSTA, P., Implementing the Experience Factory concepts as a set of Experience Bases, SEKE'2001, pp. 102-109, Buenos Aires, Argentina, Jun, 2001.
11. ALAVI, M. and LEIDNER, D., Knowledge Management Systems: Emerging Views and Practices from the field in Proceedings of the 32nd Hawaii International Conference on System Sciences, Maui, Hawaii, 1999.
12. STAAB, S. Human Language Technologies for Knowledge Management. IEEE Intelligent Systems, vol. 16, n. 6 (November/December 2001), 84-88, 2001.
13. PIROLLI, P., CARD, S.K. E WEGE, M.M.V.D, The effect of information scent on searching information visualizations of large tree structures, in: Advanced Visual Interfaces, AVI 2000, Palermo, Italy, 2000.
14. MONTONI, M., MIRANDA, R., ROCHA, A. R.. TRAVASSOS, G. H., Knowledge Acquisition and Communities of Practice: an Approach to Convert Individual Knowledge into Multi-Organizational Knowledge, In: Workshop Learning Software Organization, Banff, Canada, 2004.
15. BIRK, A., DINGSOYR, T. and STALHANE, T. Postmorten: Never Leave a Project Without It. IEEE Software vol. 19 n. 3 (May/June 1998), 43-45, 1998.
16. MARKKULA, M. Knowledge Management in Software Engineering Projects, Software Engineering and Knowledge Engineering – SEKE, Kaiserlautern, Germany, June 1999.
17. FARIAS, L., TRAVASSOS, G. H., ROCHA, A. R. C., Knowledge Management of Software Risks In: Workshop Learning Software Organization, Luzern, Switzerland, 2003.

REBUILDER: A CBR Approach
to Knowledge Management in Software Design

Paulo Gomes, Francisco C. Pereira, Paulo Paiva, Nuno Seco,
Paulo Carreiro, José L. Ferreira, and Carlos Bento

CISUC - Centro de Informática e Sistemas da Universidade de Coimbra,
Departamento de Engenharia Informática, Universidade de Coimbra,
3030 Coimbra, Portugal
pgomes@dei.uc.pt

Abstract. Knowledge generated during the software development process can
be a valuable asset for a software company. But in order to take advantage of
this knowledge, the company must be able to store this knowledge for later use,
which can be achieved through the use of knowledge management tools. This paper provides an overview of a computational system for management and reuse of
software design knowledge. We present a Case-Based Reasoning approach combined with a lexical resource: WordNet. We explain how knowledge management
is performed and how is the stored knowledge reused.

1 Introduction

In general, knowledge generated in the software development process is not stored, and
consequently can not be reused later in other projects. The reuse of software development knowledge can improve productivity and the quality of software systems. Another
advantage of storing and reusing this kind of knowledge, is that it minimizes the loss
of know-how when a member of the development team leaves the company. Storage,
management and reuse of software development knowledge enables also the sharing of
know-how among development teams and across different projects.

Software development has several phases [1]: analysis, design, implementation,
testing and integration. From these phases, we focus in the design phase, during which
the structure and behavior of the system is specified. Design is a complex an ill-defined
task [2], making it hard to model and automate the process. Most of the times, software
engineers reuse knowledge generated during the design phase in other projects that they
are working on. We are interested in studying the management of design knowledge in
a software development company, involving several software designers.

Most of the decisions concerning software design are made using the designers'
experience. The more experience a designer has, the better s/he can perform its job.
Reasoning based on experience is a basic mechanism for designers, enabling them
to reuse previous design solutions in well known problems or even in new projects,
sometimes generating innovative or creative solutions. In artificial intelligence there is
a sub area called Case-Based Reasoning (CBR, see [3, 4]) that uses experiences, in the
form of cases, to perform reasoning. Case-Based Reasoning (CBR) can be viewed as

G. Melnik and H. Holz (Eds.): LSO 2004, LNCS 3096, pp. 31–42, 2004.

a methodology for developing knowledge-based systems that uses experience for reasoning about problems [5]. We think that CBR is a suited methodology for building a design system that can act like an intelligent design assistant.

We developed a computational system that can perform three tasks: store, management and reuse of software design knowledge. To achieve these goals, we propose a system based on CBR. This reasoning framework is flexible enough to comply with different knowledge types and reasoning mechanisms, enabling the software designer to use whatever design assistant s/he wants to use. We also integrated a lexical resource - WordNet [6] - which enables several semantic operations like indexing software objects and computing semantic distances between concepts.

The next section describes the architecture of our system - REBUILDER. We then detail some key issues of REBUILDER: knowledge base (section 3), design knowledge management (section 4) and design knowledge reuse (section 5). Section 6 describes and example of REBUILDER's use, providing more information about the system. Finally section 7 discusses several important issues concerning design knowledge management in REBUILDER.

2   REBUILDER

REBUILDER comprises four main modules: the UML (Unified Modelling Language [7]) editor, the knowledge base manager, the knowledge base (KB), and the CBR engine. It also shows the two different user types: software designers and KB administrators. Software designers use REBUILDER as a CASE (Computer Aided Software Engineering) tool, and the reuse capabilities of the system. A KB administrator as the function of keeping the KB updated and consistent. The UML editor is the interface between REBUILDER and the software designer, while the KB manager is the interface between the KB administrator and the system.

The UML editor is the front-end of REBUILDER and the environment where the software designer develops designs. Apart from the usual editor commands to manipulate UML objects, the editor integrates new commands capable of reusing design knowledge. These commands are directly related with the CBR engine functionalities and are divided into two main categories: KB actions, such as connect to KB and disconnect from KB; and cognitive actions, such as retrieve design, adapt design using analogy or design composition, verify design, evaluate design, and actions related with object classification.

The KB Manager module is used by the administrator to manage the KB, keeping it consistent and updated. This module comprises all the functionalities of the UML editor, and adds case base management functions. These are used by the KB administrator to update and modify the KB. The available actions are: create KB, open KB, close KB, case library manager (which comprises actions to manipulate the cases in the case library, like adding new cases, removing cases, or changing the status of a case), activate learning (gives the KB administrator an analysis about the contents of the case library), and system settings.

The KB comprises four different parts: the case library, which stores the cases of previous software designs; an index memory used for efficient case retrieval; a data type taxonomy, which is a taxonomy of the data types used by the system; and WordNet [6], which is a general purpose ontology. This module is described in more detail in the next section.

The CBR Engine is the reasoning module of REBUILDER. As the name indicates, it uses the CBR paradigm to establish a reasoning framework. This module comprises five different parts: Retrieval, Analogy, Design Composition, Verification, and Learning. These modules are detailed in section 5.

3 Knowledge Base

The KB comprises WordNet, a case library, the case indexes and the data type taxonomy. In REBUILDER, a case describes a software design, which is represented in UML through the use of class diagrams. Figure 1 shows an example of a class diagram representing part of an educational system. Nodes are classes, with name, attributes and methods. Links represent relations between classes. Conceptually a case in RE-BUILDER comprises: a name used to identify the case within the case library; the main package, which is an object that comprises all the objects that describe the class diagram; and the file name where the case is stored. Cases are stored using XML/XMI (eXtended Mark-up Language), since it is a widely used format for data exchange. UML class diagram objects considered in REBUILDER are: packages, classes, interfaces and relations. A package is an UML object used for grouping other UML objects. A class describes an entity in UML and it corresponds to a concept described by attributes at a structural level, and by methods at a behavioral level. Interfaces have only methods, since they describe a protocol of communication for a specific class. A relation describes a relationship between two UML objects.

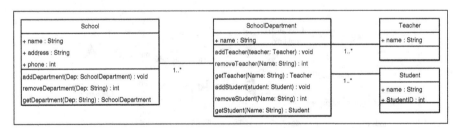

Fig. 1. An example of an UML Class diagram (*Case1*), the package classification is *School*.

WordNet is used in REBUILDER as a common sense ontology. It uses a differential theory where concept meanings are represented by symbols that enable a theorist to distinguish among them. Symbols are words, and concept meanings are called synsets. A synset is a concept represented by one or more words. If more than one word can be used to represent a synset, then they are called synonyms. The same word can have more than one different meaning (polysemy). WordNet is built around the concept of synset. Basically it comprises a list of word synsets, and different semantic relations between synsets. The first part is a list of words, each one with a list of synsets that the word represents. The second part, is a set of semantic relations between synsets, like *is-a* relations, *part-of* relations, and other relations. REBUILDER uses the word synset list and four semantic relations: *is-a*, *part-of*, *substance-of*, and *member-of*. Synsets are classified in four different types: nouns, verbs, adjectives, and adverbs. REBUILDER uses synsets for categorization of software objects. Each object has an associated synset, named context synset, which represents the object meaning. The object's context synset can be used for computing object similarity (using the WordNet semantic relations), or it can be used as a case index, allowing the rapid access to objects with the same classification. The synset associated with the object is determined automatically by the system using word sense disambiguation methods (see [8]).

As cases can be large, they are stored in files, which makes case access slower then if they were in memory. To solve this problem we use case indexes. These provide a way to access the relevant case parts for retrieval without having to read all the case files from disk. Each object in a case is used as an index. REBUILDER uses the context synset of each object to index the case in WordNet. This way REBUILDER can retrieve a complete case, using the case root package, or it can retrieve only a subset of case objects, using the objects' indexes. This allows REBUILDER to provide the user the possibility to retrieve not only packages, but also classes and interfaces. To illustrate this approach, suppose that the class diagram of Figure 1 represents *Case1*. Figure 2 presents part of the WordNet structure and some of the case indexes associated with *Case1*. As can be seen, WordNet relations are of the types *is-a*, *part-of* and *member-of*, while the index relation relates a case object (squared boxes) with a WordNet synset (rounded boxes). For instance *Case1* has one package called *School* (the one presented in Figure 1), which is indexed by synset *School*. It has also a class with the same name and categorization, indexed by the same synset, making this class available for retrieval.

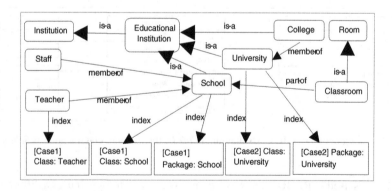

Fig. 2. A small example of the WordNet structure and case indexes.

The data type taxonomy is a hierarchy of data types used in REBUILDER. Data types are used in the definition of attributes and parameters. The data taxonomy is used to compute the conceptual distance between two data types.

4   Knowledge Management

REBUILDER stores and manages design knowledge gathered from the software designers activity. This knowledge is stored in a central repository, which is managed by the KB administrator.

The KB manager module is used by the administrator to manage the design cases. The basic responsibilities of the administrator are to setup the system and to decide which cases should be in the case library. Another task that s/he has to perform is to revise new diagrams submitted by the software designers.

Deciding the contents of the case library is not an easy task, especially if the case base has a large number of cases. In this situation the KB manager provides a set of case base maintenance policies that s/he can use to determine which are the cases that should be deleted or added to the case library (for details see [9]).

When a diagram is submitted by a software designer as a candidate to a new case to be added to the case library, the administrator has to check some items in the diagram. First the diagram must have synsets associated to the classes, interfaces and packages. This is essential for the diagram to be transformed into a case, and to be indexed and reused by the system. Diagram consistency and coherence must also be checked. REBUILDER provides a verification and evaluation mechanism that can help the administrator in two different ways: verification can identify certain syntax and semantic errors, or it can point out unusual items in the diagram and draw the administrator's attention to them; evaluation assesses the design properties and characteristics, presenting them as guidelines for the diagram's evaluation. This is performed using several object-oriented metrics [10]. Finally the administrator can use the case base maintenance policies described before to help him to decide if the submitted diagram should be added to the case library or not.

The KB Manager module is used by the administrator to manage the KB, keeping it consistent and updated. This module comprises all the functionalities of the UML editor, and it adds case base management functions to REBUILDER. These are used by the KB administrator to update and modify the KB. The list of available functions are:

KB Operations: create, open or close a KB.

Case Library Manager: Opens the Case Library Manager, which comprises functions to manipulate the cases in the case library, like adding new cases, removing cases, or changing the status of a case.

Activate Learning: gives the KB administrator an analysis about the contents of the case library. REBUILDER uses several case base maintenance policies to determine which cases should be added or removed from the case library.

Settings: adds extra configuration settings which are not present in the normal UML Editor version used by the software designers. It also enables the KB administrator to configure the reasoning mechanisms.

5   Knowledge Reuse

Reuse of UML class diagrams can be done in REBUILDER in three different ways: using retrieval, using analogy or using design composition. The retrieval mechanisms searches the WordNet structure looking for similar cases and then ranks and presents them to the designer. Analogy takes as input an UML class diagram and tries to complete it using analogical mapping and knowledge transference. Design composition generates a new class diagram through the integration of different pieces of cases, using the target diagram for guidance in this process. The next sub sections describe each one of these reuse mechanisms.

5.1   Retrieval

Retrieval in REBUILDER comprises two phases: retrieval of a set of relevant cases from the case library, and assessment of the similarity between the target problem and the retrieved cases.

The retrieval phase is based on the WordNet structure, which is used as an indexing structure. The retrieval algorithm uses the classifications of the target problem object as the initial search probe in WordNet. This algorithm is flexible enough to retrieve three different types of UML objects: packages, classes and interfaces, depending on the type of object selected as target problem. For example, if the designer selects a package as the target problem, the retrieval algorithm uses the package's synset as the initial search probe. Then the algorithm checks if there are any packages indexes associated with the WordNet node of that synset. If there are enough indexes, the algorithm stops and returns them. Otherwise, it explores the synset nodes adjacent to the initial one, searching for package indexes until the number of found indexes reaches the number of objects that the user wants to be retrieved. Suppose that the N best objects are to be retrieved, $QObj$ is the query object, and $ObjectList$ is the universe of objects that can be retrieved (usually $ObjectList$ comprises all the library cases), then the algorithm is described in figure 3.

The second step of retrieval is ranking the retrieved objects by similarity with the target object. Since there are three types of target objects (packages, classes and interfaces) we have developed a specific similarity metric for each type of objects (for more details on these metrics see [11]). These metrics allow the system to distinguish objects with the same synsets but presenting different views about the same concept.

Package Similarity Metric: this metric is based on four different aspects: the similarity between packages' synsets, similarity between packages' dependencies[1], similarity between packages' class diagrams, and similarity between the sub-packages (a recursive call to this metric). Basically this metric assesses structure similarity and semantic similarity of packages and it's objects.

Class Similarity Metric: the class similarity metric is based on three items: synset similarity of classes being compared, inter-class similarity comprising the assessment of relation similarity between classes, and intra-class similarity which evaluates the similarity between classes' attributes and methods.

Interface Similarity Metric: the interface similarity metric is the same as the class similarity, except in the intra-class similarity, which is based only in method similarity, since interfaces do not have attributes.

---

[1] Dependencies are a type of UML relations that can exist between packages, expressing a package's dependency on another package.

$ObjsFound \leftarrow \varnothing$
$PSynset \leftarrow$ Get context synset of $QObj$
$PSynsets \leftarrow \{PSynset\}$
$ObjsExplored \leftarrow \varnothing$
WHILE($\#ObsFound < N$)AND($PSynsets \neq \varnothing$)DO
    $Synset \leftarrow$ Remove first element of $PSynsets$
    $ObjsExplored \leftarrow ObjsExplored + Synset$
    $SubSynsets \leftarrow$ Get $Synset$ hyponyms
    $SuperSynsets \leftarrow$ Get $Synset$ hypernyms
    $SubSynsets \leftarrow SubSynsets - ObjsExplored - PSynsets$
    $SuperSynsets \leftarrow SuperSynsets - ObjsExplored - PSynsets$
    $PSynsets \leftarrow$ Add $SubSynsets$ to the end of $PSynsets$
    $PSynsets \leftarrow$ Add $SuperSynsets$ to the end of $PSynsets$
    $Objects \leftarrow$ Get all objects indexed by $Synset$
    $Objects \leftarrow Objects \cap ObjectList$
    $ObjsFound \leftarrow ObjsFound \cup Objects$
ENDWHILE
$ObjsFound \leftarrow$ Rank $ObjsFound$ by similarity
RETURN the first N elements from $ObjsFound$

Fig. 3. The case retrieval algorithm used in REBUILDER.

5.2 Analogy

The analogy mechanism relies in a set of cases given by the retrieval phase. From these cases, the n best ones are selected for generation of new diagrams. This number is chosen by the user and represents the number of alternative solutions required. Then, for each case, the analogy module tries to map each object in the target diagram to an object in the case diagram. In this process structural relations are used as constraints, transforming this process in a structural matching algorithm, in which node matching is based on semantic similarity of objects' synsets. This semantic similarity is based on the WordNet distance between synsets. The result of this process is a mapping between target and case objects, which is then used for transferring the knowledge from the case diagram to a new diagram (which is a copy of the target diagram). Knowledge transference is performed in two steps: first attributes and classes are transferred from case classes to the new diagram classes, and then new objects and relations are transferred from the case diagram to the new diagram. The final result is a new class diagram based on the target diagram. For more details on the analogy process see [12].

5.3 Design Composition

The design composition is a different way of generating new diagrams based on the merging of different case pieces. Design composition starts with a set of retrieved cases, which are then used to generate the new class diagrams. There are two different composition strategies: best case composition (BCC) and best complementary set of cases composition (BCSCC).

The main idea of the BCC strategy is based on selecting the best retrieved case, mapping it to the target diagram, and transferring the knowledge to a new diagram. If there are unmapped target objects, then this strategy tries to find matching objects in other retrieved cases. This goes on until, all the target objects are mapped or no more retrieved cases can be used.

The BCSCC strategy is based on the idea of complementary cases, regarding the target diagram. This strategy starts by mapping every retrieved case to the target diagram, yielding a mapping, which is then used for grouping the retrieved cases in sets. These sets are generated based on how well the cases of a set, map the target diagram. The preference is to have sets, whose cases merged, completely map the target diagram. Then, each one of these sets can give origin to a new diagram. As in analogy, only the n best sets originate new diagrams. Sets are ranked by the degree of mapping of the target diagram.

6   Example of Use

This section describes an example that illustrates how the system can be used by a software designer. This example is about the designer client of REBUILDER, showing how design knowledge is reused.

Suppose that a designer is starting the design of a information system for a high school. S/he has already the system's analysis done, and some initial entities are extracted by the designer and drawn in the REBUILDER system. Figure 4 shows the initial class diagram, representing one of the system's modules (scheduling). This module is responsible for handling the information data about teachers, classes and rooms timetables.

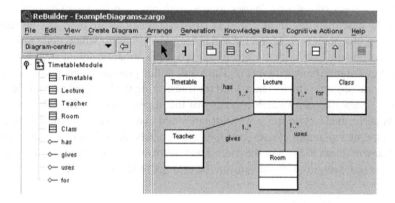

Fig. 4. The initial diagram used by the designer as target problem.

One of the tools available to the designer is the retrieval of similar designs from the case library. Imagine that s/he selects the package object and clicks on the retrieval command. REBUILDER retrieves the number of diagrams defined by the designer (in this situation three cases). Figure 5 presents part of one of the retrieved cases (the most similar one), notice that in the diagram's name there is the similarity score with the target design.

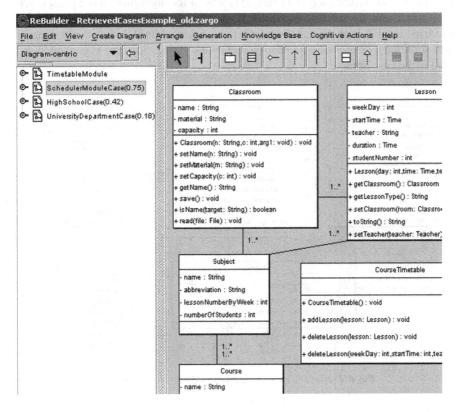

Fig. 5. The most similar case from the retrieved ones, the number in brackets is the similarity score.

The retrieved designs can help the designer exploring the design space, aiding the assessment of the different alternative designs. Or she can go further and use the adaptation mechanisms of REBUILDER to generate new designs. Suppose that the designer selects design composition, figure 6 shows part of a diagram generated by this mechanism. As can be seen, it used the most similar case (case in figure 5) to build this new case, and then completed it with the missing objects.

Generated diagrams can have some inconsistencies, which can be fixed using the verification module. For example, suppose that, in the generated diagram (figure 6) the relation between class *Teacher* and class *Timetable* is out of context. The verification module checks four different knowledge sources to assess the relation's validity: Word-Net, design cases and verification cases. In WordNet, the system looks for a relation between the *Teacher* synset and the *Timetable* synset. If it is found then the relation is considered valid. Otherwise, the system searches the design cases for a similar relation (a relation of the same type between the synsets of classes *Teacher* and *Timetable*). If the algorithm fails to find it, the next step is looking in the verification cases. It searches for a verification case describing the validity of a similar relation. A verification case can have two outcomes: success or fail. This way, if the algorithm finds a similar verification case and the outcome is success, the relation is considered valid, otherwise is considered invalid. If in the end the relation is considered invalid, then the designer is asked for a judgement about the relation and a new verification case is generated and stored in the case library.

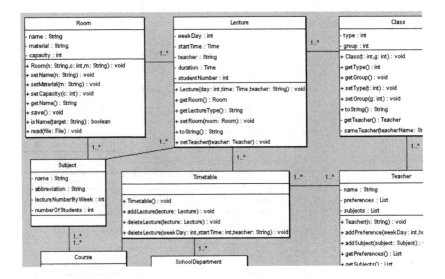

Fig. 6. Part of a diagram generated by design composition.

After verification, if the designer considers the diagram correct and ready for being stored in the KB, for later reuse, then she can submit the diagram to the KB administrator. This new diagram goes into a list of unconfirmed cases of the case library. The KB administrator has the task of examining these diagrams more carefully, deciding which are going to be transformed into cases, going to the list of confirmed cases (ready to be reused by REBUILDER), and which are going to the list of obsolete cases not being used by the system.

7   Discussion

This paper describes REBUILDER, a system that manages software design knowledge gathered during the development process. REBUILDER is also used as a platform for knowledge reuse. If we analyze deeper the implications of software reuse in REBUILDER, it can be seen that inexperienced designers profit a lot from the reuse of design knowledge, avoiding mistakes made in previous systems. From the point of view of experienced designers, the system can help them exploring different alternative designs. This exploration can be very useful for innovative or creative design.

From the company's viewpoint, REBUILDER can be a very useful tool for minimizing the loss of know-how. Part of the software engineers' experience is kept in the organization in the form of design cases. For the software development process the management and reuse of design knowledge can lower the development time and increase the software quality.

A limitation of our approach is that the company should adapt the software development process in order to fully use all the advantages of REBUILDER. The organization should adapt it's development process with the goal of developing software through reuse. Of course, REBUILDER can also be used in different ways, going from a CASE tool to a complete Knowledge Management tool integrated with a CASE tool.

There is another important limitation to our approach, which relates to WordNet. From our experience, concepts defined in WordNet are sufficient to index cases and objects when the designer is working at a conceptual level. Objects represent abstract concepts and do not necessarily represent classes to be implemented. A problem arises when the designer goes into the implementation (or detailed) design, where the objects must represent classes and interfaces to be implemented. To address this problem we added to WordNet the Java class hierarchy. Several software specific concepts, in this case relating to Java language, where added to WordNet hierarchies along with *is-a* links connecting them. These concepts allow the indexing of many software specific objects, that are present at the detailed design level.

References

1. Boehm, B.: A Spiral Model of Software Development and Enhancement. IEEE Press (1988)
2. Tong, C., Sriram, D.: Artificial Intelligence in Engineering Design. Volume I. Academic Press (1992)
3. Kolodner, J.: Case-Based Reasoning. Morgan Kaufman (1993)
4. Aamodt, A., Plaza, E.: Case–based reasoning: Foundational issues, methodological variations, and system approaches. AI Communications 7 (1994) 39–59
5. Althoff, K.D.: Case-based reasoning. In Chang, S.K., ed.: Handbook on Software Engineering and Knowledge Engineering. Volume 1., World Scientific (2001) 549–588
6. Miller, G., Beckwith, R., Fellbaum, C., Gross, D., Miller, K.J.: Introduction to wordnet: an on-line lexical database. International Journal of Lexicography 3 (1990) 235 – 244
7. Rumbaugh, J., Jacobson, I., Booch, G.: The Unified Modeling Language Reference Manual. Addison-Wesley, Reading, MA (1998)
8. Gomes, P., Pereira, F.C., Paiva, P., Seco, N., Carreiro, P., Ferreira, J.L., Bento, C.: Noun sense disambiguation with wordnet for software design retrieval. In Xiang, Y., Chaib-draa, B., eds.: 16th Conference of the Canadian Society for Computational Studies of Intelligence (AI 2003). Volume 2671 of Lecture Notes in Computer Science., Halifax, Canada, Springer (2003) 537–543
9. Gomes, P., Pereira, F.C., Paiva, P., Seco, N., Carreiro, P., Ferreira, J.L., Bento, C.: Evaluation of case-based maintenance strategies in software design. In Bridge, D., Ashley, K., eds.: Fifth International Conference on Case-Based Reasoning (ICCBR'03), Trondheim, Norway, Springer (2003)

10. Rosenberg, L.H., Hyatt, L.E.: Developing a successful metrics programme. In: ESA 1996 Product Assurance Symposium and Software Product Assurance Workshop, ESTEC, Noordwijk, The Netherlands, European Space Agency (1996) 213–216
11. Gomes, P., Pereira, F.C., Paiva, P., Seco, N., Carreiro, P., Ferreira, J.L., Bento, C.: Case retrieval of software designs using wordnet. In Harmelen, F.v., ed.: European Conference on Artificial Intelligence (ECAI'02), Lyon, France, IOS Press, Amsterdam (2002)
12. Gomes, P., Pereira, F.C., Paiva, P., Seco, N., Carreiro, P., Ferreira, J.L., Bento, C.: Combining case-based reasoning and analogical reasoning in software design. In: Proceedings of the 13th Irish Conference on Artificial Intelligence and Cognitive Science (AICS'02), Limerick, Ireland, Springer-Verlag (2002)

COTS Evaluation Supported by Knowledge Bases

Abdallah Mohamed, Tom Wanyama, Günther Ruhe,
Armin Eberlein, and Behrouz Far

[1]University of Calgary, 2500 University Drive NW, Calgary, AB, T2N 1N4, Canada
{mohameda,wanyama,far}@enel.ucalgary.ca, ruhe@ucalgary.ca
[2]Computer Engineering Department, American University of Sharjah, UAE
eberlein@enel.ucalgary.ca

Abstract. Selection of Commercial-off-The-Shelf (COTS) software products is a knowledge-intensive process. In this paper, we show how knowledge bases can be used to facilitate the COTS selection process. We propose a conceptual model to support decision makers during the evaluation procedures. We then describe how this model is implemented using agent technologies supported by two knowledge bases (KB): the COTS KB and the methods KB. The model relies on group-decision making and facilitated stakeholder negotiations during the selection process. It employs hybrid techniques, such as Bayesian Belief Networks and Game Theory, to address different challenges throughout the process. In addition, the paper also describes how the COTS knowledge base can be used at three levels of usage: global (over the internet), limited (between limited number of organizations) and local (within a single organization).

1 Introduction

In order to improve the software processes and products, there is an increasing need for accumulating, managing, disseminating, and reusing knowledge all the way through the process of developing new software systems [11]. A good example for knowledge aggregation and reuse during software development can be found during the process of developing a COTS based system. Generally, COTS software components are ready-made software products that are acquired and used as-is. During the last decade, they have received a lot of industry attention due to their potential for time and effort saving [8]. However, developers are faced with the problem of ensuring that COTS products perform the functionality they claim to have at acceptable levels of quality, which is best described as the problem of getting the 'right' knowledge at the 'right' time. Several people in industry have stated clearly that if COTS products were selected improperly, the whole project would be more costly and time consuming. Therefore, selecting the 'right' COTS product requires a robust decision support model that considers different stakeholder opinions and other constraints, and that is supported by a well established knowledge-base that includes stakeholders' experiences as well as up-to-date relevant knowledge.

Generally, it is possible that different stakeholders' preferences might be inconsistent and changing over time. Under such situations, there is a need for a COTS evaluation model that is flexible during aggregation of stakeholders' opinions, and that allows evaluating different scenarios easily. The model should handle trade-offs

G. Melnik and H. Holz (Eds.): LSO 2004, LNCS 3096, pp. 43–54, 2004.

between different perspectives so as to obtain a single product that satisfies all stake-holders. This is in fact achieved through negotiations, traditionally carried out using the *consensus approach* [13]. Within this approach, stakeholders have to reach agreement on the evaluation criteria and their relative importance. Then, the devel-oper team has to evaluate the functionality of different COTS candidates against the given criteria. Finally, the results for the evaluation process are aggregated in order to select the most convenient COTS. However, this approach has a lot of drawbacks. Firstly, it does not offer any means for trying out different scenarios to deal with con-flicting stakeholders' preferences. Secondly, it does not deal with the situation where one (or more) stakeholder changes his/her preferences after the negotiation process without the involvement of other stakeholders. Thirdly, the uncertainty and interde-pendencies inherent in the evaluation process are usually not addressed. Fourthly, reusing information from previous evaluation processes is usually not considered.

In this paper, we propose a conceptual model for COTS evaluation that circum-vents the above mentioned shortfalls of traditional models. We then describe how this model can be implemented by a system that uses agent technologies supported by two kinds of knowledge bases (KB) which are of key importance: the COTS Knowledge Base (CKB) and the Methods Knowledge base (MKB). The evaluation system simu-lates the evaluation process, allowing users to try out different scenarios and deter-mine their impact on the evaluation outcome. The system also addresses changing requirements and stakeholders' preferences. In addition, our proposed system deals with the inherent uncertainty and requirements of interdependencies by using a bayes-ian belief network (BBN) to estimate the quality of each COTS candidate from differ-ent stakeholders' perspectives.

One of the challenges that we faced, while developing our approach, is to link our ideas and suggested procedures to the real-world. To deal with this point, we heavily studied the lessons learned from COTS-based software development repository pro-vided by CeBASE (Center of Empirical Software Engineering)[2] and tried to address the stated issues. Mainly, CeBASE repository is a very rich source of real-world ex-periences and practical knowledge collected from different COTS-based projects over private industry and government. For example, it may contain hypothesis, good/bad practices, success stories or things to be avoided. The lessons-learned are submitted by different users and validated by on of the CeBASE experts.

Mainly, this paper is organized as follows: section 2 presents how the proposed system helps as a decision support system to address challenges inherent in the COTS selection process. Section 3 describes a conceptual model to be used during the evaluation process. In section 4, we show how this model can be implemented using an agent-based system supported by the mentioned types of knowledge bases, CKB and MKB. Moreover, we show the possible benefits gained from using this system. Finally, section 5 includes the conclusion and the suggestions for future work.

2   A Decision Support System for COTS Selection

A good Decision Support System (DSS) should be combined with firm knowledge modeling and management [12]. Moreover, it should be able to overcome many chal-lenges inherent in the decision making process. In his paper [10], Ruhe has described these challenges for the process of COTS evaluation and selection. An ideal DSS should be able to address all these challenges perfectly. In our proposed system, we tried to cover as many as possible of those difficulties. Typical challenges are shown in Table 1 along with the techniques used in the proposed system to address them.

Table 1. The challenges of COTS selection process and how they are addressed.

Problem Characteristics		Proposed Procedure
Related to	Description	
Stakeholders	Typically, there are different stakeholders with different (and sometimes conflicting) views about the system to be developed.	- We employ the game theory along with agents assigned to stakeholders to facilitate a semi-automatic negotiation between them - We suggest using a knowledge base to provide necessary relevant information to different stakeholders which harmonizes their decisions
Dynamic Changes	System requirements are changing all the time due to stakeholders' continuous progressive understanding.	Using agents allows applying requirements changes faster to the selection process. It also can show any inconsistency that results from such changes and propagate them quickly to other stakeholders.
Dynamic Changes	Every 8-9 months, a new version for the COTS products is released with new (or modified) features.	Although it is difficult to keep track of all the changes in a real-time way, we suggest using a knowledge base that is updated continuously with the latest information regarding relevant COTS products to current domain.
Uncertainty	There is a large uncertainty about requirements, vendors, and the impact of COTS products on the system due to their "black box" nature	We tried to handle this issue as much as possible by using techniques that deals with uncertain and incomplete data, for example, we suggest using a bayesian belief network to estimate the quality of each COTS product. Nevertheless, we are still working on solving this problem more conveniently.
Constraints	There are several constraints that should be considered when choosing the best COTS product	In our approach, the negotiation process is controlled by some constraints such as the maximum cost or the underlying technology of the products. Nevertheless, some other constraints are more qualitative and uncertain such as the products' reliability and performance. We intend to cover this part in a future research.
Problem complexity	This problem is of high complexity due to the existence of many different COTS alternatives to select from.	Although the knowledge base should contain enough information about available COTS products relevant to a certain domain, we cannot claim that maintaining such knowledge base is easy. Sometimes, it takes more effort to maintain it than searching for end evaluating available COTS products in the market.
Objectives	When considering the selection problem, several incomparable objectives have to be considered. For example, the cost-benefit ratio, the reputation and trustworthy of the vendors, and the covered functionality.	In our proposed system, we have addressed only the covered functionality and the quality of the selected COTS product. However, we intend to extend our approach to cover all other objectives in a future research.

3 Conceptual Model for COTS Evaluation

We believe that COTS evaluation process is based upon the fact that relative importance of evaluation criteria depends upon the perspective of each individual stakeholder. For example, the System Design Team might be interested in the system needs and architectural issues, whereas the customers are more interested in the domain issues related to their organizations and relative constraints, such as budget limits. We illustrate these differences in perspective in the proposed conceptual model shown in Figure 1. In the model, COTS alternatives are presented, along with relevant information, through a KB, which will be split later on into the COTS knowledge base (CKB) and the methods knowledge base (MKB). The KB gets its knowledge from different sources such as domain experts and vendors documents, as well as from previous evaluation processes. The *"update"* feedback loop aims at storing the results of previous evaluation processes to enable continuous learning, and hence, reduce the time and effort needed for future evaluation processes. Ideally, all the knowledge regarding COTS products functionality, quality, cost and other issues should be stored. However, this is very difficult to implement, at least in the current time. The COTS products are evaluated according to the needs and preferences of individual stakeholders, who are provided with feedback from the KB about the actually available COTS features. The evaluation process is carried out within the aggregation component, provided by the KB, by assessing COTS product features according to stakeholders' preferences. Different stakeholder preferences may lead to two situations. Firstly, all stakeholder preferences point to the same COTS product, and thus we don't have any problem selecting the product. The second situation is the one in which the stakeholders' preferences point at different COTS products, and thus a negotiation process is carried out, within the negotiation component under certain constraints. The goal of this negotiation process is to deliver the best ranking for the selected products, addressing as many as possible of the combined needs of all stakeholders.

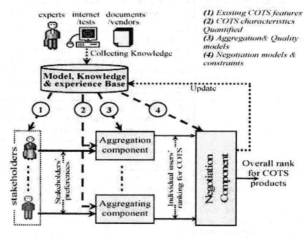

Fig. 1. COTS evaluation conceptual model.

4   Agent-Based System for COTS Evaluation

4.1   Why We Use Agents

COTS evaluation process has a number of characteristics that make it appropriate to use agent technology for the evaluation decision support system. These are:

- COTS evaluation is not a cleanly separable action, but is more permeative: it exists in multiple forms and at subtly different levels. For example, stakeholders make decisions on the following issues before the final evaluation process:
  1. Evaluation criteria that meet the needs of their respective organizations.
  2. Relative importance of the evaluation criteria.
  3. Support developing system in house or using COTS.

  This amounts to a distributed decision making problem since each stakeholder has decisions to make before being able to participate in the evaluation process.

- COTS evaluation is carried out when system requirements are still subject to change. This means the evaluation goes on as stakeholders develop deeper understanding of the system under development. In addition, stakeholders assimilate information about COTS alternatives as the evaluation process progresses. This leads to two major issues:
  1. Difference in the rate at which stakeholders acquire relevant information,
  2. Changing stakeholder preferences.

- COTS evaluation benefits tremendously from previously conducted evaluation processes. However, stakeholders can only gain from historical data that were generated by roles similar to their own role(s) in the current evaluation.

The above characteristics require that an appropriate COTS evaluation DSS has, among others, the following capabilities:

1. Distributed problem solving capabilities so as to offer decision support to stakeholders as they develop their views and preferences.
2. Handling iterative decision making both at individual and group level.
3. Evaluation of products without views of some stakeholders and inclusion of those views (views of previously absent stakeholders) when they are available (flexibility and modularity).
4. Distributed learning in order to offer efficient and customized decision support to different stakeholders (customization of the DSS to stakeholders).

Agent technology makes it easy to develop and use a DSS that offers the above capabilities [4]

4.2 An Overview of the Proposed System

We suggest using an agent based system to realize our COTS evaluation conceptual model. Figure 2 is a high level layout of the system with the following components:

1. Methods Knowledge Base (MKB) that provides stakeholders' agents, through the administrator agent, with the knowledge required to use properly different methods and techniques during the evaluation and negotiation processes.
2. COTS Knowledge Base (CKB) that stores information quantitatively about different COTS candidates. This will be discussed in more detail later on in this paper
3. Several agents that represent stakeholders involved in the evaluation process. All stakeholders are assigned agents to ensure getting the best results from the COTS evaluation process. Two roles are assigned to these agents: first, to collect corresponding stakeholder preferences to be used in the evaluation process; and second, to evaluate alternative products according to the collected views of the individual stakeholders and the data obtained from the CKB.

4. An administrator agent, maintained by the project administrator, to manage and coordinate the different tasks throughout the evaluation process (e.g. the negotiation phase).
5. COTS expert agent which has mainly two roles: first, to provide COST experts a fast and easy means to access and manage the CKB. We mean by the COTS expert the person who is responsible of managing and maintaining the CKB to keep it up to date with the latest information about COTS products. The second role of the COTS expert agent is to pass on the needed information about COTS products to the stakeholders' agents to perform a sound evaluation process.

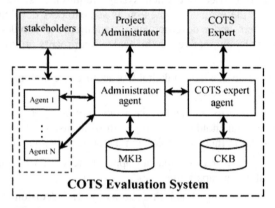

Fig. 2. High level structure of our evaluation system.

4.3   The Benefits of the Proposed System

We believe that by using the proposed system, several benefits will be achieved:

- This system can be used for automatic documentation for different tasks during the evaluation process. Each agent should document its set of goals, plans, tasks, and results. This eases understanding and learning from previous evaluation processes
- When conflict occurs between stakeholders in ranking COTS alternatives, it easy to determine the source and impact of these conflicts before resolving them. This saves time and resources, because negotiation is carried out only if deemed necessary.
- Agent technology allows for easy semi-automation of the negotiation process. Therefore, negotiation results are obtained faster and are mainly dependant upon product characteristics and stakeholder preferences. This contrasts with the *consensual approach* where the negotiation results may depend upon the negotiation skills of stakeholders. This does not mean that the proposed system is intended to remove all negotiations between stakeholders, but rather to give them extra facilities to make faster robust decisions.
- With negotiation automated, it is possible to simulate the COTS selection process, try out different scenarios and weigh their impact on the outcome of the COTS evaluation process.

- The agent-based negotiation process does not require stakeholders to agree upon evaluation criteria or their relative importance. Therefore, it is possible for the decision support tool to accommodate issues related to changing requirements and changing stakeholder needs and preferences.
- Implementing this system as a web-based system allows inheriting many advantages associated with web technologies. For example, stakeholders do not have to be in the same physical place to carry out a sound COTS selection process.
- Having a knowledge base (i.e., CKB) to store and retrieve information during different evaluation processes involves a lot of advantages. For example, it reduces overall required evaluation time and effort. We will discuss that in more detail in the following section.

4.4   Knowledge Bases

Different type of knowledge, models, experiences or lessons learned should be included in LSO knowledge base [11]. In the context of this paper, we split our knowledge base into two, upon which the agents depend to evaluate COTS products. These are the COTS Knowledge Base (CKB) and the Methods Knowledge Base (MKB). In the next two subsections, we will discuss in detail these two knowledge bases.

4.4.1   COTS Knowledge Base (CKB)

In [1], Boehm and Basili stated a hypothesis that almost 99% of all executing computer instructions come from COTS products. Morisio et al [8] suggest that for COTS projects there should be a consulting team whose responsibility is to gather and store information about COTS products. This information can be related to the latest COTS updates, or to the previous selection processes. As a whole, this means that having a repository for COTS products with enough information about them is becoming a necessity. In our proposed approach, we suggest having a CKB as a repository of available COTS products and their characteristics. We believe that having these characteristics stored in a quantified form would facilitate and speed up investigating different scenarios, including different aspects and views, for the final selection. However, maintaining and updating such a knowledge base is challenging. Usually, COTS products undergo new releases once or twice a year [1] either by adding new features or modifying existing ones. Hence, we should be very careful about what type of information is to be stored in the CKB. Typically, we should focus on longer lasting features (i.e., those ones which are least probably to change in every release). Nevertheless, all the relevant product features should be up-to-date during the actual development process. Although not the focus of this paper, we intend to address this issue in a future research.

In our proposed system, we use a quantitative information repository of COTS components to help software system developers to more easily and quickly search for and evaluate different COTS alternatives (Figure 3). In general, our approach has multiple layers for sorting and storing information about the products in a very organized way, for example, the *quality features'* layer and the *functional requirements'* layer. In this paper, we only focus upon the quality features of COTS products. However, the same idea can be adapted to store COTS functionality and other features.

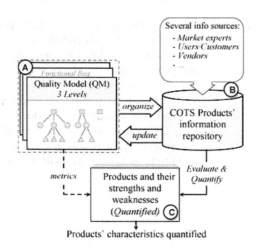

Fig. 3. The COTS Knowledge Base (CKB).

The idea of such repository is very simple. In Figure 3, information about each COTS product in the system database is stored in Component B according to a specific pattern provided by Component A. The stored information is evaluated for correctness by an expert(s); then quantified according to some metric defined by Component A; and finally stored in Component C.

Component A: This component represents the pattern with which the information about a COTS product should be stored. It includes different layers for different categories of COTS features. As mentioned, we will focus upon product quality features as an example of how this component is built. The quality model (QM) included in this component is divided into 3 levels: the very high abstract level (L1), the detailed level (L2), and the attribute level (L3) [7]. L1 and L2 represent the high level description of the quality features and are domain independent. They are built according to some global quality standards (e.g., ISO/IEC 9126 [3] and McCall [6] quality models). On the other hand, L3 is the level where certain metrics are provided to measure the attributes affecting the quality features at L2. L3 is domain and application dependent. It represents how L2 characteristics are actually implemented within COTS products. Building L3 should include careful market studies by experts to find out what is available. In addition, Component B continuously updates Component A with the actual attributes available in the market. For example, quality characteristics at L1 and L2 may be "*Reliability*" and "*Recoverability*", while an attribute at L3 may be "*how a COTS handles errors in a given system*".

Component B: this component represents a COTS products' information repository. The information is stored according to certain templates provided by Component A. The CKB is an open system, meaning that it allows different stakeholders (e.g., end-users, customers, vendors, and market experts) to participate and to give their feedback about COTS components. The system has three main interfaces for getting information from different stakeholders:

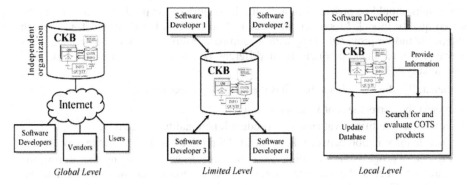

Fig. 4. Diffierent levels for using the CKB.

– An interface for the vendors to submit a detailed description of their products
– An interface available to the public to submit (e.g., through the internet) any experience they have about the product.
– An interface for the software organizations which use the system to have their knowledge, experiences, and test results stored in the system.

The information stored in component B is subjective and is not certified yet. It is stored based upon the subjective view of the people who submitted it.

Component C: this component represents a repository for certified and quantified COTS product features. They are stored according to the patterns and metrics provided by component A. Component C provides quantified information about each COTS product, including its weaknesses and strengths. This allows quick and easy comparisons to be made between different products, especially given that all the data is stored according to the same pattern.

The proposed CKB can be plugged into any COTS evaluation and searching process, such as the system presented in [7] or the system presented in this paper. In fact, it can be used at *one* of three levels (Figure 4):

1. **Local level:** It can be maintained and managed locally by a certain software organization, which stores the history of its COTS selection processes. This will make future COTS acquirement for a specific domain much easier, faster and cheaper.
2. **Limited level:** It can be used as a centralized database between different organizations having an agreement to submit their evaluation results to the CKB.
3. **Global level:** It can be maintained and managed by an independent organization which provides services through a website. This organization should be responsible for testing and ensuring the accuracy of any information regarding product functionality and quality. We assume that financial support for such project is available, for instance from advertisements, from charging vendors who wants to get their product into this KB, or from charging users who search the KB. Of course, the starting budget for such a project will be relatively high, but we believe that with time, this project would be very profitable.

Regardless of level, there should be a search engine capable of searching the database of products and their features according to different criteria and/or keywords.

The results should be provided, along with the quality of the product, according to the stored quality model. Moreover, in order to find the best COTS product, the search engine should be provided along with a "compare utility" that performs comparisons between the resultant products from different perspective (e.g., quality, cost, and functionally).

Generally, this knowledge base has the following capabilities:

- Assess the correctness of vendors' claims.
- Provide a quantified evaluation for product functionality and quality.
- Provide information between different COTS products in a comparable way.
- Provide a progressive searching capability for products, meaning that during the searching process, the user can provide further criteria to narrow down the number of results. The search criteria may include:

4.4.2 Methods Knowledge Base (MKB)

This knowledge base, illustrated in Figure 5, has two components. The first component stores the algorithms needed to carry out the evaluation process. For example, in this paper, we rely on bayesian belief networks (BBN) [5] to carry out the evaluation process for individual COTS quality features. The second component is used to facilitate the negotiation process between different stakeholder agents. The negotiation component has three layers; the first layer being the negotiation protocols layer. It includes several rules and methods for the formation of *payoff matrices* and *coalition* [9] between agents. These rules and methods produce input data for the second layer, the negotiation algorithm layer. The second layer includes methods used during the negotiation phase. In the context of this paper, we suggest using the Game Theory [9] to carry out the negotiations. The third layer represents the learning part, using information related to the selection process quality as feedback to improve agents' future capabilities.

- **The "COTS Evaluation Algorithm" Component.** This component of the MKB contains information about methods used to evaluate different COTS products. Since we have focused upon quality features in the CKB, we will now focus upon selecting a method suitable for evaluating the quality features in the MKB. For evaluating the quality of different COTS alternatives, we need a method that:

- Can be used to model and reason about uncertain and incomplete data.
- Can capture linguistic information about different quality features (e.g. *"the product's ease-of-use"* is high).
- Can be used to model inter-relationships between problem variables.

We suggest using BBNs to handle this situation. BBNs are used to model or map real-world situations, which involve uncertain interacting events. They are based upon the Bayesian probability theory. A BBN consists of a direct acyclic graph containing "nodes", which represent different problem variables (events), and are connected by "causal links" to show their dependency relationships. When a node has an effect on another node, the first one is called the "parent node" and the latter one is called the "child node". Each parent node (event) has a conditional probability table (CPT) to show its probability of occurrence according to its child nodes. The CPT is determined by domain experts and historical data.

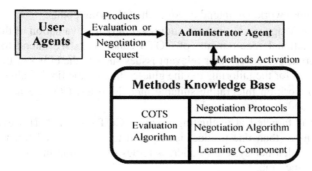

Fig. 5. The Methods Knowledge Base (MKB).

- **The "Negotiation Algorithm" Component.** We suggest using Game theory techniques to handle the negotiations. Products evaluation scores are modeled, according to individual stakeholders' preferences, as payoffs of players (stakeholders), because these scores represent benefits stakeholders get when a particular product is selected. Since agents are in full knowledge of each others utility, we model the negotiation problem as an n-person general-sum cooperative game with complete information.

If it is determined that the preferences of all stakeholders point at the same COTS product, then there is no need for negotiations between the agents. Ranking of other alternatives is determined by the deviation between their scores and those of the 'best' product. In such a situation, the game is said to have a *core*. The core is defined as set of un-dominated, feasible solution configuration. That is, each element of the core represents a solution configuration acceptable to all players. Otherwise, a game theory solution process is carried out to determine stakeholder Pareto optimal payoffs [9]. The beauty of using game theory negotiation algorithm is the fact that such algorithms are independent of the utility function of stakeholders. Therefore, any multi attribute decision making method can be used for products evaluation algorithm.

5 Conclusions and Future Work

This paper reviews a new conceptual model for COTS evaluation. It presents a part of an ongoing research aiming at developing a sound method for COTS selection. We believe that using our approach will give great support to decision makers during COTS selection process. The main focus was on the KB that supports the evaluation process. However, the KB at the global level would be of limited value unless it is possible to establish a community of interested users around it. We also explained how to carry out the other procedures to perform the selection process. The proposed approach has some advantages over similar approaches since: firstly, it uses two knowledge bases, CKB and MKB, to help continuous accumulating, managing and reusing of relevant knowledge. Secondly, it employs agent technology to facilitate negotiations between different stakeholders and providing them with quick alternative scenarios to select from. In addition, we suggest using a hybrid of techniques to address uncertainty and stakeholders varying preferences.

As for the future work, we intend to cover the following points:

- In the proposed approach, we have addressed only the evaluation of the functional and non-functional requirements of COTS candidates. We intend to extend the current approach to cover other relevant issues such as the effect of the amount of effort required for the tailoring and the glue-coding on the final evaluation results.
- We plan to work on integrating suitable models to test COTS candidates at both the product and the system levels.
- This paper is targeted at evaluating a single COTS product. However, in some situations, more than one product is required to cover needed functionality. We intend to broaden our system to address issues of selecting multiple COTS products at the same time.
- We are working on developing guidelines to allow easy management and maintenance for the CKB. Moreover, we intend to define the enabling techniques (e.g. measurements, experiments, etc) [11] for such knowledge base in details.

Acknowledgement. The authors would like to thank the Alberta Informatics Circle of Research Excellence (iCORE) and the International Council for Canadian Studies (ICCS) for its financial support of this research.

References

1. Basili, V.,Boehm, B.:COTS-Based Systems Top 10 List,IEEE Computer, Vol.34, No.5. (2001)
2. CeBASE COTS Lessons Learned Repository, available at http://www.cebase.org
3. International Organization for Standardization: Software Product Evaluation - Quality Characteristics and Guidelines for Their Use. Geneve, Switzerland: International Organization for Standardization (1991)
4. Jennings, N.R., Faratin, P., Johnson, M.J., O'Brien, P., Wiegand, M.E.: Using Intelligent Agents to Manage Business Processes. Proceedings of PAAM (1996) 345-360.
5. Jensen, F.V.: An Introduction to Bayesian Networks. Univ. College London Press, London (1996)
6. J. A. McCall. Concepts and definitions of software quality. Factors in Software Quality, NTIS Vol 1, (1977).
7. Mohamed, A., Ruhe, G., Eberlein, A.: Selecting COTS Components for Product Lines. Proceedings of the 4th ASERC Workshop on Quantitative and Soft Computing Based Software Engineering (2004)
8. Morisio, M., Seaman, C.B., Parra, A.T., Basilli, V.R., Kraft, S.E., Condon, S.E.: Investigating and Improving a COTS-Based Software Development Process. ICSE'00. Limmerick, Ireland (2000)
9. Owen, G.: Game Theory. W.B. Saunders Company (1968)
10. Ruhe, G.: Intelligent Support for Selection of COTS Products. Proceedings of the Net.ObjectDays (2002), Erfurt, Springer (2003) 34-45.
11. Ruhe, G.: Learning Software Organisations. In Handbook of Software Engineering and Knowledge Engineering (S.K.Chang.ed.), Vol 1.World Scientific Publishing (2001)663-678.
12. Ruhe, G.: Software Engineering Decision Support - A New Paradigm for Learning Software Organizations. Proceedings of the 4th Workshop on Learning Software Organizations, Chicago, Springer (2003) 104-113.
13. Schwab, D.P., Herbert, G. H.: Assessment of a Consensus-Based Multiple Information Source: Job Evaluation System. Journal of Applied Psychology, Vol.71, No.2 (1986) 354-356.

Embedding Experiences
in Micro-didactical Arrangements

Eric Ras and Stephan Weibelzahl

Fraunhofer Institute for Experimental Software Engineering (IESE)
Sauerwiesen 6, 67661 Kaiserslautern, Germany
{eric.ras,stephan.weibelzahl}@iese.fraunhofer.de

Abstract. Experience-based Information Systems (EbIS) enable organizations
to capture, store and reuse knowledge and experiences for continuous competence development. However, there are several shortcomings that seem to limit
the usage of the stored knowledge. Focusing on technical issues, the stored experiences consist mainly of contextual knowledge provided by domain experts,
while declarative and procedural knowledge is required in addition to facilitate
learning for novices. Moreover, these systems do not support learning in an optimal way because they do not activate learning processes. We present an approach that enriches retrieved experiences with additional learning elements in
so-called micro-didactical learning arrangements, created by a pedagogical
agent based on cognitive learning goals and an instructional design model. The
advantages of this approach are twofold: first, the applicability of experience
packages increases by adding learning elements to the package; second, the application of the experience and the newly gained knowledge in practice deepens
the learning effect.

1 Introduction

Continuous competence development is essential to keep track with the requirements
of today's work environments. This trend can be observed especially in the Information and Communication Technologies sector with its increasing flood of information,
rapid deterioration and hence ageing of knowledge, as well as the continuously changing requirements for problem understanding and solving. As a result, these facts require lifelong learning to remain competitive in the information society.

Today, learning is less a reaction to 'being learned' but more the reaction to varied
requirements of learning situations and learning environments. The short innovation
cycles in Software Engineering lead to many learning situations where new knowledge
is required to solve new challenges during daily work.

In the future, learning within an organization will balance out structured, directed
learning and unstructured, autonomic learning. Autonomic learning consists of learning without direct teaching. Learners define their own learning goals according to
given situations and select the learning steps as well as their sequence to reach the
goals. Autonomic learning is more a way of explorative learning than learning based
on given procedures and rules. Directed learning will be launched by the organization
to communicate and change their strategy, culture, products and services, which in-

G. Melnik and H. Holz (Eds.): LSO 2004, LNCS 3096, pp. 55–66, 2004.

volves individuals, teams or the entire organization. Autonomic learning originates within the organization, initiated by individuals and communities of practice.

The increasing number of Knowledge Management Systems (KMS) led to research and developments focusing mainly on capturing, structuring, and packaging knowledge for reuse. One of the domains where KMS's were profitably implemented is Software Engineering [22], a quickly changing, knowledge-intensive business involving many people working in different phases and activities. However, organizations frequently encounter problems identifying the content, location and use of knowledge. As a result 50 to 60 percent of KM deployments failed because organizations did not have a good KM deployment methodology or process, if any at all [17]. Regarding the deployment process, learning is considered to be a fundamental part of Knowledge Management (KM) since employees must internalize (learn) shared knowledge before they can use it to perform specific tasks [22]. It was assumed that KMS's could solve the problem of continuous competence development by providing intelligent retrieval mechanisms and innovative presentations techniques. KMS's focuses mainly on the knowledge, (i.e., the product of learning processes), and less on learning processes itself and the needs of individuals. A recent study stated that 'next generation' KMS developments should focus on designing KM technologies for people and not make people to adapt to KM technologies [17]. Designing KM technologies for people means supporting people in their learning processes to ensure that the provided knowledge can be transferred back to the work process. Enhancing learning means more than sequencing 'chunks' of knowledge. It requires an understanding of learning goals and processes, and the different types of learners and their competence levels.

An interview-based study showed that perceived connections between KM and e-learning are not operationalized, i.e., the integration ideas are rarely implemented in practice. KM addresses learning mostly as part of knowledge sharing processes and focuses on specific forms of informal learning (e.g., learning in a community of practice) or to providing access to learning resources or experts [9]. In addition to these interviews, an outcome of a follow-up workshop was that future KM initiatives should shift their focus from knowledge sharing to support actual learning from others and applying the experiences of these people [8].

In this paper, we present an approach that enriches retrieved experiences (i.e., applied knowledge) with additional learning elements in micro-didactical learning arrangements in order to enable learning from others' captured knowledge. These arrangements are created by a pedagogical agent based on learning goals and associated educational learning patterns.

2   Experience-Based Information Systems (EbIS)

While knowledge is frequently seen as the range of learned information or understanding of a human or intelligent information system, experience is considered to be "knowledge or practical wisdom gained through human senses, from directly observing, encountering, or undergoing things during the participation in events or in a particular activity" [25, p.24]. Experience Management (EM) can be seen as a sub-field of KM that aims at supporting the management and transfer of relevant experiences

[6, 25]. The software system used for managing, storing, retrieving and disseminating these experiences is called an Experience-based Information System (EbIS) [15] that is based on the *Experience Factories* concept [5]. Another type of systems that are not based on the EF concept is *Lessons Learned Systems* (LLS) [27]. Amongst the definitions for lessons learned the most complete definition as stated by Weber et al. [27, p.3] is: "A lesson learned is knowledge or understanding gained by experience. The experience may be positive, as in a successful test or mission, or negative, as in a mishap or failure. Successes are also considered sources of lessons learned. A lesson must be significant in that it has a real or assumed impact on operations; valid in that it is factually and technically correct; and applicable in that it identifies a specific design, process, or decision that reduces or eliminates the potential for failures and mishaps, or reinforces a positive result." [23]. In this paper we use the term *experience package* (EP) which includes both experiences embedded within EbIS's and lessons learned within LLS's.

We argue that experience packages that are retrieved by EbIS's are often inadequate for learning and competence development for several reasons. First, the experience base might be incomplete, outdated or might just contain wrong information. This problem has been addressed by several knowledge elicitation and maintenance approaches (see [6] for an overview). Second, users might refuse to apply an experience package, because of a lack of confidence. There is a chance that the quality of packaged experiences is also influenced by contradictory interests (e.g., commercial interests). Thus, it might be unclear whether applying the packaged experience might involve a certain risk. A good and transparent quality assurance process might alleviate this problem. Finally, even if the EB has a high coverage and precision, and even if the users have enough confidence in the quality of the information, the packages might still be inappropriate for learning due to the fact that the learning issues are not considered by the EbIS. Often, users need additional information about the subject domain, because experts provided the experience without giving extensive explanations of the background and because the users lack knowledge of domain concepts. Our approach aims at closing this gap by enriching the experience packages with learning elements based on didactical considerations.

3 Learning Based on Packaged Experiences

One reason why Software Engineering knowledge is usually captured from experts is that their knowledge is assumed to be concise, correct and complete. Further, by finding out what kind of knowledge is considered essential by the experts, we hope to get information about what should be learned by novices. A problem that occurs when expert knowledge is used for teaching novices is that there is not only a quantitative difference between expert and novice knowledge bases, but also a qualitative difference, e.g., the way in which knowledge is organized [11].

The following sections provide an overview of the different knowledge types and related knowledge stages and how we can learn from expert knowledge. Finally, we derive requirements for micro-didactical learning arrangements.

3.1 Knowledge Types

Anderson developed a model of the architecture of human knowledge. He classifies knowledge not according to its content but according to its state in the person's long-term memory. Two types of knowledge were defined [4,13]:

- Declarative knowledge consists of 'knowing about' – e.g., facts, impressions, lists, objects and procedures,, and 'knowing that' certain principles hold. Declarative knowledge is based on concepts that are connected by a set of relations forming a network that models the memory of a person. This leads to the conceptual and theoretical understandings that remain long after many facts are forgotten. For instance, declarative knowledge items in the domain of Software Engineering might be: a definition of 'test case', a listing of defect types, a detailed explanation of key testing principles.
- Procedural knowledge consists of 'knowing how' to do something, i.e., skills to construct, connect and use declarative knowledge. Learners are doing tasks, such as understanding and processing relationships between items (e.g., facts or objects) and creating new connections between them. Procedural knowledge contains the discrete steps or actions to be taken, and the available alternatives to perform a given task. Procedural knowledge consists also of 'if-then' rules that describe conditions when to perform certain actions in a specific situation. These rules are abstract, modular (i.e., they can be combined), goal-oriented, and operate on the basis of declarative knowledge. With sufficient practice, applying the rules of procedural knowledge may become an automatic process, thus allowing the person to perform a task without conscious awareness. For instance, procedural knowledge items in the domain of Software Engineering might be: a method for deriving test cases from requirements, a method for classifying defects choosing the right reading technique to perform an inspection.

Both declarative and procedural knowledge can be abstract or concrete. The knowledge can be connected to more or less concrete information that can be described technically, e.g., by semantic networks. Nevertheless, knowledge about experienced situations or evaluating facts or determining circumstances in given situations, cannot be classified as declarative or procedural knowledge. Therefore, a third form of knowledge, conditional or contextual knowledge describing 'when, where and why', has extended the spectrum of knowledge in cognitive science [10]. In the context of didactical design, Tennyson and Rasch [26] defined contextual knowledge as another type of knowledge:

- Contextual knowledge consists of 'knowing when, where and why' to use or apply declarative or procedural knowledge. Contextual knowledge is created by reflecting on the usage of declarative and procedural knowledge in practice in different contexts. Contextual knowledge enables the individual to be aware of commonalities between situations, and of the appropriateness or applicability of principles or procedures in a new context.

In summary, three types of knowledge have been presented. Packaged experiences, i.e., documented experiences, consist mainly of contextual knowledge. They originate in most cases from expert memories and they lack declarative basis background knowledge and detailed procedural knowledge, resulting in them being ineligible for learning purposes. The next section details the problem mentioned above and focuses especially on barriers that exist when individuals are learning from expert knowledge.

3.2 Learning from Expert Knowledge

The standard method for transferring knowledge from experts to novices is the 'copy-model': expert knowledge is considered as learning material and they are transferred directly to the learner by using an appropriate medium. Even if this model is commonly applied in many different educational contexts and KMS's, it does not comply with the structures and processes of human information processing [3]. What makes the transfer of expert knowledge or experiences difficult? Firstly, from a cognitive science point of view, new knowledge is always related to existing knowledge in human memories. This means that novices might have problems in relating new expert knowledge to their existing 'basics'. Secondly, learning is a special case of information acquisition and information storage. The learning process is dependent first on the quality of the information to be learned and second on the cognitive activities of learning. If those activities do not take place because of the problem stated above, the efficiency of information acquisition and storage is decreased. Thirdly, there is not only a quantitative difference between expert and novice knowledge bases, but also a qualitative difference, i.e., the organization of knowledge [11]. Cognitive schemata from experts cannot be transferred to the memories of novices. This fact results from a compilation process that is performed when new knowledge is learned: updating or forgetting of old knowledge, creating new relations or rules between knowledge items and aggregating knowledge items etc. Fourthly, asking experts about their knowledge results often in an enumeration of many facts, methods and principles explained in a complex manner. Experts forgot about how they learned those knowledge chunks, and they are unable to explain why they choose certain activities to perform them in a certain manner. The applied knowledge is somehow 'routine' [11]. Finally, transferring past experiences made by others requires more than only contextual knowledge, in particular problem-solving strategies for a specific context and knowing 'when, where, and why' knowledge should be used. It requires a strong anchoring with declarative and procedural knowledge.

The goal of effective knowledge transfer is to guide a novice through so-called knowledge stages to become an expert. Fitts and Posner defined three different stages [12]: The goal during the first *cognitive stage* is to build up basic conceptual knowledge and to integrate the knowledge into a semantic network. By solving problems in this stage, the person accesses simple concepts and content specific rules that are represented as declarative knowledge. In the second *associative stage*, domain specific rules are created. These 'if-then' rules are based on associations between conditions and specific operations, and they broaden procedural knowledge in the current context of the problem to be solved. If the 'if'-part of the rule is fulfilled, the 'then'-part is automatically used for problem solving. The third *autonomous (automatic) stage* is reached after many years of practice. The rules have a high degree of association because of many applications. This results in a replacement of many rules by high-level and simple rules. These simple rules have often a reduced 'if' and 'then' part. A characteristic of these rules is that they cannot be verbalized, i.e., the rules cannot be explained to others and they determine autonomous activity and behavior in general. This evolution process makes the transfer of knowledge and connected rules between novices and experts difficult.

The next sections propose an approach how to bridge the gap between novice and expert knowledge levels, resulting from many compiling cycles of knowledge evolution in experts' memories.

3.3   Enabling Learning from Packages Experiences

The main purpose of an EbIS is to provide the right experience package to solve a problem in a certain situation. Often, the packaged experiences originate from applied expert knowledge, documented by the experts themselves. As described in the previous sections, novices might have problems to apply these experiences in practice.

The central goal of our approach is to embed experts' experience packages related to the Software Engineering domain into *micro-didactical learning arrangements* that enable cognitive learning processes and that allow less experienced persons to acquire the necessary skills to apply the experience packages in practice.

Such a learning arrangement consists of a learning offer that allows learning in context. The experience is enriched with additional so-called learning elements. A learning element is an atomic chunk of knowledge, either declarative, procedural or contextual, that represents content about facts, processes, rules and principles and augments specific cognitive learning activities by reading, searching, orientating, summarizing and reflecting. In the following, the requirements of such an arrangement are listed:

- A micro-didactical arrangement contains learning elements to all three types of knowledge and thus ensures that contextual knowledge is anchored with declarative and procedural knowledge.
- An arrangement follows the constructivist and the pedagogical principle of autonomous learning, i.e., explorative learning. Explorative learning is less a didactical design principle, but it ensures that the learners deal explicitly with the problem to be solved; the learners choose their own learning goal; the learners are collecting new knowledge by themselves, construct their own cognitive schemata and strengthen the associations between different knowledge types; the learners perform learning by-doing to get new insights in complex circumstances and principles and acquires necessary skills for applying the embedded experience.
- Explorative learning does not take place as a linear process from one topic or one difficulty level to another but more in a cyclical manner. Knowledge on different topics is acquired in parallel. Changing between topics could be useful for a better understanding of the topics directly related to the problem. Such a cyclical procedure is typical observed when complex problems have to be solved. Explorative learning is essential to understand the relationships between different sub-domains, to enhance the orientation within the domain by building up individual cognitive schemata.

- An arrangement is created automatically by a so-called pedagogical agent. A pedagogical agent uses a set of micro-didactical patterns based on an instructional model, a Software Engineering ontology and a semantic network for learning elements (see next section).
- An arrangement is conform to current e-learning standards and this ensures the compatibility to other platforms, like Learning Content Management Systems (LCMS).

The following section describes the design of our approach: a model for competence levels with associated knowledge stages is defined, a set of predefined learning goals, a taxonomy for learning elements that are used for enriching packages experiences is provided, and the creating process for micro-didactical arrangements is elaborated.

4 Enabling Learning in EbIS

By referring to the knowledge stages described above, we define a *novice* as a person in the cognitive knowledge stage who starts to build up basic declarative knowledge. A *practitioner* is somebody who is currently in the associative stage, i.e., creating more associations between declarative knowledge and identifying 'if-then' rules to broaden the procedural knowledge in the current context of the problem to be solved. An *expert* is a person whose knowledge has reached an autonomous stage. Experts are able to create or adapt their rules automatically by informal learning on the job and applying current knowledge in practice. The following sections describe how we can enrich packaged experiences by learning elements and how we can address the requirements listed in Section 3 to create micro-didactical arrangements. Our approach focuses especially on knowledge acquisition for novices and practitioners.

4.1 Educational Goals

Educational goals differ widely in dependence of the target audience and the knowledge of the learners. For instance, novices should usually learn the basic facts and definitions of a topic, before bothering them with details and inconsistencies. Practitioners are interested in getting hints and instructions on how to perform a given task in the first place. Thus, in order to provide suitable learning material, an adequate learning goal has to be specified. In our approach, we refer to Bloom's taxonomy of educational goals [5,15], which is widely accepted and applied in various topic areas including Software Engineering [1].

Bloom defines and describes six performance levels that differ in terms of the complexity from a cognitive point of view. The lowest level is called *knowledge* and aims at the acquisition of facts and definitions. The learner should be able to recall information such as dates, events and places. The next level, *comprehension*, goes beyond knowledge, as the learner is required to understand the meaning of the information. Learners should be able to interpret and compare facts and summarize ideas. The *application* level aims at using the acquired information, methods and concepts to solve problems. Theories are applied in new situations. The *analysis* level comprises the ability to identify underlying patterns and components. On the *synthesis* level learners are able to use old ideas to create new one, to generalize from given facts and to draw conclusions. Finally, learners that reached the *evaluation* level are able to assess the value of theories, make choices based on reasoned argument and recognize subjectivity.

Our approach addresses only the first three levels of this taxonomy, because these are important for reaching the upper levels and can be taught directly, while the fourth to sixth level require a longer term and deeper insight into a subject matter.

4.2 Taxonomy of Learning Elements

In order to select the most suitable learning elements from the repository, we assign each element to a learning element type derived from another taxonomy introduced by Meder [20]. According to this taxonomy, learning elements belong to one of four types: First, they might provide an *Explanation* (e.g., definition, description, example). Second, they might serve as *Orientation* (e.g., overview, summary, history). Third, a learning element might be *Action* knowledge that contains information on how to perform a task (e.g., procedure, checklist, rule, principle). Finally, it might be a *Reference* to a source (e.g., document reference, annex reference, glossary reference). These learning element types can be categorized in terms of Bloom's educational learning goals. *Knowledge* and *Comprehension* are goals related to the cognitive knowledge stage (i.e., declarative knowledge). The *Application* goal is part of the associative knowledge stage (i.e., procedural knowledge).

Each learning goal requires a different learning activity that focuses on different aspects of cognitive schemata. Table 1 provides an overview of the assignment of learning elements to goals. Meder claims that the list of elements has been applied successfully but might require extensions for new domains.

Table 1. Overview of educational goals and associated learning elements

Knowledge	Comprehension	Application
Definition	example	procedure
description	counterexample	administrative direction
theorem	summary	instruction
reference	history	social direction
	overview	principle
	scenario	strategy
		checklist
		law
		rule

Based on this categorization every atomic learning element is now related to a high level educational goal. The next section describes the relations between the learning elements that are used by the pedagogical agent to create the learning arrangements.

4.3 Learning Elements and Their Relations

Learning elements (LE's) are stored in the learning element base (LEB). The LE's that are used in our system have been created during recent projects related to Software Engineering learning content. Each learning element is described by means of a metadata set (see Fig. 1). The metadata description is based on the Learning Object Metadata standard (LOM) [14]. LOM specifies the syntax and semantics of Learning Object Metadata, defined as the attributes required to fully and adequately describe a learning object. Within the metadata description relations to the Software Engineering (SE) domain ontology are coded. We distinguish between two types of references: references describing the learned concept(s) after using the LE and the references listing the prerequisite concept(s) for using this LE, i.e., knowledge that should be known before using the LE. The ontology consists of key SE-concepts (i.e., keywords) that are connected by relations such as: *is-a*, *part-of*, *consumes*, *produces*, etc.

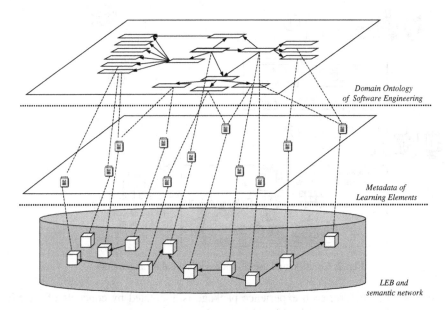

Fig. 1. Learning elements and their relations

4.4 Creation Process of Micro-didactical Arrangements

By providing a set of educational goals, a learning element taxonomy, and their classi-fication to knowledge types, we are now able to describe the process of creating a micro-didactical arrangement.

After the occurrence of a problem during daily work (see step 1 in Fig. 2), the user searches for suitable experiences in the repository to solve the problem. The retrieved and selected experience is forwarded to a pedagogical agent (see step 2). The user selects a learning goal by taking the decision on which level she or he wants to acquire knowledge. The pedagogical agent selects an appropriate pattern from the pattern base (PB) according to the type of experience, i.e., technology, process or product package, and the selected learning goal. Patterns are instances from an instructional model that is based on the 4C/ID approach introduced by Merriënboer et al [21]. The focus of this model is on learning task-specific skills. We apply the model for enabling the construction of individual cognitive schemata and to ensure the applicability of experience related knowledge into practice. According to the selected learning goal and the experience type, learning tasks are selected to learn necessary skills for applying the experience.

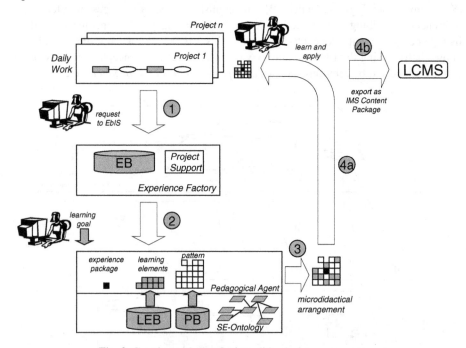

Fig. 2. Creation and use of micro-didactical arrangements

As described before, each experience package is annotated by concepts of the SE domain ontology. The agent is able to retrieve LE's that refer to the same concepts as the experience package and to infer prerequisite LE's by using the metadata description of the LE's. Then, the agent inserts the experience and the LE's into the pattern (see step 3). The agent uses the rhetoric-didactical relations, selects and sequences the LEs according to the selected learning tasks. The produced micro-didactical arrangement is provided to the user (see step 4a). The arrangement supports explorative learning in a cyclical way and the construction of cognitive schemata. The package experience is the central element of the arrangement and the trigger for learning. Depending on the selected goal, the user can decide which learning task to take first, i.e., whether he or she wants to acquire background knowledge (basics) first, or to get an orientation in the SE domain by browsing a graphical representation of the ontology, or to read examples and to try parts of them in practice. The learner can decide whether the appropriate knowledge level is reached that is prerequisite for understanding or applying the experience package. An option is, to make the micro-didactical arrangement conform to the *Sharable Content Object Reference Model* (SCORM) and to export it as IMS Content Package in order to make it available to conventional Learning Content Management Systems (LCMS) (see step 4b). SCORM is a reference model for learning content and provides the framework and detailed implementation reference that enables content, technology, and systems using SCORM to 'talk' to each other, thus ensuring interoperability, re-usability and manageability [2].

5 Summary and Future Work

In this paper we stated the barriers when people are learning from expert knowledge from a cognitive and didactical point of view. We propose an approach that enables novices and practitioners to learn from packaged expert knowledge, by providing a set of learning goals, a taxonomy for learning elements, and an agent who combines learning elements with experiences to micro-didactical learning arrangements according to an instructional model. The advantages of this approach are twofold: first, the applicability of experience packages increases by embedding the experience into a learning arrangements; second, the application of the experience and the new gained skills deepens the learning effect and strengthens the cognitive schemata.

Future work will focus on further developing and evaluating educational patterns in practice and using the results for adapting the instructional model that is used by the agent for creating patterns. Skill taxonomies and learning tasks will be developed that enforce the construction of cognitive schemata for the SE domain. Another issue will be to observe current development of e-learning standards and specifications to ensure the interoperability of micro-didactical arrangements with LCMS.

References

1. Abran A., Bourque P., Dupuis R., MooreDonald J. W.: Guide to the Software Engineering Body of Knowledge (SWEBOK). IEEE Press, Piscataway (NJ). Retrieved on 2004/02/28, http://www.swebok.org/
2. ADL: Sharable Content Object Reference Model (SCORM) Version 2004, (2004), Retrieved 2004/02/20, http://www.adlnet.org
3. Anderson, J. R.: Kognitive Psychologie. Spektrum der Wissenschaft, Heidelberg, (1988)
4. Anderson, J. R.; Rules of the mind. Hillsdale, Erlbaum, New York (1993)
5. Basili, V.R., Caldiera, G., Rombach, D.: Experience Factory. In Marciniak, J.J. (ed.), Encyclopedia of Software Engineering, John Wiley & Sons, vol 1, (1994), 469–476
6. Bergmann R.: Experience Management: Foundations, Development Methodology, and Internet-Based Applications. Springer, (2002)
7. Bloom B. S., Engelhart, M. D., Furst, E. J., Hill, W. H., Krathwohl, D. R.: Taxonomy of educational objectives: The classification of educational goals: Handbook 1 cognitive domain. Longmans, Green and Company, New York (1956)

8. Efimova, L., Swaak, J., Converging Knowledge Management, Training and e-learning: Scenarios to make it work. Journal of Universal Computer Science, vol. 9, no. 6 (2003), 571-578
9. Efimova, L., Swaak, J.: KM and (e)-learning: towards an integral approach? Proc. KMSS02, EKMF, Sophia Antipolis (2002), 63-69
10. Enns, C. Z.: Integrating Separate and Connected Knowing: The Experiential Learning Model. Teaching of Psychology 20(1), (1993), 7-13
11. Ericsson, K. A., Krampe, R. T., Tesch-Römer, C.: The role of deliberate practice in the acquisition of expert performance. Psychological review 100, (1993), 363-406
12. Fitts, P. M., Posner, M. I.: Human performance. Brooks Cole, Belmont, CA (1967)
13. Gagne, R. M., Briggs, L. J., Wager, W. W.: Principles of instructional design. (3rd ed.). Holt, Rinehart and Winston, Incorporated, New York (1988)
14. IEEE Learning Technology Standards Committee: Learning Object Metadata Standard. Retrieved on 2004/02/26, http://ltsc.ieee.org/wg12/
15. Jedlitschka A.,Nick M.: Software Engineering Knowledge Repositories. In Empirical Methods and Studies in Software Engineering:Experiences from ESERNET, (2003),55-80
16. Krathwohl, D. R., Bloom, B. S., Masia, B. B.: Taxonomy of educational objectives: The classification of educational goals. Handbook ii, Affective domain, David McKay Company, Incorporated, New York (1964)
17. Lawton G.: Knowledge Management: Ready for Prime Time? Computer, vol. 34, no. 2, (2001), 12–14
18. Mädche, A.: -VISION- A roadmap Toward Next Generation Knowledge Management. Presentation, Prague, VISION EU Project, IST-2002-38513, (2002), Retrieved on 2004/02/20, http://km.aifb.uni-karlsruhe.de/fzi/presentations/docs/1035178906.ppt
19. Mann W. C., Thomson S. A.: Rhetorical Structure Theory: A Theory of Text Organization. Technical Report RS-87-190, Information Science Institute, USC ISI, USA (1987)
20. Meder, N.: Didaktische Ontologien, Retrieved on 2004/02/21, http://www.l-3.de/de/literatur/download/did.pdf
21. Merriënboer van, J. J. G., Clark, R. E., & de Croock, M. B.: Blueprints for complex learning: The 4C/ID* model. Educational Technology, Research and Development, 50(2), (2002)
22. Rus, I., Lindvall, M.: Knowledge Management in Software Engineering. IEEE Software, May/June (2002), 26-38
23. Secchi, P., Ciaschi, R., Spence, D.: A Concept for an ESA lessons learned system. In P. Secchi (Eds.), Proceedings of Alerts and LL: An Effective way to prevent failures and-problems, Tech. Rep. WPP-167, Noordwijk, The Netherlands: ESTEC, (1999), pp. 57-61
24. Steinacker A., Seeberg C., Fischer S., Steinmetz R.: MultiBook: Meta-data for Webbased Learning Systems. Proceedings of the 2nd International Conference on New Learning Technologies, (1999)
25. Tautz C., Customizing Software Engineering Experience Management Systems to Organizational Needs. PhD thesis, University of Kaiserslautern, Germany, 2000. Fraunhofer IRB Verlag, (2001)
26. Tennyson, R. D., Rasch, M.: Linking Cognitive learning theory to instructional prescriptions. Instructional Science, 17, (1988), 369-385
27. Weber, R., Aha, D.W., Becerra-Fernandez, I.: Intelligent lessons learned systems. International Journal of Expert Systems Research & Applications, Vol. 20, No. 1, (2001), 17-34

Learning Software Maintenance Organizations

Kleiber D. de Sousa, Nicolas Anquetil, and Káthia M. de Oliveira

UCB – Catholic University of Brasilia
SGAN 916 Módulo B – Av. W5 Norte
Brasilia – DF – 70.790-160, Brazil
kleiber@fnde.gov.br, {kathia,anquetil}@ucb.br

Abstract. Developing and maintaining software systems is a knowledge intensive task. One needs knowledge of the application domain of the software, the
problem the system solves, the requirements for this problem, the architecture
of the system and how the different parts fit together, how the system interacts
with its environment, etc. More often than not, this knowledge is not documented
and lives only in the head of the software engineers. It is, therefore, volatile and
an organization may repeatedly pay professionals to rediscover a knowledge it
previously acquired and lost. In recognition of this fact, knowledge management techniques such as Postmortem Analysis are being used to help salvage
this knowledge. Traditionally, Postmortem Analysis has been applied at the end
of software development projects with a focus on organizational aspects such as
how to improve the execution of a process. In this paper, we present the application of Postmortem Analysis in a new context: for software maintenance projects.
We also apply it, not only for process improvement, but to discover knowledge
on the software maintained itself.

1 Introduction

To maintain legacy software systems, software engineers need knowledge on many different domains: application domain, system's architecture, particular algorithms used,
past and new requirements, experience on the execution of a particular software process, etc. To help managing this knowledge, techniques such as the Postmortem Analysis (PMA) are starting to be used in software projects [13, 3]. PMA is a technique by
which a team gather after the end of a project to try to identify which aspects of the
project worked well and should be repeated, and which worked badly and should be
avoided [16]. These positive and negative aspects of the project must then be recorded
to help in the future projects. PMA may be used for example in the Experience Factory
[2] to improve a software process.

A study of the literature (see for example [3, 15, 16]) shows that PMA has been
mainly used in software development projects with a particular view on process improvement. In this paper, we propose to use the same technique for software maintenance projects. Studies (e.g. cited in [13, 14], or [6, 7]) show that during software
maintenance, software engineers use different kinds of knowledge: knowledge about
the software process, but also about the system being maintained, the organization using the software, etc. Based on these facts we propose to use PMA, not only to improve
the maintenance process, but also to gain more knowledge on the system maintained.

G. Melnik and H. Holz (Eds.): LSO 2004, LNCS 3096, pp. 67–77, 2004.

In the following sections we first introduce Postmortem Analysis and its use in software engineering (section 2), then we discuss the importance of knowledge in software maintenance (section 3). In section 4, we present our approach of maintenance Postmortem Analysis. Finally, in section 5 we present our conclusions and ongoing works.

2   Postmortem Analysis

2.1   Definition

It is popular wisdom that one should not make the same mistake twice[1]. The same applies to organizations, where one member should not repeat another member's mistake. To avoid repeating mistakes, software engineers may use knowledge management techniques to help them identify what went well or wrong in the execution of their daily work.

A well advocated knowledge management technique is the Postmortem Analysis (PMA). A PMA simply consists in "[gathering] all participants from a project that is ongoing or just nished and ask them to identify which aspects of the project worked well and should be repeated, which worked badly and should be avoided, and what was merely 'OK' but leaves room for improvement" [16]. The term Postmortem implies that the analysis is done after the end of a project, although, as recognized by Stalhane in the preceding quote, it may also be performed during a project, after a signi cant mark has been reached.

There are many different ways of doing a PMA, for example [8] differentiate their proposal, a "lightweight postmortem review", from more heavy processes as used in large companies such as Microsoft, or Apple Computer. A PMA may also be more or less structured, and focused or "catch all". One of the great advantages of the technique is that it may be applied on a small scale with little resources (e.g. a two hours meeting with all the members of a small project team, plus one hour from the project manager to formalize the results). Depending on the number of persons participating in the PMA, it may require different levels of structuring, from a relatively informal meeting where people simply gather and discuss on the project, to a more formal process as proposed in [4].

It is important to remember that postmortem analysis is not sufficient to form a complete politic of knowledge management (also known as Experience Factory [2] in the context of software engineering). There are various steps implied in knowledge management: collecting the data (experiences), analyzing it, recording it, disseminating the knowledge, etc. In this framework, postmortem analysis is mainly a useful tool to elicit the knowledge, i.e. to discover the relevant pieces of experience obtain from a project. Other important steps as "packaging" of the knowledge (record the experience in a reusable form), or disseminating it, are not considered by the PMA.

2.2   Postmortem Analysis in Software Engineering

As already mentioned, Postmortem Analysis is a commonly recommended practice for software engineering projects [13, 3].

---

[1] "Anyone can make a mistake. A fool insists on repeating it." — Robertine Maynard

Three facts emerged as near constants in the articles reporting use of PMA:

- It is mostly used for process or managerial improvement.
- It is mostly used in software development context.
- It is mostly used at the end of projects.

In the literature, PMAs are mainly viewed as process improvement tools. For example, Stalhane et al. start their paper [16] with the affirmation: "An obvious way to improve a software development process is to learn from past mistakes." Other authors [3, 8, 11, 15, 17] assume the same point of view, either explicitly or implicitly.

In the same way that PMA is always related to process improvement, it is always cited in the context of software development (either explicitly or implicitly). For example, Kerth [11] in discussing whether to call the activity Postmortem ("after death") Analysis or Postpartum ("after birth") Analysis, argues: "a software effort is more like a birthing experience than dying experience — after all the goal is to create something new". This view mainly holds for development projects, if we consider maintenance, particularly corrective maintenance, the goal may not be to create anything new.

Finally, PMA appears to be mostly performed at the end of projects (hence the name). One problem with this approach is that for long projects, the team only remembers "the large problems that are already discussed — things that have gone really bad" [16], however, despite recognizing the problem, the article does not propose any specific solution. Another problem raised by Yourdon [17] is the high turnover which may cause key team members to disappear, with their own experience, before the end of the project. The solution proposed (but not described) by Yourdon is to conduct mini-postmorta at the end of each phase of the projects. One of the objectives of this paper is to describe how we implement Yourdon's idea of intermediary mini-postmorta.

3 Knowledge for Software Maintenance

Maintenance results from the necessity of correcting errors in a system (20% of the maintenance projects according to [14]), or of adapting software systems to an ever changing environment. In most cases, it can be neither avoided nor delayed much: one has little control on the promulgation of new laws or on the concurrence's progresses. Organizations must keep pace with these changes, and this usually means, modifying the software that supports their business activities. Lehman [12] established in his first law of software evolution that "a program that is used, undergoes continual change or becomes progressively less useful." Software maintenance is not a problem in the sense that one cannot and should not try to solve it. Software maintenance is a fact and a necessity.

One of the main problems in software maintenance is that of loss of knowledge on the systems being maintained. Software maintenance is a knowledge intensive activity. Maintainers need knowledge of the system they work on, of its application domain, of the organization using it, of past and present software engineering practices, of different programming languages (in their different versions), programming skills, etc.

Among these different knowledge needs, knowledge about the system maintained emerge as a prominent necessity. Studies report that 40% to 60% of the software maintenance effort is devoted to understanding the system [13, p.475], [14, p.35]. Jørgensen and Sjøberg [10] showed that sheer maintenance experience is not enough to reduce the frequency of major unexpected problems after a maintenance, whereas application experience does.

In a preceding study [6, 7] we analyzed the different kinds of knowledge used by maintainers. We first defined an ontology on the knowledge used in software maintenance. This ontology is composed of 98 concepts divided into 5 sub-ontologies:

Skills: Concepts of various computer science technologies, languages, tools, etc.

Application domain: Concepts of a high level representation of a domain that can be instantiated for any possible domain (it contains concepts, properties of these concepts, tasks and restrictions).

Modification: Concepts about the maintenance activities, resources used, modification requests (and their causes), or input/output artifacts. This is the sub-ontology that deals more specifically with concept relating to the maintenance process.

System: Concepts on software systems, their artifacts, hardware where the system is installed, its users, or the technologies used in its development.

Organization structure: Concepts on an organization, directives it defined, its composing units where different functions are performed by human resources.

We then investigated the usefulness of these concepts studying maintainers while they were maintaining a system. Table 1 shows the detailed results where one may observe that all kinds of concepts are used, not limited to the maintenance process (which is one of the concepts in the Modification sub-ontology). The study also showed that concepts from the system and skill sub-ontologies are among the most frequently used (not shown in the table).

Table 1. Number of concepts used in software maintenance experiments.

	Concepts		
	Identified	Used	
Skill	38	26	68%
Application domain	4	2	50%
Modification	30	23	77%
System	23	13	57%
Organizational structure	3	3	100%

Concurrently to this knowledge necessity, legacy software systems are known to suffer from a chronicle lack of documentation. This lack results in suboptimal maintenances, gradually deteriorating the system's structure (Lehman's second law of software evolution [12]). Due to this lost of structure, the system becomes each time more complex to understand and modify which leads to more difficult maintenance. It is therefore important to discover this knowledge, to record it, and to make it available to the software maintainers in their activities.

Another closely related work by Deridder [5] proposes an ontology and a tool to populate this ontology that would help record important concepts, association, etc. during the development of a software system. This store of information would then be used to help maintenance. The ontology defined appears to be a very high level one. Deridder objective seems more to focus on the representation of the knowledge and possibly automatic reasoning on it than on the actual extraction and use of this knowledge to help maintenance.

4 Software Maintenance Postmortem

We saw, in section 2, that PMA, in software engineering, has been mainly used (a) in the context of software development, (b) at the end of the projects, and (c) to collect lessons learned on the process (for process improvement). We also saw, in section 3, that software maintenance is a knowledge intensive activity with a particular emphasis on knowledge on the software system maintained and its application domain. We propose, therefore, to use the PMA technique to help manage the knowledge learned during maintenance projects. This knowledge may be on the maintenance process (how it was executed, what tools or technique worked best), or the particular system maintained (how subsystems are organized, or what components implement a given requirement).

To define this new PMA model, we had to consider three important aspects that will be detailed in the following subsections: (i) when to insert PMA during the execution of a typical maintenance process, (ii) what knowledge should we look for in the PMA, and (iii) how to best extract this knowledge from the software engineers.

4.1 When to Perform PMA during Maintenance

Maintenance projects may be of widely varying size, they may be short in the correction of a very localized error, or very long in the implementation of a new complex functionality, or correction of a very diluted problem (e.g. the Y2K bug). For small projects, one may easily conduct a PMA at the end of the project without risking loosing (forgetting) important lessons. But for larger projects (as proposed by Yourdon [17]), it is best to conduct several PMAs during the project so as to capture important knowledge before it becomes so integrated in the participants' mental models that they cannot clearly remember the details.

To identify the points, in a maintenance project, where we could perform PMA, we used the ISO 12207 [1] maintenance process. It is a basic process for maintenance projects with the following activities: process implementation, problem and modification analysis, modification implementation, maintenance review/acceptance, migration, and software retirement.

Process implementation: The activity includes tasks to document the maintenance process, establish procedures for modification requests, establish the configuration management process, ...
Problem and modification analysis: The activity includes tasks to replicate the problem, analyze it, develop options to solve it, and obtain approval for one option.
Modification implementation: The activity includes tasks to implement the modification such as: requirements analysis, architectural design, detailed design, coding, and testing.

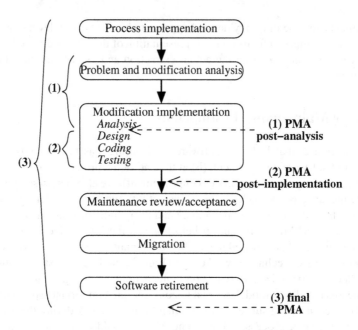

Fig. 1. Overview of the ISO 12207 Maintenance process [1] with the intermediary and final PMAs and their respective scope.

Maintenance review/acceptance: The activity includes tasks to review the modification with the authorizing organization and obtain approval for it.

Migration: The activity includes tasks to plan the migration of the modified system, notify when, why, and how the migration will happen, train the users, review the impact of the new system, etc.

Software retirement: The activity includes tasks similar to the preceding activity but focused on the old system to be retired instead of the new one to be implanted.

To be of use, the intermediary PMAs should be conducted at the end of significant marks, evenly distributed during the project. In a large project, analysis of the modification (how it may be done, what parts it would impact, how to fit it in the existing architecture), and actual implementation (detailed design, coding, testing) would consume the major part of the project time, while other activities as validation or migration should be shorter. We identified two main points where one could perform the intermediary PMAs (see also Figure 1):

– After the analysis of the modification which includes the first two activities (Process implementation and Problem and modification analysis) and the initial tasks of the third activity (Modification implementation: requirement analysis).
– After the implementation of the modification which includes the rest of the third activity (Modification implementation).

A third PMA would then be conducted at the end of the project to review all its aspects and the most recent activities no yet considered in the intermediary PMAs.

Other points where to perform PMAs could be considered, for example the important Maintenance review/acceptance activity. However, we considered that a PMA after this activity would probably be very close in time after the second PMA (post-implementation) and before the third one (final), therefore duplicating the effort for little return.

4.2   What Knowledge to Look for in Maintenance

Depending on the specific scope (see Figure 1) of each PMAs (intermediary or final), we may hope to discover information on specific issues. For example, information on the testing techniques used will presumably be best discovered during the second PMA (post implementation).

It is clear from previous work on PMA, that it is a successful technique to discover lessons learned from the execution of a process and thereby improve its next execution. During each intermediary PMA, we will seek new information on the tasks and activities that occurred before this PMA. The final PMA will look for information on the execution of the whole process.

However, we also wish to discover new knowledge learned on the system, its application domain, or other issues not related to the maintenance process. To identify what information we could hope to discover in each PMA, we considered the particular tasks reviewed in these PMAs as well as the list of concepts useful to software maintenance as defined in the ontology we proposed in an earlier work [6, 7] (see also section 3).

For example, the first PMA (post analysis, see Figure 1) occurs after: (i) the Process implementation activity, (ii) the Problem and modification analysis activity, and (iii) the Requirements analysis task from the Modification implementation activity.

In the Implementation process activity (i), the only task typically performed for each new maintenance project is to develop plans and procedures for conducting the activities of the project. To execute this task the manager usually takes into account his/her experience from previous projects with a similar domain, size, and team. The knowledge category we identified for this activity is, therefore, knowledge about the process execution, what tasks and activities are needed. This means that the first PMA should focus on discovering knowledge from this particular category.

The Problem and modification analysis activity (ii) starts when the maintainer analyzes the modification request to determine its impact on the organization, on the existing system, and on other systems that interacts with it (this is done considering the type of maintenance — corrective, adaptive, etc. —, the scope of the project — size, cost, time to modify —, and its criticality). From this analysis the maintainer defines options for implementing the modification. Based on the analysis report the manager estimates the effort to do the maintenance and sets the time limit for the project. With this information, s-he obtain approval to do the modification. The knowledge category we identified for this activity are: detailed knowledge on the modification request, how the impact analysis was performed, the different options developed for implementing the modification, the organizational structure (what parts of the organization uses the software), and how the time frame to implement the modification was defined and negotiated. We used the ontology of concept used in maintenance to identify specific concepts relating to the modification request and knowledge about the organization structure. This way, the first PMA may be focused to instantiate these particular concepts.

Finally, the Requirements analysis task (iii), part of the Modification implementation activity includes updating the system documentation related to the problem being solved. Performing this task, the maintainer uses specific requirement elicitation techniques and tools to better collect and register the user requirements. During this task, the maintainer should learn about different concepts of the domain, business rules, and also about who are the users and which parts of the organization uses the system and why. All this information should be captured in the PMA. We have therefore the following categories of knowledge for this task: knowledge on the documents and the software components modified, knowledge on the requirement elicitation techniques and tools used, and knowledge on the application domain itself. Again, the ontology on the concept used in maintenance helped us, for example by defining a taxonomy of all types of documentations of a system that can be changed during a maintenance.

The knowledge category to consider in the two other PMAs are defined similarly, based on the tasks and activity each PMA reviews. The list of knowledge categories may be consulted in Table 2, whereas examples of how we plan to discover information in each category is given in the next section.

Table 2. The three maintenance PMAs and the knowledge categories they focus on.

PMA	Knowledge category
(1) Post analysis	Details on the modification request
	Organizational structure using the software
	Options for implementing the modification
	Negotiation of time limit to do the modification
	Effort estimation for the modification
	Documents modified
	Requirement elicitation technique used
	Tools used
	Application domain
	Details on the requirements
(2) Post implementation	Programming languages & tools used
	Programming techniques used
	Software components modified
	Systems interrelationship
	Analysis/design inconsistencies
	Re-engineering opportunities detected
	Artifacts traceability
	Database design
	Design patterns used
	Testing technique used
	Process and support documentation modified
(3) final	Negotiations with other technological departments
	Modification monitoring
	Maintenance process
	Application of the PMAs

4.3 How to Perform PMA during Maintenance

Finally, we had to define a method that would help the software engineer remember all they could have learned in the various knowledge domain considered (process, system, application domain, ...). For this we decided to perform the PMAs in two steps: First, we designed a questionnaire as a means to pre-focus their mind on the bits of information we want to discover (i.e. the knowledge categories defined for each PMA in the previous section). This questionnaire is distributed among the software engineers that will participate in a PMA session. In a second step, we conduct a PMA session where the same topics are brought up again to effectively discover the lessons learned. The actual PMA session may take various forms (for example, see [16]): semistructured interviews, KJ session, using Ishikawa diagrams, or using a combination of the last two. The choice of the PMA session type depends on the facilitator of the PMA who may choose considering the team size, the importance of the maintenance, its size, etc.

...

Category: Negotiation of time limit to do the modification

- How was the time limit negotiated with the client? Do you think the method was satisfactory? Why?
- The time frame initially proposed by the client was realistic given the size of the modification? Why? Was it the result of a previous maintenance?

Category: Application domain

- What business concepts were involved in this maintenance?
- What business rules were involved in this maintenance?
- Did you discover any new requirement or application domain concept during this maintenance?
- If the modification request was due to a requirement modification, what law, measure, status, etc. caused the change of requirement? What is the context of the change?

...

Fig. 2. Excerpt of the post-analysis questionnaire.

The use of questionnaires is also recommended by Collier [4], or Humphrey [9, pp.185–96]. The questionnaires are composed of one or more questions for each category of knowledge defined for that PMA. Questions are also designed to instantiate the concepts defined in the ontology of knowledge used in maintenance. Figure 2 shows some questions from the PMA post analysis questionnaire. There are two possible uses of the questionnaires. They may be used only to revive the memory of the PMA participants on the various categories of knowledge sought. In this approach, the actual answers would not be considered in the PMA session. Another approach, that we actually used, is to use the answers to the questionnaires to help the facilitator focus the PMA session on the topics that appear most likely to bring new knowledge.

We have, thus far, experimented our proposal only with semi-structured interviews, although KJ sessions were already used in a different context in the same organization. Semi-structured interviews are a systematic way to follow an agenda and allow the interviewer to find out more information on any issue that was not adequately answered in the questionnaire. The results have been showing some interesting knowledge bits, as the necessity to involve technical counterparts in the negotiation with the client, or the identification of a requirement which changed repeatedly.

5 Conclusion

To discover, document, and disseminate new knowledge, gained during software projects, is considered a fundamental activity for software organizations trying to improve their practice. For software maintenance organizations this involves uncovering not only the lessons learned on the software processes executions, but also the knowledge acquired on the legacy systems maintained, their application domains, the organizations that use them, etc.

In this paper we presented an approach that uses Postmortem Analysis (PMA) at the end of maintenance projects to discover all this knowledge. We showed that PMA is traditionally used (a) in the context of software development, (b) at the end of the projects, and (c) to collect lessons learned for process improvement. We designed a PMA approach (a) for maintenance projects, (b) with PMA sessions during and at the end of long maintenance projects, and (c) that allows to collect knowledge on other topics than the software process.

Future plans for the research involves deploying our PMA approach on a larger scale in a governmental agency for testing, and defining a dissemination method that would allow to take better advantage of the knowledge gained.

Acknowledgment

This work is part of the "Knowledge Management in Software Engineering" project, which is supported by the CNPq, an institution of the Brazilian government for scientific and technological development.

References

1. ISO/IEC 12207. *Information technology — Software life cycle processes*. ISO/IEC, 1995.
2. Victor R. Basili, Gianluigi Caldiera, and H. Dieter Rombach. *Encyclopedia of Software Engineering*, volume 1, chapter The Experience Factory, pages 469–76. John Wiley & Sons, 1994.
3. Andreas Birk, Torgeir Dingsøyr, and Tør Stålhane. Postmortem: Never leave a project without it. *IEEE Software*, 19(3):43–45, may-jun. 2002.
4. Bonnie Collier, Tom DeMarco, and Peter Fearey. A defined process for postmortem review. *IEEE Software*, 13(4):65–72, jul.-aug. 1996.
5. Dirk Deridder. Facilitating software maintenance and reuse activities with a concept-oriented approach. Technical report, Programming Technology Lab - Vrije Universiteit Brussel, may 2002.

6. Marcio Greyck Batista Dias, Nicolas Anquetil, and Káthia Marçal de Oliveira. Organizing the knowledge used in software maintenance. In Ulrich Reimer, Andreas Abecker, Steffen Staab, and Gerd Stumme, editors, *WM2003: Professionnelles Wissensmanagement – Erfahrungen und Visionen*, number ISBN 3-88579-357-1, pages 65–72. Lecture Notes in Informatics, Gesellschaft für Informatik, Bonn, April, 3rd 2003. Presented at the Learning Software Organizations Workshop.
7. Marcio Greyck Batista Dias, Nicolas Anquetil, and Káthia Marçal de Oliveira. Organizing the knowledge used in software maintenance. *Journal of Universal Computer Science*, 9(7):641–58, 2003.
8. Torgeir Dingsøyr, Nils Brede. Moe, and Nytrø Øystein. Augmenting experience reports with lightweight postmortem reviews. *Lecture Notes in Computer Science*, 2188:167–181, 2001. PROFES 2001, Berlin, Germany.
9. Watts S. Humphrey. *Introduction to the Team Software Process*. SEI Series in Software Engineering. Addison-Wesley Longman, Inc., 1999.
10. Magne Jørgensen and Dag I.K. Sjøberg. Impact of experience on maintnenance skills. *Journal of Software Maintenance: Research and Practice*, 14(2):123–46, Mar. 2002.
11. Norman L. Kerth. An approach to postmorta, postparta & post project review. On Lione: http://c2.com/doc/ppm.pdf. Last accessed on: 06/01/2003.
12. M.M. Lehman. Programs, life cycles and the laws of software evolution. *Proceedings of the IEEE*, 68(9):1060–76, sept. 1980.
13. Shari L. Pfleeger. What software engineering can learn from soccer. *IEEE Software*, 19(6):64–65, nov.-dec. 2002.
14. Thomas M. Pigoski. *Practical Software Maintenance*. John Wiley & Sons, Inc., 1996.
15. Linda Rising. Patterns in postmortems. In *Proceedings of the Twenty-Third Annual International Computer Software and Applications Conference*, pages 314–15. IEEE, IEEE Comp. Soc. Press, Oct. 25–26 1999.
16. Tor Stålhane, Torgeir Dingsøyr, Geir K. Hanssen, and Nils Brede Moe. Post mortem – an assessement of two approaches. In *Proceedings of the European Software Process Improvement 2001 (EuroSPI 2001)*, oct. 10–12 2001.
17. Ed Yourdon. Minipostmortems. *COMPUTERWORLD*, march 19 2001.

How to Manage Knowledge
in the Software Maintenance Process

Oscar M. Rodríguez[1], Aurora Vizcaíno[2], Ana I. Martínez[1],
Mario Piattini[2], and Jesús Favela[1]

[1] CICESE, Computer Science Department, México
{orodrigu,martinea,favela}@cicese.mx
[2] Alarcos Research Group. University of Castilla-La Mancha,
Escuela Superior de Informática, España
{Aurora.Vizcaino,Mario.Piattini}@uclm.es

Abstract. The software maintenance process involves a lot of effort and costs. In fact, this stage is considered the most expensive of the software development life-cycle. Moreover, during maintenance a considerable amount of information needs to be managed. This information often comes from diverse and distributed sources such as the products to be maintained, the people who work in this process, and the activities performed to update the software. However, very few software companies use knowledge management techniques to efficiently manage this information. Appropriate knowledge management would help software companies improve performance, control costs and decrease effort by taking advantage of previous solutions that could be reused to avoid repeating previous mistakes. This work presents a multiagent system designed to manage the information and knowledge generated during the software maintenance process; using web technologies to support this management. The system has different types of agents, each devoted to a particular type of information. Agents use different reasoning techniques to generate new knowledge from previous information and to learn from their own experience. Thereby the agents become experts in the type of knowledge they are responsible for. Additionally, agents communicate with each other to share information and knowledge.

Keywords: Knowledge management, software maintenance, agents

1 Introduction

Knowledge is fast becoming the key to survival and competitive advantage [12]. Many innovative companies have long appreciated the value of knowledge to enhance their products and customer services. Therefore, a huge investment is being done in the field of knowledge management, for example, Berztiss in [5] claims that by the year 2004 the cost of knowledge management is expected to reach USD 10,200,000,000.

The software organizations, encouraged by the idea of improving costs, schedules and quality of their products, and improved customer satisfaction, are also interested in knowledge management [22]. Some reasons of this interest are that:

G. Melnik and H. Holz (Eds.): LSO 2004, LNCS 3096, pp. 78–87, 2004.

a) Software Engineering is a knowledge-intensive work where the main capital is what has been called the "intellectual capital". Unfortunately, the owners of this intellectual capital are often the employees instead of being the company as we might expect. Employees, from their experience, obtain tacit knowledge, which is richer and more valuable than explicit knowledge, but that cannot be easily expressed or communicated [13]. Thereby, software organizations depend greatly on knowledgeable employees because they are the key to a project's success.

b) Software development is a constantly changing process. Many people work in different phases, activities and projects. Knowledge in software engineering is diverse and its proportions immense and steadily growing [15]. Organizations often have problems identifying the resources, localizations and use of knowledge.

Both reasons are also applicable to a specific process of the software life cycle: this is software maintenance where the problems mentioned above could be even more significant. Maintainers have to face legacy software, written by people from other units, which often has little or no documentation describing the features of the software [24].

Thus, a well-known issue that complicates the maintenance process is the scarce and distributed documentation that exists related to a specific software system, or even if detailed documentation was produced when the original system was developed, it is seldom updated as the system evolves.

Storing knowledge helps to reduce these problems since it decreases dependency on employees' cognition because at least some of their expert knowledge has been retained or made explicit. Moreover, storing good solutions to problems or lessons learned avoids repeating mistakes and increases productivity and the likelihood of further success [22]. However, for information to be usable it needs to be modelled, structured, generalised and stored in a reusable form, to allow for effective retrieval [1].

This work describes how to manage distributed knowledge and information generated during the software maintenance process in order to improve maintainers' work and efficiency. The content of this paper is organized as follows: Section 2 outlines the tasks performed during the software maintenance process and justifies why knowledge management should be used in this process. Section 3 presents a multi-agent system designed to encourage and facilitate the reuse of previous experience in software maintenance organizations, using a global web repository. Finally, conclusions and future work are presented in Section 4.

2 Software Maintenance

Many studies [17,19] have demonstrated that most of the overall expenses incurred during the life-cycle of a software product occur during the maintenance process. During this process different types of maintenance could be required: corrective, perceptive, adaptive or preventive. Each type of maintenance has its own features but all of them follow a similar process, summarized in Figure 1; the maintenance engineer receives the requirements that the modification should fulfil. Then, s/he identifies which parts of the system should be modified, which modules could be affected by this modification and plan what activities have to be performed. The maintainer, unconsciously, takes advantage of his/her experience to carry out all of these tasks. And, in the case of his/her experience not being enough, the engineer would consult other resources that are often two: a person who has already solved a similar problem or has worked with that software previously or the engineer analyses the source code which means to dedicate a lot of time to this activity.

To carried out the present work, two case studies were performed [20]. In these studies, maintenance engineers were observed performing their work. The study helped us to identify scenarios that show that on many occasions, organizations had documents or people with the information or knowledge necessary to support or help other colleagues in their activities, but either the former did not know what the latter was working on, or the latter did not know that other documents or people could have provided useful information to help them to complete the assignment.

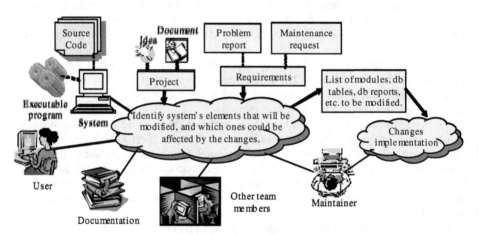

Fig. 1. Basic aspects of the process that the maintenance engineer performs at the moment of implementing changes on the system, as well as the knowledge sources that help him to do these tasks.

This fact has already been commented on by other authors, such as Szulanski [23] who found that the number one barrier to knowledge sharing was "ignorance": the sub-units are ignorant of the knowledge that exists in the organization, or the sub-units possessing the knowledge are ignorant of the fact that another sub-unit needs such knowledge. Sometimes the organization itself is not aware of the location of the pockets of knowledge or expertise [14].

After studying the results of the case studies, the question of how to help the maintainers to identify knowledge sources that could help them to carry out their work, or to improve it by decreasing costs, time or effort, arose. The scenarios identified in these studies also showed us how a knowledge management system can support some of the necessities that maintainers have while they perform their job. The analysis of these scenarios and the findings of the studies provided some basic characteristics that a knowledge management system to support software maintenance teams should fulfill. These characteristics were used to define a multi-agent architecture which is described in the next section.

3 A Multi-agent System to Manage Knowledge during the Software Maintenance Process

A knowledge management "program" in an organization often consists of three parts: a strategy, processes and tools. Next we describe how we tackle these three aspects in order to obtain a suitable knowledge management approach.

The knowledge management strategy in organizations can be defined based on their goals, and how they proceed to achieve them. Software development organizations are concerned with controlling costs, meeting deadlines or/and improving quality. To achieve this they look for means to facilitate the work of their software engineers [7]. In our case, we are interested in a strategy based on making easier for maintenance engineers to find knowledge and information that could facilitate their work. Moreover, we think that by reusing proven good solutions or lessons learned, engineers will increase their expertise and their work will have more quality with less costs and effort.

The second part consists of *processes* or organizational activities to assist in knowledge management. These will usually be methods for collecting and distributing knowledge. We consider that the best option to tackle this aspect is to have a separate section of the organization in charge of these processes such as an Experience Factory (a term introduced by Basili et al in [2]). Otherwise, we would have to face different problems such as how to motivate maintenance engineers to capture their knowledge into the system and manage it and, of course, how to reward this work.

Finally, there are many *tools* to support knowledge management and different classifications of them. A generic classification to information retrieval applications that could be also applied to knowledge management tools consist in dividing these into "active" or "passive" [8]. The first are those that notify users when it is likely that they will require some kind of knowledge without their request. Passive tools require a user to actively seek knowledge without any system support.

We consider active tools more appropriated for the software maintenance domain since, as was previously mentioned, maintainers seldom know all the knowledge that the organization has, and for this reason, they do not know what they can or should search for. Therefore, the system should automatically show information that can be useful for a maintainer who is working on a specific project.

On the other hand, thanks to the huge use of The World Wide Web as a medium for the dissemination of information, a new branch of Software Engineering has arisen, named Web Engineering, concerned with establishing sound principles, techniques, and tools for the development and maintenance of systems, services and applications over the Web.

As the web becomes the preferred medium for the deployment of software applications CASE tools are migrating to the web and several others have been developed. The use of the web as a platform for the support of software development offers several advantages:

- Ubiquitous access. Web repositories can be accessed from any computer connected to the Internet, including portable devices.
- Simple integration of tools. The web is based on simple, open protocols that can be easily integrated in CASE tools to enable their interoperability. At the lowest level of integration a tool can export content to HTML or semantically richer XML documents.

- Support for distributed software development. Large-scale software systems are increasingly being developed by distributed teams of specialists that need to communicate and coordinate their activities. The web offers a simple middleware for the deployment of workflow and groupware tools that support collaboration.

Because of this, we chose web servers as repositories for products and processes information. The centralized storage of this information facilitates configuration management, quality control, project tracking, and the management of maintenance requirements.

Applications manipulating Web data require both, documents or information retrieved from the Web, and metadata about this information. In order to specify and manage meta-data we used the standard MOF proposed by the OMG [16] and described in [24].

Based on the aspects just discussed and the findings of the case study presented in [20], we have identified the following requirements for our system:

- The tool should be active.
- The tool should support access to different and distributed sources of knowledge.
- The tool should support the search for solutions to similar problems and lessons learned from distributed locations (web repository).
- The tool should support the identification of modules or files which could be affected by the changes performed.
- The tool should enable the integration with other CASE tools and other software maintenance repositories.

3.1 Architecture of the System

In order to design the multi-agent architecture the MESSAGE (Methodology for Engineering Systems of Software agents) [6] methodology was used. It proposes different level of analysis. At level 1 analysis focuses on the system itself, identifying the types of agents and roles, which are described in the next paragraphs. The architecture has five main types of agents (see Figure 2): staff, product, client, project and directory agents.

The *staff agent* handles information related to the activities that the maintenance engineer (ME) performs. Its main role is to provide support to the ME in the accomplishment of his job. It monitors the ME activities, and based on this, requests the KMA to search for knowledge sources that can help the ME to perform his job. The staff agent collaborates with the KMA and KSMA that are located in its same container, and with the product and project agents that are in charge of the products and projects to which the ME is assigned.

The *product agent*, as the name suggests, manages information related with a product, including its maintenance requests, the staff members that are assigned to the product, the roles that they play, and the main elements that integrate the products (documentation, source code, databases, etc.). There is one product agent per product to be maintained. The main role of this agent is to monitor the activities that the staff members perform on each element that integrate the product. For example, which elements they consult or modify, which maintenance requests or error reports they manage, etc. In this way, the product agent has knowledge that can be used to identify, for instance, who is modifying or consulting some element of the product at each moment. This information can be used to infer which staff members know about each element of the product, also the level of knowledge they have about that particular element. To accomplish its job, this agent collaborates with several other agents, such as: the KMA and KSMA (located in its same container), the project agents that are in charge of the maintenance requests or error reports related to the product, and the staff agents of the MEs assigned to the product.

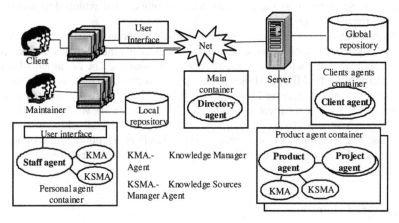

Fig. 2. Agent based architecture for a software maintenance knowledge management tool.

There is one *project agent* per project. The project agent has information about the tasks that must be performed to attend a maintenance request or error report, the time that these tasks could consume, the staff members assigned to them, the state of each task, etc. The main role of this agent is to monitor the progress of the project, informing to each staff member the tasks that they must perform. To complete its job, this agent collaborates mainly with the staff agents of the MEs assigned to the project.

The *client agent* manages information related to the maintenance requests or error reports performed by one client. There is one agent of this kind per client. Its main role is to help the client when he sends an error report or a maintenance request, directing it to the corresponding product agent. Another important activity of this agent is to inform to the client of the state of the maintenance requests or error reports sent previously by him. To do these activities, this agent collaborates mainly with the product and project agents.

The *directory agent* manages information required by agents to know how to communicate with other agents that are active in the system. This agent knows the type, name, and direction of all active agents. Its main role is to control the different agents that are active in the system at each moment, to do this, the directory agent must communicate with the staff, client, product, and project agents.

Two auxiliary types of agents are considered in the architecture, the *Knowledge Manager Agent* (KMA) and the *Knowledge Source Manager Agent* (KSMA).

The KMA is in charge of providing support in the generation of knowledge and the search of knowledge sources. These kinds of agents are in charge of managing the knowledge base in the global web repository. The staff KMA generates new knowledge from the information obtained from the MEs in their daily work. For example, if a ME is modifying a program developed in the Java language, the KMA can infer that the ME has knowledge about this language, and, add his/her name to the knowledge base as a possible source of knowledge about Java. On the other hand, the product KMA generates knowledge related to the activities performed on the product. It could identify patterns on the modifications done to the different modules, for example, it could identifies if there are modules or documents that are modified or consulted when a specific module is modified, and in this way, it could detect which modules or programs can be affected by the changes done on others, and which documents are related with these last ones.

Finally, the KSMA has control over the knowledge sources, such as documents. It knows the physical location of those sources, as well as the mechanisms used to consult them. Its main role is to control the access to the sources. The documents located in the workspace of the MEs, or those that are part of a product, such as the system or user documentation, are accessed through this agent. The KSMA is also in charge of the recovery of documents located in places different from its workspace. If those documents are managed by another KSMA, the first KSMA should communicate with the last one to request the documents. These kinds of agents mainly collaborate with other KSMA, and with the staff or the product agents that are in its same container.

3.2 Agents Collaboration

As we mentioned before, agents must collaborate with others in order to complete their jobs. In this section we present two examples of how this occurs. The first example shows how the ME is informed about the tasks that he must perform in a project when he starts to work on it. As Figure 3 shows, when the staff agent requests to be registered in the directory, the directory agent identifies in which product (or products) is the ME working. Then, the directory agent informs to the product agent that the ME has been registered in the system. After that, the product agent identifies the projects to which the ME is assigned, and informs to the corresponding project agents that the ME is working on the system. Finally, the project agent informs to the staff agent the tasks that must be performed by the ME.

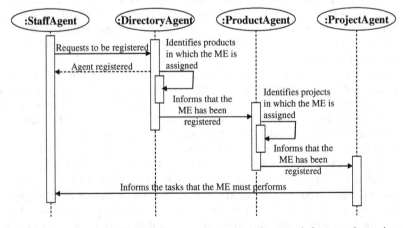

Fig. 3. Sequence diagram indicating how agents communicate to inform to the maintenance engineer the tasks he must perform.

The second example shows how the staff agent and the KMA communicate between them to support the ME in the search of knowledge sources that can help him. As Figure 4 shows, the staff agent captures each event that is trigged by the ME on the graphical user interface (GUI). When the staff agent identifies that the ME is working on a specific task of a project, it obtains information about that task. For example, the type of project (maintenance request or error report), the product or module to be modified or in which the error was presented, etc. Later, the staff agent asks the KMA to search for knowledge sources that know about that product, module, kind of modification or error, the language in which the product or module was developed, etc. The KMA searches the knowledge base for knowledge sources that can have information related to the topics of the task to be performed. Once the KMA finds the sources, it informs the staff agent about them. Next, the staff agent notifies the ME of the relevant sources that were found.

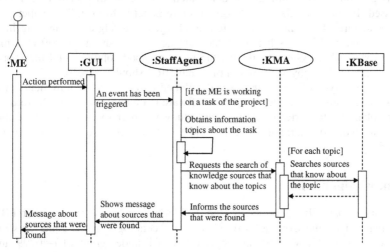

Fig. 4. The staff agent and the KMA communicate each other to help the ME search knowledge sources relevant to the problem at hand.

3.3   Some Aspects of Implementation

The platform chosen to implement the multiagent system is JADE [3] which is a FIPA compliant agent platform, implemented in Java and developed as an open source project. JADE has been used in the development of other systems in the domain of knowledge management [4, 9, 11, 18].

This platform provides a Java API that simplifies the development of agents that run in the environment of the platform. A JADE platform could be constituted from several agents containers, each one of which could be located in a different host, this facilitates the development of distributed multiagent systems.

One of JADE's main characteristics is the support of ontologies and content languages. JADE provides a mechanism to define ontologies and content languages in a manner that makes possible to convert, between ontology's elements and its content language representation, in a transparent way for developers. The above facilitates the definition of the language with which agents will communicate, and enables the easy handling of complex interactions between them.

On the other hand, as Figure 2 shows, the tool has two types of repositories of information. One is where local information related to specific tasks is stored and the other is a global web repository where more generic knowledge is stored. The data are classified following an ontology for software maintenance proposed by Ruiz et al in [21], which is an extension of that of Kitchenham [10].

4 Conclusions and Future Work

Knowledge is a crucial resource for organizations. It allows companies to fulfil their mission and to become more competitive. The management of knowledge and how it can be applied to software development and maintenance has received little attention from the software engineering research community so far. However, software organizations generate a huge amount of distributed knowledge that should be stored and processed. In this way, they would obtain more benefits from it. This paper presents the architecture of a multi-agent system in charge of storing and managing information, expertise and lessons learned which are generated during the software maintenance process. The system facilitates the reuse of good solutions and the sharing of lessons learned. Thereby, the costs in time and effort should decrease.

A first prototype of the system was developed based on the requirements obtained from two case studies carried out in two software maintenance groups. As future work we are planning to perform another case study in order to evaluate where the tool makes the work of maintainers easier and to what degree costs and effort are decreased.

Acknowledgements

This work is partially supported by the TAMANSI project (grant number PBC-02-001) financed by the Consejería de Ciencia y Tecnología of the Junta de Comunidades de Castilla-La Mancha, and by CONACYT under grant C01-40799 and the scholarship 164739 provided to the first author.

References

1. Althoff, K-D., Birk, A., and Tautz, C. (1997). The Experience Factory Approach: Realizing Learning from Experience in Software Development Organizations. In proceedings of the 10th German Workshop on Machine Learning (FGML 1997), University of Karlsruhe, 6-8.
2. Basili, V. R., Caldiera, G., and Rombach, H. D. (1994). The Experience Factory. In Encyclopedia of Software Engineering, Marciniak, J.J., and Wiley, J., (Eds.) pp 469-476.
3. Bellifemine, A., Poggi, G., and Rimassa, G. (2001). Developing multi agent systems with a FIPA-compliant agent framework. Software Practise & Experience, (2001) 31: 103-128.
4. Bergenti, Federico; Poggi, Agostino and Rimassa, Giovanni. (2000). Agent Architectures and Interaction Protocols for Corporate Memory Management Systems. Proceedings of the 14th European Conference on Artificial Intelligence, Workshop on Knowledge Management and Organizational Memories. pp. 39-47.
5. Berztiss, A. T. Capability Maturity for Knowledge Management (2002) Proceedings of the 13th International Workshop on Database and Expert Systems Applications (DEXA'02), pp 162-166.

6. Caire, G., Coulier, W., Garijo, F., Gómez, J., Pavón, J., Leal, F., Chainho, P., Kearney, P., Stark, J., Evans, R., Massonet, P. (2001). Agent Oriented Analysis Using MESSAGE/ UML in Agent Oriented Software Engineering, pp. 119-135.

7. Dingsoyr, T., and Conradi, R. (2002). A Survey of Case Studies of the Use of Knowledge Management in Software Engineering. International Journal of Software Engineering and Knowledge Engineering. Vol. 12, No 4, 391-414.

8. Dingsoyr, T., and Royrvik, E. (2003). An Empirical Study of an Informal Knowledge Repository in a Medium-Sized Software Consulting Company. In Proceedings of the 25th International Conference on Software Engineering (ICSE'2003), pp 84-92.

9. Gandon, Fabien. (2002). A Multi-Agent Architecture For Distributed Corporate Memories. Proceedings of the Sixteenth European Meeting on Cybernetics and Systems Research.

10. Kitchenham, B.A., Travassos, G.H., Mayrhauser, A., Niessink, F., Schneidewind, N.F., Singer, J., Takada, S., Vehvilainen, R. and Yang, H. (1999). Towards an Ontology of Software Maintenance. Journal of Software Maintenance: Research and Practice. 11, pp. 365-389.

11. Knowledge On Demand (KOD), IST Project, IST-1999-12503, http://kod.iti.gr/, http://www.kodweb.org.

12. Macintosh, A. (1997). Position paper on Knowledge Asset Management http://www.ntgi.net/ntgi/y2k/kmfr.html

13. Meeham, B., and Richardson, I. (2003). Identification of Software Process Knowledge Management. Software Process Improvement and Practice, pp 45-55.

14. Nebus, J. (2001). Framing the Knowledge Search Problem: Whom Do We Contact, and Why Do We Contact Them? *Academy of Management Best Papers Proceedings*, pp h1-h7.

15. Oliveira, K.M, Anquetil, N., Dias; M.G, Ramal, M., Meneses, R. (2003) Knowledge for Software Maintenance. Fifteenth International Conference on Software Engineering and Knowledge Engineering (SEKE'03), San Francisco, 1-3 July, pp 61-68.

16. OMG Meta Object Facility (MOF) Specification, v. 1.3 RTF, sep-1999. In http://www.omg.org.

17. Pigoski, T.M. (1997): Practical Software Maintenance. Best Practices for Managing Your Investment. Ed. John Wiley & Sons, USA.

18. Poggi, Agostino; Rimassa, Giovanni and Turci, Paola. (2002). An Intranet Based Muti-Agent System for Corporate Memory Management. Proceedings of the Sixteenth European Meeting on Cybernetics and Systems Research.

19. Polo, M., Piattini, M., and Ruiz, F. (2002):Using a Qualitative Research Method for Building A Software Maintenance Methodology. In Software Practice & Experience. John Wiley and Sons. Vol. 32, Nº 13, 1239-1260.

20. Rodriguez, O. M., Martinez, A. I., Favela, J, and Vizcaino, A. (2003). Administración de Conocimiento como soporte al Mantenimiento de Software. Avances en Ciencias de la Computación. ENC 2003. Tlaxcala, México, 8-12 September. pp 367-372.

21. Ruiz, F., Vizcaíno, A., Piattini, M. and García, F. (2003). An Ontology for the Management of Software Maintenance Projects. Sent to the *International Journal of Software Engineering and Knowledge Engineering*.

22. Rus, I., and Lindvall, M., (2002). Knowledge Management in Software Engineering. IEEE Software, May/June, pp 26-38.

23. Szulanski, G., (1994). Intra-Firm Transfer of Best Practices Project. *American Productivity and Quality Centre*, Houston, Texas, pp 2-19.

24. Vizcaino, A., Favela, J., Piattini, M., García, F. (2003). Supporting Software Maintenance in Web Repositories through a Multi-Agent System. In Menasalvas, E., Segovia, J., and Szczepaniak, P. S. (Eds.) First International Atlantic Web Intelligence Conference (AWIC'2003). LNAI 2663, pp 307-317.

Learning from HOMER,
a Case-Based Help Desk Support System

Thomas R. Roth-Berghofer[1,2]

[1] Knowledge-Based Systems Group, Department of Computer Science,
University of Kaiserslautern, P.O. Box 3049, 67653 Kaiserslautern
[2] Knowledge Management Department
German Research Center for Artificial Intelligence DFKI GmbH,
Erwin-Schrödinger-Straße 57, 67663 Kaiserslautern, Germany
thomas.roth-berghofer@dfki.uni-kl.de

Abstract. The HOMER help desk support system, developed in the
course of the INRECA-II project, is an example of applying Case-Based
Reasoning to problems of a software-intensive organization. This paper
discusses, in retrospect, HOMER with respect to change management processes at DaimlerChrysler and various feedback and learning possibilites
that the help desk support system provided for itself, the help desk personnel, and the supported IT infrastructure of the car development department in Sindelfingen.

1   Introduction

Help desks are installed in many companies to help customers, which have problems with the company's products and services. But customers are not the
only users of help desks. Often, companies set up internal help desks to provide support regarding IT related problems. One such internal help desk was
the CAD/CAM help desk at DaimlerChrysler in Sindelfingen, which supported
about 1,400 engineers who were developing Mercedes-Benz cars. At the Sindelfingen location alone, more than 600 mostly complex problems had to be solved
each month [2].

In the meantime, the organisational structure has changed considerably. Together with the engineers, the help desk has moved to a new location. That is
why I refer to the situation in 1998 in the following in retrospect.

At that time, the engineers worked on workstations using 38 different applications in average. Each year one third of the hardware was replaced with newer
models and each software had about one major and up to four minor updates
each year. Since the number of help desk personnel remained constant and the
help desk operation was a central and very time-critical operation, it was obvious that some kind of computer-support, going beyond classical trouble-ticket
systems, was needed.

Case-Based Reasoning (CBR) is a suitable technology to support help desks
in their daily routine [11, 10, 1]. In case-based decision support and, particularly,
in help desk support, experience is reused in the classical sense of Case-Based

G. Melnik and H. Holz (Eds.): LSO 2004, LNCS 3096, pp. 88–97, 2004.

Reasoning, i.e., by employing cases of rule type [8], which consist of a problem description and a solution part. Case-Based Reasoning, in short, solves a problem by retrieving a similar problem and applying its solution to the current problem.

One major advantage of CBR, in contrast to model-based reasoning, is that it is possible to start with an initial domain model and experience repository and to incrementally enhance its competence. This way, CBR lessens the burden put on developers and users of such a system.

In general, help desk applications focus on a particular domain such as technical devices of a certain kind or a set of software components. No other topic outside this domain is dealt with. This implies that a number of highly specific terms is used such as names of components, functions and modules.

The support department of an organization is the major entry point for feedback regarding a company's products and services. Especially, when a help desk team is supported by a software system, the organization has the opportunity to learn from successes as well as failures. A case-based decision support system such as HOMER[1] provides structured analysis of the problem domain, enriched with trouble-ticket system protocols.

In the next section, the general help desk scenario is described. In section 3, HOMER is put in relation to the general help desk scenario together with some words on the structure of the domain model. Basically, learning means handling change. Hence, in section 4, change management and the change problem are addressed, before I describe various learning possibilities that HOMER opened in section 5. The paper closes with some concluding remarks.

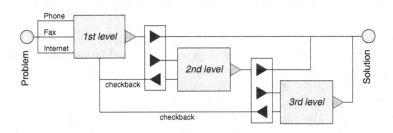

Fig. 1. Workflow of a typical support organization [9]

2 General Help Desk Scenario

Figure 1 illustrates the typical structure of support organizations, often consisting of three levels of support. The *first level support* (*Call Center*) takes incoming customer calls via phone, fax, or the Internet, and tries to solve simple requests immediately. The staff of the first level normally consists of somewhat experienced users; they are often part-time employees such as students. Their main task is to accept the problems rather than to solve them. It is more important

---

[1] Hotline mit Erfahrung, engl. hotline with experience.

that these people have rather good communication skills to calm down upset customers, or simply to provide the information where to find more information about particular products.

First level help desks work under strict time constraints. The help desk personnel is given a certain amount of time (ranging from a few minutes to a quarter of an hour) to solve a problem. If they are not able to help within the given time frame, the help desk operators record everything they did so far and escalate the respective calls to the second level. The adherence to the given time constraints is carefully observed by the respective management.

The *second level*, generally, gets its tasks by means of a workflow system, called *trouble-ticket system*. The second level staff is more skilled (fulltime) personnel than that of the first level. They work at the problem using the information recorded by the first level staff. If the problem is solved the solution is entered into the workflow system, and the first level staff communicates this information back to the customer. If required they check back to the first level or directly to the customer to get more information on the subject. If they are also not able to solve the problem they escalate the call as well.

The *third level* normally is not located at the company. It comprises manufacturers of third party products such as printers or hard disks, or software developers of special components. The third level staff can check back for more information as well. As soon as the problem is solved, the solution is communicated to the first level support that informs the customer.

3   Homer: Case-Based Second Level Help Desk Support

The HOMER system was one of the application results of the INRECA-II[2] project with its main goal to improve the development process of industrial Case-Based Reasoning applications. HOMER, besides other deployed applications, showed the successful use of the INRECA methodology [1].

The CAD/CAM help desk in Sindelfingen was principally structured as described above [3]. The first level was composed of several groups. The *system help desk* provided support on operating system and simple hardware problems. The *application help desks* were specialized on certain software and could give support on their usage and functionality. The second level consisted of *system administrators* and *application specialists*. Problems that could not be solved by them were transferred to the hardware and software vendors, some of which had representatives in-house.

The operators at the second level help desk used several software tools (developed by themselves) to support them during help desk operations. Even though these tools aided the help desk operators in performing their tasks, they did not give support in diagnosing the problem and could not serve as a knowledge repository. Thus, the HOMER system was developed.

---

[2] INRECA-II: Information and Knowledge Re-engineering for Reasoning from Cases (Esprit contract no. P22196).

In the course of the project, it was decided to use an object-oriented approach to model the domain, in contrast to a flat attribute-value representation that was also discussed at the start of the project. While the effort necessary to create such an object-oriented model was obviously higher, it was also useful in guiding the help desk operator while describing and entering cases, and during similarity calculation. The decision to use a structured domain model approach opposed to a shallow approach depended also on the intended users of that system, which were experienced help desk operators in this case.

As starting point for modelling, the domain of printer/plotter problems was chosen. On the one hand, this domain was easy to understand by all of the project participants, thus minimizing communication problems in the project team. On the other hand, the printing infrastructure with its servers, format conversion tool, and different printers and plotter of various sizes was as complex as the software problems that were modelled in a second step.

Choosing the vocabulary during knowledge acquisition can be performed in two ways: First, it can be derived from cases. This case driven approach is called the *functional* or *bottom up approach*. The second kind is called *reminding approach* or *top down* approach. It is domain driven and often depends on experts. During the development of HOMER, a mixed approach was employed, as it is common in practice. The trouble-ticket system (with more than 17,000 trouble-tickets addressing the whole range of IT-related problems of the CAD/CAM department) was the main information source to start modelling with. Even when there was no list of symptoms recorded in the trouble-tickets, the help desk operators were reminded of prior problem solving episodes that were used to construct episodic cases. Those informal cases, in turn, were used by the CBR system administrator to identify important concepts and to develop the domain model.

For the HOMER application, the classical problem part of a case was further decomposed into the components *failure* (with its subcomponents topic, subject, and behaviour), and *situation*. This distinction was very convenient because it separated the initial problem description of an end-user from the current situation description. An additional advantage was that this model was in full accordance with the approach the help desk operators were accustomed to in solving problems.

The first thing a help-desk operator gets from an end-user nearly always is a (subjective) failure description that might or might not have something to do with the actual cause of the problem. Those descriptions already were recorded in the trouble-ticket system before the project started. The *failure* in the domain model was split up into a *topic*, characterising the area in which the problem was located such as network or printing, a *subject*, which named the physical object that the failure was related to such as a specific software or a certain printer, and a *behaviour* that described the way the subject (mis-) behaved such as crashes or wrong print size.

The *symptoms* contained the minimum amount of information that allowed a help desk operator to diagnose the cause of the problem. The *solution* contained the fault, i.e., the cause of the problem, and the remedy, i.e., the actual solution of the problem.

The HOMER case, additionally, recorded administrative information about the author of that case, i.e., who solved the problem, and about the time it usually took to solve the problem, i.e., to apply the remedy.

The detailed decomposition of the each case was an important source for refactoring efforts with respect to the domain model and the IT infrastructure of the department. It helped in many cases to find the root causes for recurring problems.

4   Handling Change

A help desk support system such as HOMER is, as any software system, part of its environment. But more than an ordinary software system, a knowledge-based system is explicitly tied to its application domain. The knowledge of a knowledge-based system is changed by learning. In general, we are interested in the events that lead to environment state changes or in the changes themselves. We must recognize them and evaluate if, what, how, and how much they affect the organization in order to counteract their effects, i.e., to learn from them. In principle, this is the goal of *change management*.

4.1   Change Management

Change management is a scientific field of its own. It mainly deals with organizational and managerial issues. Technical issues must be integrated or synchronized with them (cf. [4]). The term 'change management' is not as fixed in its meaning as one would think. Nickols [6] describes three basic views on change management.

Change management is often understood as an area of professional practice. Many consultants and firms make their money in this area, with considerable variation among the practitioners.

Viewing change management as a body of knowledge, it consists of models, methods, techniques, and other tools. Its contents are drawn from psychology, sociology, business administration, economics, industrial engineering, systems engineering, and the study of human and organizational behaviour.

The task of managing changes – the third view on change management and the viewpoint taken here – consists of two parts: *making changes* and *responding to changes*. Changes always should be made in a planned and systematic way. They take place within the organization, and the organization has full control over the process. But internal changes could be triggered by external events. The organization usually has no or only little control over external changes, such as changes in legislation, or changes regarding its competitors. It has only two options: the organization's response can be *reactive* (the organization endures changes) or *proactive* (the organization anticipates changes).

4.2   The Change Problem

Managing change means moving from one state to the other, in particular, from a problem state to some solved state. The transition should be planned and executed in an orderly fashion. Therefore, problems must be analyzed, goals set, and means and ends discussed. In this context, a problem is nothing more than a situation requiring action but in which the required action is not known. The required action is the solution to that problem. The *change problem* is *some future state to be realized, some current state to be left behind, and some structured, organized process for getting from the one to the other* [6]. It can be of large or small scope. It can focus on individuals or groups, on one or more divisions or departments, the entire organization, or one or on more aspects of the organization's environment.

The analysis of a change problem will, at various times, focus on defining the outcomes of the change effort. It will focus on identifying the change necessary to produce these outcomes and on finding and implementing ways and means of making the required changes. Thus, in simpler terms, the change problem can be treated as smaller problems having to do with the *how*, the *what*, and the *why* of change.

The change problem is often expressed, at least initially, in the form of a how-question. Their formulation is *means-centered*, with the goal state more or less implied. Examples are: "How do we get people to be more open, to assume more responsibility, to be more creative? How do we introduce self-managed teams in department W?" For the help desk team, one could formulate such questions as "How can we reduce the number of calls?" Or, more specifically: "How can we avoid regular overflow of the printing spooler on server X?"

To focus on *ends* requires the posing of what-questions such as "What are we trying to accomplish? What changes are necessary?" Ends and means are relative notions, not absolutes. That is, something is an end or a means only in relation to something else. Thus, chains and networks of ends-means relationships often have to be traced out before one finds the 'true' ends of a change effort. In this regard, why-questions prove extremely useful. To ask why-questions is to get at the ultimate *purposes of functions*, and to open the door to finding new and better ways of performing them. Examples are: "Why do we do what we do? Why do we do it the way we do?" Rephrased for the help desk: "Why do we solve problem P this way?"

Problems may be formulated as how-, what-, and why-questions. Which formulation is used, depends on where in the organization the person posing the question is situated, and where the organization is situated in its own life cycle. All of these questions had to be answered in the course of the development of HOMER as for any other software project.

How-questions tend to cluster in *core units* (systems and operations) where coordination is achieved through standardization, that is, adherence to routine. What-questions tend to cluster in *buffer units* (upper management and staff or support functions) where coordination is achieved through planning. People in *perimeter units* (sales, marketing, and customer service) tend to ask what-

and how-questions. They achieve coordination through mutual adjustment. The what- and why-questions were extremely important during the development phase of the help desk project. During the utilization those questions were answered repeatedly and in regular intervals. The why-questions are typically the responsibility of top management, which is not directly responsible for day-to-day operations and results.

Managing such kinds of changes in and by organizations requires a broad set of skills [6]. In a help desk project *people* and *systems skills* are particularly required. Organizations are first and foremost social systems. Without people there can be no organization. Thus, the skills most needed in this area are those that typically fall under the heading of *communication* or *interpersonal skills*.

Additionally, two sets of systems skills must be mastered: systems analysis and the set of skills associated with General Systems Theory. Systems analysis deals with *closed* systems. Closed systems have no purpose of their own and are incapable of altering their own structure. The second set of skills deals with *open*, purposive systems, carrying out transactions with other systems. In a way, the help desk operators had to deal with HOMER as a closed system in their daily business when adding new cases. As soon as a new case could not be expressed with the available domain model, they had to deal with HOMER as an open system. They had to think about other software systems in order to suggest an appropriate extension of the domain model to the CBR system administrator.

Especially in knowledge acquisition, those skills are of utmost importance because keeping knowledge to oneself is a major problem in every knowledge acquisition (and, in general, knowledge managment) effort. Organizational measures, such as incentives for documenting knowledge, had to be taken to support knowledge engineers who had to be very skilled particularly in communication skills, not only during development, but also during utilization of HOMER.

Change management looks at the whole organization as the subject of change. A help desk organization, with or without software support, must be embedded in the change processes of an organization to get all the information relevant to its proper functioning. Information sources are, for example, domain experts, handbooks, manufacturer newsletters, specialized literature, and magazines. Of course, not every information source is relevant to the system. The relevant information sources form the borders of the environment of a knowledge-based system. Well-structured information sources make it a lot easier to keep a particular system up and running[3].

5   Learning from HOMER

Knowledge acquisition supplies the help desk support system with knowledge needed within its decision steps. Hence, knowledge acquisition is part of the

---

[3] In a figurative sense, this could be seen as a requirement regarding experts. If experts are 'well-structured', they help to keep a system up and running and do not hinder. This is another situation where good people skills are very helpful.

learning process. It is a task that must be ongoing throughout the lifetime of a case-based reasoner if it should be successful [1].

To handle change effectively, i.e., to learn, it is necessary to know the environment of the help desk system with its information sources. To know where the information comes from, of course, does not guarantee to recognize changes coming from those sources. The changes themselves are not usable by a knowledge-based system. The changes must be transformed from information that is somehow *relevant* to the system into knowledge that is directly *accessible* by the system. For the handling of changes, Event-Condition-Action (ECA) rules [7] seemed to be most appropriate. ECA rules separate events, which trigger the computation of possibly complex conditions, from these conditions. Events can be as simple as timer-based events that just trigger regular checks or remind of regular meetings [9].

After HOMER was up and running, one major challenge was to keep the case base consistent, i.e. regarding the cases of the case base and regarding the case base in relation to the environment. One main source of change were the help desk operators who could enter new cases into the case base if they did not find appropriate cases. Those cases were marked as *unconfirmed* [3]. This served two purposes. First, new knowledge was available to other help desk operators as soon as it was entered into the system (a requirement for this project). And second, the other operators could see at first glance if a case was new and that they could not fully rely on those cases. On the other hand, such information could be particularly interesting because it was new and, thus, topical. The CBR system administrator also had a closer look at the IT infrastructure when there were more new cases than usual or some kind of cases was retrieved more often.

The use of unconfirmed cases was also very important for winning over the help desk operators. Taking this measure helped to build up trust in the application's advice, thus increasing the overall trustworthiness of HOMER. In order to store the status of a case, the case structure, originally consisting of problem and solution, was enhanced by a component that we called *administrativa*. This case component not only stored if a case was confirmed, it also recorded the author and date of the case. This gave the help desk operators a clue on how old a case was and, much more important from the help desk operators' point of view, who entered the information. The latter information determined the degree of reliability of the case, the help desk operators had. An additional effect was that a help desk operator, who was confronted with a problem similar to one of the cases, could simply ask the author of the respective case for advice.

Another kind of changes was provided by feedback e-mails from the help desk operators to the CBR system administrator. Every time operators found incorrect cases, they (had to) tell the administrator about it (best commented on with the expected results or with some hints on corrections). On a regular basis, the administrator checked those cases and corrected them whenever necessary.

Environmental changes were easy to handle in this closed environment. Update and upgrade schedules existed and allowed the operators to plan ahead extensions of the knowledge base or removal of outdated knowledge.

The help desk personnel could also learn at a higher level of abstraction. At regular time intervals, the team members came together and discussed the cases in the case base. They used the opportunity to analyze the cases independently from daily routine. Together with the CBR system administrator, who was responsible for approving unconfirmed cases, they generalized and joined cases and/or enhanced the domain model appropriately.

In many ways, organizational learning with respect to the help desk seems to me similar to function enhancing maintenance, which aims at the implementation of further functionality into a software system [5]. Here, the analysis of recurring problems is aimed at enhancing the IT infrastructure in such a way that problems do not recur, by technical means such as installing new printer drivers as well as by educational measures such as sending end-users to additional software seminars.

The management of the CAD/CAM department indeed understood how important it was to embed the HOMER help desk support system not only into technical but also into the organisational and managerial workflows of Daimler-Chrysler. By regularly reporting about their experience to other departments, the learning process has been made explicit. HOMER was also transferred to another production site where the same printer/plotter infrastructure was about to be installed, allowing for successful reuse of the respective part of the case base not only for problem solving but also as training material.

6   Concluding Remarks

Case-Based Reasoning commonly is seen as a technology that is able to handle change easily because learning is part of its design. The HOMER help desk support system showed the utility of such a technical 'device'. It had not only direct positive effects on the help desk personnel but also was a platform for further organisational learning.

From my experience, the support team always should be a controlling or, at least, it should be a reviewing instance of an organization. Problems most of the time are simply first visible to the support department. Understanding that, DaimlerChrysler installed feedback loops in order to monitor and improve the overall IT infrastructure for the CAD/CAM engineers. Also, feedback loops inside the help desk organization as well as between the end-users and the help desk were installed to tap and utilize this powerful source of change.

Before HOMER was installed at the CAD/CAM help desk at DaimlerChrysler, the recurrence of problems was not recognized very well. This was partly due to the work load at the help desk, but also due to the way in which the problems and solutions were recorded in the trouble-ticket system. This made a structural analysis of the IT infrastructure impossible and symptoms of different problems could not be related to each other.

After HOMER was up and running, the help desk operators could handle more calls. They could concentrate on root causes that were related to the infrastructure, such as incompatible drivers and file format conversions, and those that were related to the engineers as well as the help desk personell and system administrators. Here, proper training helped to reduce the number of calls.

Acknowledgments

I have to thank Harald Holz for talking me into writing this paper.

References

1. Ralph Bergmann, Klaus-Dieter Althoff, Sean Breen, Mehmet Göker, Michel Manago, Ralph Traphöner, and Stefan Wess. *Developing Industrial Case-Based Resoning Applications: The INRECA Methodology*. Lecture Notes in Artificial Intelligence LNAI 1612. Springer-Verlag, Berlin, second edition, 2003.
2. Mehmet Göker and Thomas Roth-Berghofer. Development and utilization of a case-based help-desk support system in a corporate environment. In Klaus-Dieter Althoff, Ralph Bergmann, and L. Karl Branting, editors, *Case-Based Reasoning Research and Development: Proceedings of the Third International Conference on Case-Based Reasoning, ICCBR'99, Seeon Monastery, Germany*, pages 132–146, Berlin, 1999. Springer-Verlag.
3. Mehmet Göker, Thomas Roth-Berghofer, Ralph Bergmann, Thomas Pantleon, Ralph Traphöner, Stefan Wess, and Wolfgang Wilke. The development of HOMER – a case-based CAD/CAM help-desk support tool. In Barry Smyth and Pádraigh Cunningham, editors, *Advances in Case-Based Reasoning, Proceedings of the 4th European Workshop, EWCBR'98, Dublin, Ireland*, pages 346–357, Berlin, 1998. Springer-Verlag.
4. Mehmet H. Göker and Thomas Roth-Berghofer. The development and utilization of the case-based help-desk support system HOMER. *Engineering Applications of Artificial Intelligence*, 12(6):665–680, December 1999.
5. Prof. Dr. Franz Lehner. Ergebnisse einer Untersuchung zur Wartung von wissensbasierten Systemen. *Information Management*, 2:38–47, 1994.
6. Fred Nickols. Change management 101 – a primer, 2000. http://home.att.net/~nickols/change.htm [Last access: 2004-04-12].
7. Joachim Reinert and Norbert Ritter. Applying ECA-rules in DB-based design environments. In *Tagungsband CAD'98 "Tele-CAD – Produktentwicklung in Netzen"*, pages 188–201. Informatik Xpress 9, 1998.
8. Michael M. Richter. Generalized planning and information retrieval. Technical report, University of Kaiserslautern, Artificial Intelligence – Knowledge-based Systems Group, 1997.
9. Thomas R. Roth-Berghofer. *Knowledge Maintenance of Case-Based Reasoning Systems – The SIAM Methodology, volume 262 of Dissertationen zur Künstlichen Intelligenz*. Akademische Verlagsgesellschaft Aka GmbH / IOS Press, Berlin, Germany, 2003.
10. Evangelos Simoudis. Using case-based retrieval for customer technical support. *IEEE Expert*, 7(5):7–12, October 1992.
11. Evangelos Simoudis and James S. Miller. The application of CBR to help desk applications. In *Proceedings of the DARPA Workshop on Case-Based Reasoning*, pages 25–36, Washington, DC, 1991.

Tool Support for Inter-team Learning in Agile Software Organizations

Thomas Chau and Frank Maurer

University of Calgary
Department of Computer Science
Calgary, Alberta, Canada T2N 1N4
{chauth,maurer}@cpsc.ucalgary.ca

Abstract. The need for organizational learning support is common among all software development companies but is not addressed by agile software methods practitioners. The typical Experience Factory approach to address organizational learning in software companies often stresses structured and explicit knowledge as well as controlled learning mechanisms. In contrast, the Communities of Practice approach relies more on tacit knowledge and self-organization. To bridge the gap between these two conflicting approaches, this paper proposes a suite of lightweight knowledge sharing tools by which software organizations are given the flexibility to control how structured and controlled their learning processes are. Initial results from early evaluations of the proposed tools are also given.

1 Introduction

Software development is a knowledge-intensive process requiring expertise in the customers' business domain and mastery over technological skills. These knowledge requirements are common among all software development organizations but are even more demanding in those "sweet spot" business environments for agile software methods practitioners. This is due to the fact agile teams are often confronted with short development and learning times as well as unpredictable and continuous changes in both technologies and customer needs. Furthermore, for any software organizations to survive in the long term, it is imperative that they apply experience gained from past projects to similar projects in the future. This underlies the need for knowledge sharing and organizational learning support in software organizations, and among agile practitioners in particular. We use the term "Inter-team Learning" to indicate knowledge sharing across team boundaries without moving people between teams.

One approach developed by the software engineering community to address the knowledge needs and overcome the learning challenges mentioned above is the Experience Factory concept. One of its intentions is to package "experiences by building informal and formal product models…and other forms of knowledge via people, documents, and automated support" [1]. While the Experience Factory approach does not preclude the use of tacit knowledge and informal learning processes, many of its existing implementations rely more on formal and explicit knowledge for knowledge transfer [19] and controlled learning mechanisms [18].

G. Melnik and H. Holz (Eds.): LSO 2004, LNCS 3096, pp. 98–109, 2004.
© Springer-Verlag Berlin Heidelberg 2004

Encoding knowledge in structured and explicit form has the benefits of mitigating risks of knowledge loss and enabling distributed teams to collaborate in a time- and space-independent manner. It also makes knowledge available in a more reusable format if used together with controlled learning mechanisms such as formal training and organizational units that conceive and distribute knowledge to other operational units. The overall effect can help reduce duplicated effort in devising similar solutions and prevent past failures from recurring. However, these benefits are best realized in a stable business environment where there is limited variety to development tasks – not a typical scenario for agile teams. In addition, the heavy emphasis on structured and explicit knowledge over tacit knowledge and controlled learning processes over self-organizing processes contradicts agile principles [2]. An experience factory is an organizational unit that gathers experiences, makes them accessible to others (e.g. in the form of "best practices") and provides line units with support in adopting these best practices. A major risk of such a centralized approach is that its team members are often not involved in everyday software development and might lose contact with reality over time. As a result, Experience Factories or Software Process Groups are sometimes perceived by the "real" software developers as living in an ivory tower.

Given the incompatibilities between the Experience Factory approach and agile principles, how can software organizations facilitate knowledge sharing and organizational learning while remaining agile in the process? In an attempt to overcome these incompatibilities, this paper proposes a suite of lightweight knowledge management tools, MASE and EB, by which software organizations are given the flexibility to choose how structured and controlled their learning processes are.

Another approach originated in the field of organizational dynamics to address issues in organizational learning and knowledge sharing is called Communities of Practice [6]. Unlike Experience Factories, Communities of Practice are informal and self-organizing networks of professionals. They are intended for (1) helping capture and share tacit knowledge that formal system cannot capture as easily [5]; (2) reducing time seeking for expertise; (3) linking staff interested in similar knowledge domains but dispersed across organizational units; (4) connecting and coordinating isolated initiatives addressing similar knowledge areas [7]; (5) and retain talents [3,4]. Furthermore, their people-centric approach is in line with the agile principles. Despite these benefits, potential drawbacks to the Communities of Practice approach include mismatch between the communities' knowledge domains and the business' core competences as well as stagnation due to overly tight social relationships among community members that may stifle new ideas and constructive criticisms [7].

2 Tool Criteria

Instead of viewing the two conflicting approaches as a dichotomy, we concur with others [8,10] that learning processes, in practice, often lie somewhere on a continuum from highly structured processes like the Experience Factory approach at one extreme to highly unstructured processes as in the Communities of Practice approach at the other extreme. One implication of this perspective is that knowledge sharing tools need to support: (1) formal learning based on prescribed processes and (2) informal situated learning that are often found in day-to-day collaborative work. The fact that people move unconsciously "continually and effortlessly among different collaboration styles: across time, across place, and so on" [9] also demands knowledge sharing tools to accommodate more than one collaboration style like: (3) co-located and distributed teams; (4) synchronous and asynchronous activities; and (5) use of structured and unstructured information. For such tools to be useful for agile organizations they also need to support (6) the social context critical to nurturing a knowledge sharing environment - providing information needs to be as easy as accessing it and expertise can be exchanged in informal and spontaneous manners.

3   The Tools: MASE and EB

These requirements are met by our tools, MASE and EB. MASE is a process support system to be used by agile teams for project planning coordination purposes whereas EB is an experience base to be shared among all teams in the organization.

3.1   Support for Co-located and Distributed Teamwork

Both EB and MASE are implemented using Web technology which makes the tools accessible anytime anywhere by users with a browser in their computing environment. The tools do not distinguish users working at the same place from those who work at different places. Hence, both EB and MASE are capable of supporting collaborative work for both co-located and distributed teams.

3.2   Support for Unstructured and Structured Information Content

Both EB and MASE allow information to be externalized into highly unstructured as well as structured formats. Further, they make writing – providing information – nearly as easy as reading – accessing information. Unstructured information usually consists of text and graphics whereas structured information is typically stored in a database and must follow a schema. To support unstructured information content, both EB and MASE use Wiki technology for their user interfaces [12]. Wiki technology enables any users to access, create, structure, and update web pages in real-time using only a web browser. These web pages, also known as wiki pages, act like electronic bulletin board discussion topics, each with a unique name. Users apply the Wiki markup language to edit wiki pages. Wiki markup is much simpler than HTML: a list of all Wiki markup command including examples fits onto a single page.

One may argue that wiki pages are no different from any other document and will suffer from the same maintenance problems. Wiki technology mitigates this risk by automatically creating links from a wiki page to particular topic pages if the names of those topics are mentioned in that page. This helps minimize the users' effort in maintaining the relationship among the content in different wiki pages and enhances knowledge discovery. These benefits, however, are best realized if users adhere to the same terminology when contributing content to wiki pages.

Information content in a wiki page is all free-formatted text. This is not the case when users try to update a typical web page. Normally, the information content on a web page that users see is embedded among presentation information such as HTML markup elements. For the users to edit such a web page, they need to spend the extra effort to first extract the information content then begin the actual editing of the content. Sometimes, this additional effort is so time-consuming that the users give up on editing the content, thus causing knowledge content to degenerate over time. The fact that information content of web pages in EB and MASE is in free-formatted text facilitates efficient collaboration between knowledge contributors and readers.

To support structured information content, EB and MASE employ a library of plug-ins that store specific data in a database. A plug-in in EB or MASE is either presented as an input form that allows users to submit information or as a table that displays information retrieved from the database in a structured fashion. Users can include such plug-ins in any wiki pages simply by referencing their names. Currently, the libraries of plug-ins in EB and MASE include those that are specific to agile teams and generic collaboration tools like rating a specific wiki page which supports collaborative filtering. The fact that any content on any wiki pages is modifiable and that any plug-ins can be included in any wiki pages gives users the flexibility to control how structured or unstructured they want their organizational memory to be.

Storing information does not guarantee that others can find it. Retrieving information from a repository that combines structured and unstructured data often requires users to learn two different query mechanisms. To overcome the resulting usability problems, MASE provides a single full-text searching capability on any unstructured and structured content.

3.3 Support for Personal Portals

When a team member first logs into EB or MASE, she is automatically provided a personal wiki page that serves as her personal portal. She can store in her portal any content, either structured or unstructured information (or both). The content may be relevant only to her or to some subset of team members; it may not even be related to the project or task at hand. The key idea is that a team member has complete control over the type and granularity of the information content that she deems is relevant for her. Like any wiki pages, the content in the personal portal is accessible by others.

3.4 Support for Asynchronous and Synchronous Collaboration

Both EB and MASE support asynchronous collaboration by storing the state of any wiki pages one has worked on before logging out. This resembles the common practice in the real world where team members leave artifacts in a physical place for others to review or update when they work at different times.

EB and MASE also support synchronous work through integration with a real-time collaboration tool, Microsoft NetMeeting. Every time when a team member logs into EB or MASE, the tools track the network address of that team member's computer. This allows EB and MASE to display which members of a team are currently using the system, thus making all online team members aware of each other's presence. This allows for team members to easily establish informal, synchronous and spontaneous communications with one another – most likely moments when sharing of tacit knowledge take place [13].

3.5 Support for Agile Practices

As a process support system for agile project teams, MASE supports agile practices through its library of plug-ins. For project planning, project managers and customers can create iterations and user stories as structured data objects to be kept in the database and accessed through plug-ins. The developers can submit to MASE their time estimates for tasks that they assume. MASE will then suggest to both the development team and customers the appropriate size for the next iteration based on the developers' estimation accuracy from the previous iteration. Using the suggested iteration size, customers can prioritize user stories and move them from iteration to iteration or move them back to the product backlog. During the course of the project, both the customers and development team can track work progress at various granularities using the Whiteboard plug-in (project, iteration, user story) and view effort metrics for a particular individual or for the entire team.

Fig. 1. The above plug-in is named "Whiteboard" to mirror the big physical whiteboard often used by agile teams to show vital information that the entire team should know

Through the Whiteboard, developers can see the features and tasks allocated for each of the iterations in the project and track their time. Details of a user story or a task are stored in a wiki page allowing developers to annotate in free-formatted text. Leveraging MASE's integration with NetMeeting, developers can also perform distributed pair programming by sharing their code editor and thus collaborate on a design together using the shared whiteboard. Using the video and audio conferencing and multi-user text-chat features of NetMeeting, distributed team members who work at the same time can perform daily Scrum meetings.

3.6 Support for Organizational Learning

To facilitate learning based on prescribed processes, EB allows users to construct models of common tasks. Such process models can contain detailed description about common tasks and their possible decompositions in structured format. Users can also store any specific information about the model that one should pay attention to as free-formatted text. The left window in figure 2 shows the process model for a common development task, EJB Creation and Deployment. It contains descriptions of the steps one should follow in performing tasks of similar kind and some common bad practices to avoid. The process model basically acts as a type system for project tasks.

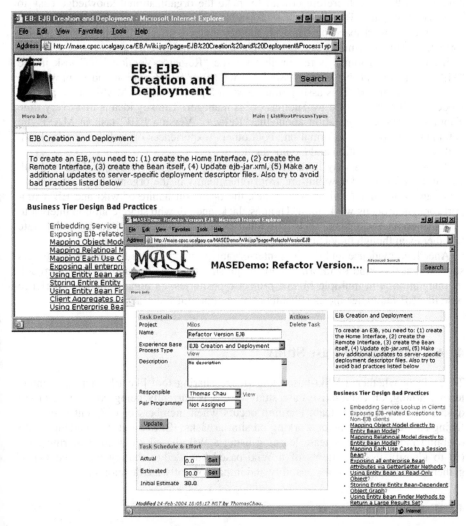

Fig. 2. The integration between EB (left) and MASE (right) can help disseminate knowledge created collaboratively by members in the organization to different project teams and can link members of different teams who are interested in similar task-related knowledge areas

Depending on how formal and controlled a company wants its organizational learning process to be, the job of process modeling can be open to anyone in the organization or it can be performed by designated roles, such as a group of knowledge brokers or, in the case of an agile organization, a group of Scrum Masters [11]. EB can support either approach.

While it is important to capture knowledge that is useful for the whole organization in process models, this measure alone is insufficient for facilitating learning based on prescribed process. Studies reveal that people often are unaware of information that may be of help to them even if such information exists in the organization's knowledge base [20]. It is therefore crucial to make the organizational knowledge easy to find. To this end, EB delivers the task-relevant information in process models to users' project workspace on demand; thereby reduces users' time in looking up information. This is demonstrated in the right window in figure 2.

It shows that Thomas is responsible for the "Refactor Version EJB" task in the "Milos" project and this task is associated with the "EJB Creation and Deployment" process model in EB. This association between a project task in MASE and a process model in EB can be made by Thomas or his manager. The key idea is that every time Thomas accesses information about the "Refactor Version EJB" task in MASE, he automatically receives information about others' experiences on tasks of similar kind, in this case, EJB Creation and Deployment.

These experiences may have been provided by others, for example Jack and Jill, whom Thomas may know but are from other teams in the organization. Since these experiences are annotated on wiki pages, the open-edit nature of wiki and EB's support for synchronous work allow Thomas, Jack, and Jill who share common interest to establish contact, exchange their individual experience and expertise, and collaborate together even though they may be dispersed across organizational units.

Anecdotal evidence and thriving inter-organizational practice that use Wiki servers suggest that this kind of informal knowledge sharing actually happens [16]. Through its integration with multiple MASE project repositories, an organizational experience base like EB facilitates the establishment of communities of practice.

4   An Explorative Case Study

To evaluate whether a Wiki-based knowledge sharing tool like EB facilitates inter-team learning, an explorative case study of EB is currently being conducted: (1) to determine whether inter-team learning occurs when members of different teams are facing common problems or working on similar tasks; (2) to elicit the challenges and enabling factors for inter-team learning using a Wiki-based knowledge sharing tool; (3) to identify usage patterns of a Wiki-based knowledge sharing tool, and (4) to gather feedback on the tool's usability and impact on software development.

4.1   Experimental Context

Participants of this study include a total of 42 senior undergraduate students of which 25 are enrolled in the course, Web-Based System, at the University of Calgary (UC) and the remaining 17 enrolled in a similar course, Internet Software Techniques, at the Southern Alberta Institute of Technology (SAIT). The 25 UC students are divided into 6 teams each consists of 4 to 5 members. Likewise, the 17 SAIT students are divided into 6 teams each consists of 3 to 4 members.

Both courses last 4 months and they expose students to the latest technologies and practices in building Web-based enterprise systems. The content of both courses are offered by the same instructor in approximately the same time period. Over the 4-

month time frame, all teams are required to complete 6 comprehensive programming assignments involving the construction of a document review system. Each assignment is to be completed in a short iteration, usually 2 to 3 weeks long. Teams are encouraged to share their individual learning and work on their assignments following agile development practices such as short iteration and pair programming.

In the first week of the study, all teams received training on using EB and MASE. When each assignment is released, dedicated KM brokers (the class instructor and teaching assistants) provide in EB information that they deem as important for all teams to know for completing their assignments. All teams have read and write access to EB and they are each given their own project information repository, MASE.

To collect data to meet the goals of the study, EB logs all use of the tool by any participants. In addition, participants will be asked to voluntarily fill out questionnaires at the end of the 4-month observation. The context and dependent variables of this study are summarized in figure 3.

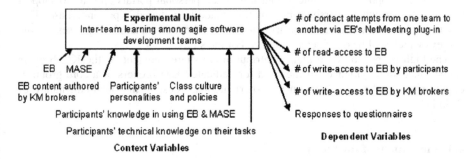

Fig. 3. Experimental Unit

4.2 Initial Results

At the time of this writing, all teams have finished two out of six assignments. About 9 weeks of data on the usage of EB have been collected and over 25,000 transactions have been recorded. Results shown in table 1 indicates that students use EB primarily to retrieve information they need for their development tasks; as bookmarks to other external online resources; and to share information.

Table 1. EB Usage Breakdown

EB Usage Breakdown	usage (%)	# of transactions
Read	82.38	22040
Bookmark to External Sites	13.16	3521
Write	4.02	1075
Search Query	0.37	98
Collaborative Work using NetMeeting	0.07	20
Total		26754

Table 2 indicates that students are contributing more content to EB than dedicated KM brokers (the course instructor and teaching assistants). However, most of the content contributed by students is in the students' personal portals.

Table 2. Breakdown of content contribution in EB by users' role

	KM Broker	Student	Total
Personal Portal Content	64	406	470
Common Information (e.g. FAQs)	464	141	605
Total	528	547	1075

4.3 Interpretation

By inspecting the individual postings made by the students to the shared content in EB, we did observed different teams offering advices to each other's problems. However, since the benefits of inter-team learning are subjective to individual perceptions, we are unable to assert whether a Wiki-based knowledge sharing tool like EB meets its goal of facilitating inter-team learning using only the available initial results.

The high proportion of content contribution on personal portals appears to support the need for providing personal information space in a shared experience base. This assertion, however, requires confirmation from the participants' responses to the surveys which will be distributed at the end of the study.

The high proportion of content contribution on shared content by the KM brokers echoes anecdotal evidences of the need for dedicated KM brokers or a core group of community members to maintain an experience base despite the open-edit nature of Wiki [7].

4.4 Limitations of the Study

A number of limitations in this study should be recognized. First, the number of participants in the study is small and the observation period is short. This is going to impact on how representative our findings will be. Second, the lack of objective measures of knowledge exchange will be an inherent limitation of the study.

5 Related Work

Existing tools which support agile practices or inter-team learning include VersionOne [14], Xplanner [15], TWiki [16], and BORE [17]. All of them are web-based tools which allow them to be used by team members working at the same place or at different locations. However, they differ in terms of their level of support for the various agile practices, capabilities in accommodating the different collaboration styles, and facilitation for organizational learning.

Both VersionOne and Xplanner support project planning and tracking. VersionOne, in particular, provides each team member with a private web page which serves as his/her own information portal. However, VersionOne pre-defines all the content in one's personal information portal showing only tasks that are assigned to the team member. In fact, all information content in both tools can only be created and browsed in a structured way. Team members cannot control the formality of the content nor can they specify their own search query for retrieving information.

TWiki also supports those agile team-related features provided by VersionOne and Xplanner but its usage is not targeted to agile development teams. It differentiates itself as a collaboration platform, not just a tool. This can be seen in the multitude of team-oriented tools it provides, such as event calendar, action tracker, drawing editor, and vote collection. As the name suggests, TWiki is developed based on the Wiki technology. Hence, TWiki and EB share a lot in common: plug-in architecture, support for unstructured and structured information content, personal portal support, and full-text search. TWiki allows a set of web pages to be grouped together, known as a TWiki Web. This indirectly facilitates the establishment of communities of practice in that a community can have its own TWiki Web. One drawback of TWiki is that it provides no direct support for online team members to be aware of each other's presence. This limits the opportunities for team members to establish informal and spontaneous encounters with one another. TWiki also does not have explicit support for modeling common tasks, making learning based on prescribed processes difficult.

Unlike the other three tools, BORE does not directly support specific agile practices. As an implementation of the Experience Factory concept, it provides a repository that contains experience collected from projects across the entire organization. These experiences are organized as cases, which are used to generate pre-defined tasks for similar projects in the future. A case is similar to a project task in nature. The generated set of tasks serves as a "best practice" guide. Project team members can diverge from the generated plan and not perform the suggested tasks if they deem the tasks to be inappropriate for the project situation at that time. In such cases, team members can submit their experiences and details of the tailored tasks in a structured format to the repository. A dedicated team of people is recommended to maintain the integrity of the cases stored in the repository. BORE's explicit support for the reuse and sharing of process knowledge facilitates learning based on prescribed process. However, it does not possess the support provided by EB in facilitating the informal and spontaneous exchange of experience and expertise in day-to-day collaboration that is critical for situated learning.

6   Open Issues and Future Work

Immediate future work includes assessing the impact of the tools on software development and inter-team learning by analyzing the usage data and responses to the perception study once the experiment completes. The next step is to involve companies to engage in further pilot studies to evaluate our approach in realistic settings.

For cultivating communities, the integration between the process models in EB and specific tasks in MASE currently only fosters community of users who are interested in task-related knowledge topics. To identify potential users who may be interested in similar knowledge topics that are not task-related, future work include developing plug-ins that group users by wiki pages that they frequently browse or contribute.

Our approach is designed specifically for agile teams and their situated environments, and so may not be appropriate for other types of projects or environments.

Since organizational learning and knowledge sharing is not just a technical but also a social problem, a major open research question is the organizational changes needed to foster the knowledge sharing culture that is essential for our tools and any other knowledge management tools to realize their benefits.

7 Conclusion

The knowledge-intensive nature of software developments underlies the need for knowledge sharing and organizational learning support for all software companies. Agile software organizations are no exception, especially if they are to survive in the long term. Typical Experience Factory approach to address organizational learning often stresses on the use of structured and explicit knowledge as well as controlled learning mechanisms. While this approach supports learning based on prescribed processes well, it contradicts agile principles. In contrast, the Communities of Practice approach's valuation on tacit knowledge and self-organizations is a good fit with agile software methods but this approach also has some inherent drawbacks. This paper describes a suite of lightweight knowledge management tools, MASE and EB, which leverages on the strengths of these two conflicting approaches and bridges their incompatibilities.

On one hand, EB supports the Experience Factory approach by allowing one to construct process models containing structured knowledge on common tasks. Through its integration with MASE, a process support system for agile teams, EB can deliver task-relevant information to knowledge workers' project workspace on demand, thereby facilitating learning based on prescribed process. On the other hand, EB also facilitates informal situated learning often found in communities of practice through its integration with MASE and its ability to accommodate different collaboration styles: co-located and distributed teamwork; asynchronous and synchronous work activities; and use of structured and unstructured information.

While the approaches of Experience Factory, Communities of Practice, and Wiki-based knowledge management tools are not new, the novelty of our approach is the integration of these concepts and tools to provide software companies a flexible mean to support their organizational learning and knowledge sharing processes, however controlled or structured they may be. By integrating these various approaches, we hope to get the most benefits without compromising the agility of software firms.

References

1. Basili, V., Caldiera, G., Romback, H. (1994), "Experience Factory", In *Encyclopedia of Software Engineering vol. 1*, J.J. Marciniak, Ed. John Wiley Sons.
2. Agile Manifesto. http://agilemanifesto.org.
3. Cohen, B., Prusak, L. (2001), *Good Company: How Social Capital Makes Organizations Work*. Boston: Harvard Business Press, p. 19.
4. Kelley, R., Caplan, J. (1993, July-August), "How Bell Labs Creates Star Performers", *Harvard Business Review*, p. 128-139.
5. Haas, R., Aulbur, W., Thakar, S. (2000), Enabling Communities of Practice at EADS Airbus, in M.S. Ackerman, V. Pipek & V. Wulf, eds, "Sharing Expertise: Beyond Knowledge Management", MIT Press, Cambridge MA.
6. Lave, J., Wenger, E. (1991), *Situated Learning: Legitimate Peripheral Participation*. Cambridge University Press.
7. Wenger, E., McDermott, R., Snyder, W. (2002), *Cultivating Communities of Practice*, Harvard Business School Press, Boston, MA.

8. Trittmann, R. (2001), "The Organic and the Mechanistic Form of Managing Knowledge", in K.-D. Althoff, R.L. Feldmann, W. Muller, eds, *Proceedings of the 3rd International Workshop on Learning Software Organizations 2001*, Springer-Verlag, Berlin Heidelberg

9. Greenburg, S., Roseman, M. (1998), Using a Room Metaphor to Ease Transitions in Groupware, in M.S. Ackerman, V. Pipek & V. Wulf, eds, "Sharing Expertise: Beyond Knowledge Management", MIT Press, Cambridge MA.

10. Bernstein, A. (2003), How Can Cooperative Work Tools Support Dynamic group Processes? Bridging the Specificity Frontier, in T. Malone, K. Crowston & G. Herman, eds, "Organizing Business Knowledge", MIT Press, Cambridge, MA.

11. Beedle, M., Schwaber, K. (2001), *Agile Software Development with SCRUM*, Prentice Hall, Englewood Cliffs, NJ.

12. Cunningham, W. Leuf, B. (2001), *The Wiki Way Quick Collaboration on the Web*, Addison Wesley, Reading, MA.

13. Ehrlich, K. (2000), Locating Expertise: Design Issues for an Expertise Locator System, in M.S. Ackerman, V. Pipek & V. Wulf, eds, "Sharing Expertise: Beyond Knowledge Management", MIT Press, Cambridge MA.

14. VersionOne http://www.versionone.net (Last Visited: September 25, 2003)

15. Xplanner http://www.xplanner.org (Last Visited: September 25, 2003)

16. TWiki http://www.twiki.org (Last Visited: September 25, 2003)

17. Henninger, S., Ivaturi, A., Nuli, K., Thirunavukkaras, A. (2002), "Supporting Adaptable Methodologies to Meet Evolving Project Needs", in D. Wells, L. Williams, eds, *Proceedings of XP/Agile Universe 2002*, Springer, Berlin Heidelberg New York.

18. Nick, M., Althoff, K.-D. (2001), "Engineering Experience Base Maintenance Knowledge", in K.-D. Althoff, R.L. Feldmann, W. Muller, eds, *Proceedings of the 3rd International Workshop on Learning Software Organizations 2001*, Springer-Verlag, Berlin Heidelberg

19. Lindvall, M., Rus, I., Sinha, S.S. (2002), "Technology Support for Knowledge Management", in S. Henninger, F. Maurer, eds, *Proceedings of the 4th International Workshop on Learning Software Organizations 2002*, Springer-Verlag, Berlin Heidelberg

20. Mahe, S., Rieu, C. (1997), "Towards a Pull-Approach of KM for Improving Enterprise in Small and Medium Enterprises", in *Proceedings of the International Symposium on Management of Industrial and Corporate Knowledge*, Compiegne.

Knowledge Acquisition and Communities of Practice: An Approach to Convert Individual Knowledge into Multi-organizational Knowledge

Mariano Montoni, Rodrigo Miranda,
Ana Regina Rocha, and Guilherme Horta Travassos

Federal University of Rio de Janeiro – COPPE
Caixa Postal 68511 – CEP 21941-972 – Rio de Janeiro, Brazil
Phone: +55-21-25628675, Fax: +55-21-25628676
{mmontoni,darocha,ght}@cos.ufrj.br, rodrigo@r2.com.br

Abstract. The implementation of knowledge management mechanisms to convert individual knowledge into organizational knowledge is important to guarantee business success in the global and dynamic economy. Besides that, there is a trend in the software industry to create a consistent body of software process knowledge across different organizations through the conversion of organizational knowledge into multi-organizational knowledge. Since software organizations do not execute software processes in the same way, the creation of such body of knowledge is a difficult task. This work presents a knowledge acquisition approach aimed to acquire organization members' knowledge and store it in a software process community of practice repository accessible through a Web-based system. The application and evaluation of knowledge captured in the context of a specific organization, and reuse of such knowledge in different contexts provides the means for converting organizational knowledge into multi-organizational knowledge.

1   Introduction

Most software organizations face risks that have great impact on organizational performance. Basili *et al.* [1], for instance, points out that many important tasks related to software development are dependent on individuals within the organization, because software processes execution requires expert knowledge from organization members that cooperate to achieve a business goal. In order to minimize such risks, recent studies [8] have demonstrated that skillful organization members should share their knowledge to establish an organizational learning cycle and to turn this intellectual capital in profits for the organization. Therefore, organizations should promote exchange of members' experiences and provide continuous learning throughout software processes. According to Houdek and Bunse [10], the institutionalization of a continuous learning cycle not only provides the means to transfer knowledge across the organization, but also reduces common errors reoccurrences and enhances the quality of both processes and products.

Software development processes are constituted of knowledge intensive activities, for instance, software requirements elicitation, identification of best practices in soft-

G. Melnik and H. Holz (Eds.): LSO 2004, LNCS 3096, pp. 110–121, 2004.

ware development, collection of experiences about project planning and risk management. The implementation of effective knowledge acquisition and management strategies is important to preserve important expertise and provide the means for knowledge exchange [2]. Therefore, a systematic methodology is essential to guide software engineers in the definition and implementation of knowledge acquisition methods and techniques [3]. According to Wangenheim *et al.* [21], by managing knowledge in a systematic form, software development organizations can have a better understanding of what they know and maximize the use of their members' knowledge.

This paper presents a knowledge management approach for acquisition and preservation of knowledge related to software processes. The approach aims to acquire, filter and package organization members' tacit and explicit knowledge in order to convert it into organizational knowledge [15]. The resulting packaged knowledge is published on a community of practice repository for the software process domain. Different organization members can then access the knowledge stored in the community of practice repository through a Web-based system. The sharing of such knowledge from members of different organizations allows them to give feedback on knowledge usefulness, correctness and reliability, and consequently provides the means to convert it into multi-organizational knowledge.

The next section presents some important characteristics considered during the definition and implementation of the knowledge acquisition process in software development organizations. The knowledge acquisition process and supporting tool are detailed in section 3. Section 4 presents the functionalities of a Web-based system to support access to knowledge stored in a community of practice repository. Finally, section 5 presents final considerations and points out future works.

2 Knowledge Management in Software Development Organizations

The identification, maintenance and transference of different types of knowledge related to software processes (e.g., software process models, best practices and lessons learned) from one project to another are important to develop software with high quality and enhance software processes [10]. Software process models, for instance, explicitly represent knowledge about software development and describe not only the software development activities, but also the software products, necessary resources and tools, and best practices related to software processes execution [9]. Therefore, efficient management of such knowledge supports organizational learning and initiatives for software process measurement and improvement [14].

The fact that most software development organizations are process-centered provides many benefits, for instance, process-centered knowledge management systems can be defined and implemented to explicitly associate software process activities with knowledge necessary to execute it [14]. Moreover, tacit and explicit members' knowledge related to software processes are valuable individual assets that must be captured and converted into the organizational level. The collected knowledge represents indicators of problems concerning the software process definition or the environment in which the software is being developed. This important knowledge can also be used to learn about the software process and to provide the means for implementing organizational changes aimed to enhance business performance [6]. In order to acquire such knowledge efficiently, it is necessary to transform arbitrary experiences declarations in structured explicit representations through the execution of activities for knowledge acquisition, packaging, dissemination and utilization [4].

Lindvall et al. [13] present some benefits of a knowledge management program institutionalization: (i) efficient reuse of documented experiences; (ii) easiness to find solutions for problems within the organization; (iii) identification and storage of valuable experiences; and (iv) facility to propose measures to improve processes execution and increase software products quality. Basili et al. [1] and Ruhe [17] point out that by structuring and explicitly representing software process knowledge, it is possible to define efficient training programs that can increase employees' productivity and foster transference of innovative software engineering technology. Landes [11] also notes that knowledge management solutions efficiently support activities of organization members with poor experience in a specific area or domain.

Although most organizations recognize the importance of managing software process knowledge, a great number of difficulties have to be dealt with that jeopardizes the establishment of a knowledge management program. For instance, it is hard to convert tacit knowledge to explicit, and it is difficult to implement knowledge management solutions in a non-intrusive way. Weber et al. [22] point out problems with knowledge management systems, for instance, inadequacy of knowledge representation formats and lack of incorporation of knowledge management systems into the processes they are intended to support.

Moreover, there is a trend in the software industry to create a consistent body of software process knowledge acceptable across different organizations [16]. Therefore, it is imperative for knowledge management systems to break the organizational boundaries. According to Wenger and Snyder [23], this can be achieved by identifying organization members groups that share common interests, practices, and subjects (a.k.a communities of practice). The integration of the communities of practice into the business allows them to reach their full potential through the generation of knowledge that reinforces and renews themselves. Moreover, communities of practice can be seen as an engine for the development of social capital leading to behavioral changes, which in turn positively influences business performance [12].

Although it is accepted that communities of practice bring value to organizations, the organic, spontaneous, and informal nature of these communities makes them resistant to supervision and interference. Wenger and Snyder [23] consider that to get communities going and to sustain them over time, managers should: (i) identify potential communities of practice that will enhance the organization's strategic capabilities, (ii) provide the infrastructure that will support such communities and enable them to apply their expertise effectively, and (ii) use nontraditional methods to assess the value of the company's communities of practice. Therefore, it is imperative to provide an infrastructure in which communities can thrive.

The next section details a knowledge management approach to support acquisition of organization members' knowledge related to software processes. Next, it is detailed the evolution of this approach to enable members of different software organizations to share common and domain knowledge.

3   Knowledge Acquisition Process: Converting Individual Knowledge into Organizational Knowledge

In order to support the acquisition, filtering and packaging of organization members' tacit and explicit knowledge related to software processes, an acquisition process was defined and a tool to support it was implemented [15]. The main objective of this approach is to capture individual knowledge valuable for the organization, such as, domain knowledge (domain theory), business knowledge (best practices, knowledge about clients and new technologies), past experiences knowledge (lessons learned, common problems), and organization members' knowledge acquired during process execution. Figure 1 depicts the knowledge acquisition process using the process modeling notation proposed by Bonfim [5].

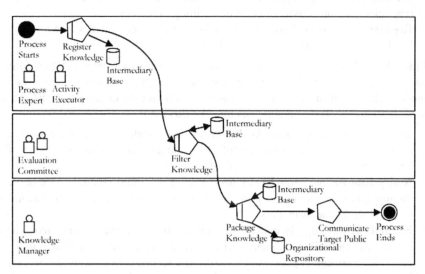

Fig. 1. Knowledge Acquisition Process

The acquisition process was defined considering some important requirements collected from the literature: (i) allow acquisition of organization members' knowledge related to software processes execution and independent of execution of specific processes, (ii) allow filtering of valuable knowledge before storing them in the organizational repository, (iii) guarantee that the representation format of the captured knowledge facilitates its reuse, (iv) guarantee that the captured knowledge content is easily understandable, and (v) guarantee that the new knowledge can be easily accessed and reused by organization members.

Next, the knowledge acquisition activities are briefly described.

- **Register Knowledge:** Expert of a specific process registers explicit knowledge about the process activities descriptions and tacit knowledge used during decision-making situations. Knowledge acquisition can be performed in two different moments: (a) acquisition independent of a process execution, and (b) acquisition during a process execution. The acquired knowledge is stored in an intermediary base to be further evaluated by an evaluation committee.

  In the first moment, the next activities must be executed:

  o **Describe Process:** The expert register knowledge about process activities descriptions, including methods, techniques, directives, and tools necessary to execute them.

  o **Register Case:** The expert register knowledge about cases related to activities execution based on his/her past experiences. A case is constituted by a group of information about a decision-making situation during a business process activity execution, and justifications of the decision made.

  In the second moment, the next activities must be executed:

  o **Identify Knowledge Type:** The organization member identifies the knowledge type related to the activity in execution willing to register.

  o **Register Knowledge Type:** The organization member provides information related to the knowledge type identified and registers the knowledge.

- **Filter Knowledge:** The evaluation committee verifies the representation format adequacy and content of knowledge items stored in the intermediary base, i.e., it must be checked if the knowledge items have value for the organization and can be reused efficiently. The next activities must be executed:

  o **Identify Knowledge Items Evaluators:** The evaluation committee coordinator identifies one or more members of the evaluation committee to evaluate the knowledge items stored in the intermediary base.

  o **Notify Knowledge Items Evaluators:** Knowledge items evaluators are notified through an email containing a link to an evaluation form on the Web that should be filled out by the evaluators.

  o **Evaluate Knowledge Items:** Each evaluator must evaluate the knowledge item considering the following characteristics: (i) correction (the knowledge item do not contain errors); (ii) completeness (the knowledge item contains all necessary information to be understood in an adequate way); (iii) consistency (the knowledge item contains coherent information); (iv) utility (packaging cost and utilization benefits relation is satisfactory); and (v) applicability (potential users of the knowledge item can apply it in an adequate way). The evaluation has four possible results: (i) approved (organization members can use the knowledge item); (ii) approved with modifications (organization members can use the knowledge item, but modifications should be done to adequate it. The evaluator should provide information concerning the modifications); (iii) not approved (knowledge item has no value for the organization); and (iv) undefined (evaluator had difficulty evaluating the knowledge item).

- o **Analyze Individual Evaluations:** Evaluation committee coordinator analyses the individual evaluations, and, if there is a consensus among them, the activity *Make Pertinent Decision* must be executed. In the other case, the activity *Execute Consensus* must be executed.
- o **Execute Consensus:** If a consensus is necessary, because the individual evaluations do not permit yet to draw a conclusion about the final evaluation of the knowledge item, each evaluator receives a notification containing his/her individual evaluation, and the other evaluators' evaluation.
- o **Discuss Evaluation:** Knowledge item evaluators discuss and reach a consensus for the final evaluation of the knowledge item. The final evaluation has four possible results: (i) approved; (ii) approved with modifications; (iii) not approved; and (iv) undefined.
- o **Modify Individual Evaluations:** After discussing about the final consensus, the evaluators should modify his/her individual evaluations to reflect the final consensus. Next, the activity *Analyze Individual Evaluations* must be executed.
- o **Make Pertinent Decision:** Evaluation committee coordinator must analyze the individual evaluations and make one of the following decisions: (i) send knowledge item to packaging activity, if final evaluation is *approved* or *approved with modifications*; (ii) remove knowledge item, if final evaluation is *not approved*; or (iii) keep knowledge item in the intermediary base, if final evaluation is *undefined*.

- **Package Knowledge:** The Knowledge Manager adapts the content of evaluated knowledge items stored in the intermediary base and reformats the representation structure so that the knowledge items can be transferred in an adequate way. Thus, this activity should be executed considering two levels: (a) conceptual level (knowledge item is packaged considering its content, i.e., involves knowledge item analyses, edition, interpretation, translation and syntheses); and (b) physic level (knowledge item is packaged considering its structure, i.e., involves restructuring the knowledge item representation format). The next activities should be executed:
  - o **Review Knowledge Item:** The Knowledge Manager reviews the knowledge item content and restructures it. The knowledge item revision involves standardization of terms contained in the knowledge item, substitution of specific terms for generic ones, and homogenization of written style. In the case the knowledge item has been approved with modifications, such modifications should then be done.
  - o **Index Knowledge Item:** The Knowledge Manager indexes the knowledge item in the organizational repository to be reused by other members during processes activities execution. The indexes should be defined based on knowledge acquisition context (e.g., knowledge sources), and knowledge application context (e.g., processes activities related to the knowledge item, key words and target public).

- **Communicate Target Public:** The Knowledge Manager communicates the target public about the availability of the new knowledge item in the organizational repository. The communication should contain information about the item content and utilization context.

In order to support the execution of the described process, the tool ACK-NOWLEDGE was implemented and integrated into other tools that support software processes in an enterprise-oriented software development environment (i.e., a software development environment that provides organizational knowledge required by software development and maintenance processes and by their management [20]). The tool ACKNOWLEDGE can be accessed from two icons located under the title bar of all tools from the software development environment. The integration of ACKNOWLEDGE to these tools avoids taking executors from their normal routine during knowledge capture and reuse. Figure 2 presents the interface of a tool to support the risk management activity [11] and the integration of ACKNOWLEDGE tool.

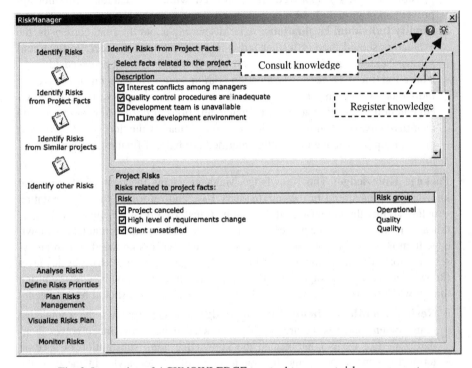

Fig. 2. Integration of ACKNOWLEDGE to a tool to support risk management

Organization members' knowledge can be acquired by clicking on the icon (⚘). A list of all knowledge types that can be acquired is presented to the user select which knowledge type is willing to register, for instance, ideas or lessons learned during the execution of the current activity. The acquired knowledge is stored in an intermediary base for further evaluation. The objective of this evaluation is to filter the intermediary base in order to identify the knowledge items relevant to the organization, i.e., the knowledge items, which reuse would improve members' activities execution, and, therefore, enhance organizational performance. By using the ACKNOWLEDGE tool, the evaluation committee coordinator selects members of the committee qualified for the filtering activity and notifies these members of the evaluation to be done. The

ACKNOWLEDGE tool also supports the filtering activity by providing collaboration mechanisms for evaluation of the knowledge items over the Internet. Once the knowledge items have been evaluated, the knowledge manager can use the ACKNOWLEDGE tool to package and index the filtered knowledge into the organizational repository. Finally, all captured knowledge can be consulted by clicking on the icon (❷). Figure 3 presents the knowledge consulting interface.

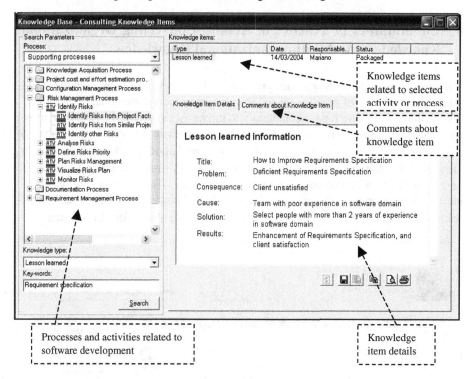

Fig. 3. Consulting interface of ACKNOWLEDGE tool

In order to facilitate the search, some consulting parameters can be specified, such as, activity or process related to software development, knowledge type, and key words. The consulting interface also allows knowledge users to register comments about knowledge items. These comments are very useful during knowledge repository maintenance since they facilitate identification of knowledge items that have real value for the organization. Moreover, the comments add value to knowledge items turning them more reliable for knowledge users, and providing the means for establishment of a continuous learning cycle.

Although, it is recognized the importance of converting individual knowledge into organizational knowledge, there is a trend in the software industry to construct a common body of software process knowledge consistent across different organizations [18]. In order to achieve this goal, the knowledge acquisition approach presented in this section evolved to allow the conversion of organizational knowledge into multi-organizational knowledge. Therefore, different software organizations' members were identified according to their common interests, practices and subjects providing the means to define a community of practice that uses and generates software process knowledge. The next section presents an approach to support communities of practice definition and development and to promote communities members social interaction beyond geographical and organizational boundaries.

4   Communities of Practice in Action: Converting Organizational Knowledge into Multi-organizational Knowledge

The knowledge acquisition approach presented in section 3 evolved through the definition of a community of practice related to software process domain, and implementation of an infrastructure for the community to thrive. At the end of the execution of the knowledge acquisition process, all knowledge is stored in a community of practice repository accessible through the Web-based system TabaCop. This system was implemented to allow members of different organizations to access and use knowledge items stored in the community of practice repository. This approach provides the means for creating a continuously evolving body of knowledge consistent across different organizations. Figure 4 presents the main interface of the TabaCop system.

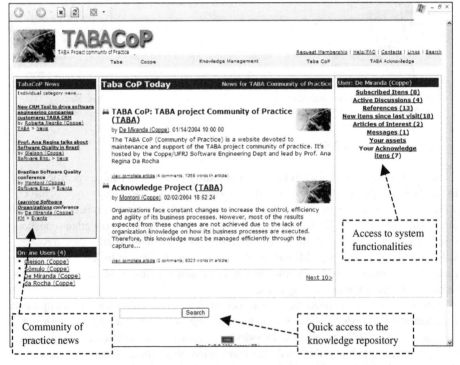

Fig. 4. Main interface of Web-based system to support access and use of knowledge stored in the software process community of practice repository

The **TabaCop** system supports the interaction of the community of practice members by providing functionalities such as discussion forums related to comprehensive topics, consulting of the knowledge repository, exchange of documents and files related to software process, synchronous and asynchronous discussions, knowledge items cross references so that knowledge located outside the repository can easily be located and accessed. Moreover, the system monitors the evolution, correction and usefulness of the knowledge repository over time.

The reuse of intellectual capital located in the software process community of practice repository facilitates the identification of valuable knowledge that could be used to support software process activities execution. Application of such intellectual capital from community of practice members, evaluation of the trustworthiness and reciprocity of the knowledge captured in the context of a specific organization, and reuse of this knowledge in different contexts allow the conversion of organizational knowledge into multi-organizational knowledge, and consequently foster the construction of a software process body of knowledge consistent across different organizations.

5 Conclusions

This paper presented a knowledge acquisition process to capture organization members' tacit and explicit knowledge related to software processes, and the functionalities of a Web-based system that supports access and reuse of knowledge items acquired from members of different organizations and stored in a software process community of practice knowledge repository.

This work is evolving in many directions. Knowledge dissemination mechanisms are being defined and implemented in order to deliver knowledge to organization members in an effective and efficient way. Different approaches for establishing knowledge maintenance politics are also being defined in order to guarantee that the captured knowledge do not become useless and to reduce knowledge redundancy. Mechanisms for facilitating knowledge recovery and visualization are also important and will be considered in the next evolution of the presented work.

The approach presented has been implemented and utilized in eighteen software development organizations of the state of Rio de Janeiro and Bahia in Brazil in the context of a university-enterprise technology transference project. The approach will also be implemented in another ten organizations of the state of Rio de Janeiro as of April 2004. An experimental study is going to be executed on these organizations aiming to demonstrate some benefits of the proposed approach, such as (i) preservation of intellectual capital, (ii) improvement of software processes execution through the diminishment of common errors and support for decision-making, (iii) promotion of organizational learning that facilitates training and knowledge exchange, and (iv) decrease of the interaction among knowledge engineers and business experts during knowledge acquisition process.

Acknowledgement

The authors would like to thank CAPES for the financial support granted. We also acknowledge K. Oliveira, K. Villela, S. Mafra and S. Figueiredo for their contributions to this project.

References

1. Basili, V., Lindvall, M., Costa, P.: Implementing the Experience Factory concepts as a set of Experiences Bases, In: Proceedings of the Int. Conf. on Software Engineering and Knowledge Engineering, Buenos Aires, Argentina, Jun, (2001) 102-109
2. Birk, A., Dingsoyr, T., Stalhane, T.: Postmortem: never Leave a Project without It, IEEE Software, May/Jun, (2002) 43-45
3. Birk, A., Surmann, D., Althoff, K.: Applications of Knowledge Acquisition in Experimental Software Engineering, IESE-Report 059.98/E, Nov, (1998)
4. Birk, A., Tautz, C.: Knowledge Management of Software Engineering Lessons Learned, IESE-Report 002.98/E, Jan, (1998)
5. Bonfim, C. S., A Tool to Support Process Modeling in Organizational Oriented Software Development Environments, Graduation Course Final Project, Federal University of Bahia, Salvador, BA, Brazil (2001).
6. Decker, B., Althoff, K.-D, Nick, M., Tautz, C.: Integrating Business Process Descriptions and Lessons Learned with an Experience Factory , In: Professionelles Wissensmanagement - Erfahrungen und Visionen (Beiträge der 1. Konferenz für Professionelles Wissensmanagement), eds. Hans-Peter Schnurr, Steffen Staab, Rudi Studer, Gerd Stumme, York Sure. Baden-Baden, Germany. Shaker Verlag, Aachen, Mar, ISBN 3-8265-8611-5, (2001)
7. Farias, L. L.: Producing Project Risk Plans in Enterprise-oriented Software Development Environments, MSc Thesis, Federal University of Rio de Janeiro, Brazil, (2002)
8. Feldmann, R. L., Althoff, K-D.: "On the Status of Learning Software Organizations in the Year 2001, K.-D Althoff, R.L. Feldmann, and W. Müller (Eds): LSO, LNCS 2176, (2001) 2-5
9. Holz H., Könnecker A., Maurer F.: Task-Specific Knowledge Management in a Process-Centered SEE, K.-D Althoff, R.L. Feldmann, and W. Müller (Eds): LSO, LNCS 2176, (2001) 163-177
10. Houdek, F., Bunse, C.: Transferring Experience: A Practical Approach and its Application on Software Inspections, In: Proc. of SEKE Workshop on Learning Software Organizations, Kaiserslautern, Germany, Jun, (1999) 59-68
11. Landes, D., Schneider, K., Houdek, F.: Organizational Learning and Experience Documentation in Industrial Software Projects, Int. J. on Human-Computer Studies, Vol. 51, (1999) 646-661
12. Lesser, E. L., Storck, J.: Communities of practice and organizational performance, In: IBM Systems Journal, Vol. 40, N. 4, (2001) 831-841
13. Lindvall, M., Frey, M., Costa, P., Tesoriero, R.: Lessons Learned about Structuring and Describing Experience for Three Experience Bases, K.-D Althoff, R.L. Feldmann, and W. Müller (Eds): LSO, LNCS 2176, (2001) 106-118
14. Maurer, F., Holz, H.: Process-centered Knowledge Organization for Software Engineering, In: Papers of the AAAI-99 Workshop on Exploring Synergies of Knowledge Management and Case-Based Reasoning, Orlando, Florida, Jul: AAAI Press, (1999)

15. Montoni, M. A.: Knowledge Acquisition: an Application in Software Development Process, MSc Thesis, Federal University of Rio de Janeiro, Brazil, Aug, (2003)
16. O'Dell, C., Grayson, C. J.: If We Only Knew What We Know: Identification and Transfer of Internal Best Practices, California Management Review (Spring 1998, Special Issue Knowledge and the Firm), Vol. 40, No. 3, (1998) 154-174
17. Ruhe, G.: Experience Factory-based Professional Education and Training, In: Proc. of the 12th Conference on Software Engineering Education and Training, March, New Orleans, Louisiana, USA, (1999)
18. Rus, I, Lindvall, M.: Knowledge Management in Software Engineering, IEEE Software, May/Jun, (2002) 26-38
19. Storck J., Hill, P.: Knowledge Diffusion Through 'Strategic Communities', Sloan management review, Vol. 41, No. 2, (2000) 63-74
20. Villela, K., Santos, G., Bonfim, C., et al.: Knowledge Management in Software Development Environments, In: Proceedings of the 14th International Conference & Systems Engineering and their Applications, Paris, France (2001)
21. Wangenheim, C., G., Lichtnow, D., Wangenheim, A.: A Hybrid Approach for Corporate memory management Systems in Software R&D Organizations, In: Proc. of the Software Engineering and Knowledge Engineering Conference, Buenos Aires, Argentina, Jun (2001) 326-330
22. Weber, R., Aha, D. W., Becerra-Fernandez, I.: Intelligent Lessons Learned Systems, International Journal of Expert Systems Research and Applications 20, No. 1 Jan (2001).
23. Wenger, E. C., Snyder, W. M.: Communities of Practice: The Organizational Frontier, Harvard Business Review, Vol. 78, No 1, Jan/Feb (2000) 139-145

Impreciseness and Its Value from the Perspective of Software Organizations and Learning

Grigori Melnik and Michael M. Richter

Department of Computer Science, University of Calgary
Calgary, Canada
melnik@cpsc.ucalgary.ca, richter@informatik.uni-kl.de

Abstract. When developing large software products many verbal and written interactions take place. In such interactions the use of abstract and uncertain expressions is considered advantageous. Traditionally, this is not the case for statements which are imprecise in the sense of being vague or subjective. In this paper we argue that such statements should not only be tolerated but, often, they can be very useful in interaction. For this purpose we relate abstraction, uncertainty and impreciseness to each other by investigating the differences and common properties. We also discuss the relation to the use of common sense implementations in Artificial Intelligence. The introduction of degrees of impreciseness leads to the question of finding an optimal level. This is interpreted as a learning problem for software organizations. The success can be measured in terms of different cost factors. The design of evaluation experiments is shown as an interdisciplinary task.

1 Introduction

Traditionally, software engineering as an engineering discipline has always required preciseness in requirement specifications, design, implementation, and other stages of the lifecycle. This is what many software engineering methodologies advocate (e.g., Waterfall, Spiral, Cleanroom etc.) and it is what formal methods[1] are for. For example, when dealing with requirements, the classic software engineering textbooks teach us that "the specification document should not include imprecise terms (like *suitable*, *convenient*, *ample*, or *enough*) or similar terms that sound exact (e.g. because they use numbers) but in practice are equally imprecise, such as *optimal* or *98 percent complete*." [7]

This is strongly related to the current debate on which approach is preferable – tayloristic or agile. We will not make any principle statements but rather take the position of those who think that the truth is somewhere in between those extremes and one has to decide how much of each approach to use based on a particular situation (application domain, relationship to the customer, development environment etc.)[2].

---

[1] A software development method is "formal" if it is a formal system in the sense of mathematical logic. This means that there is a formula language with a precisely defined syntax, there is a fixed meaning to the formulae, and there is a calculus to analyse or transform the formulae without recurring to the meaning (adopted from [3]).

[2] Barry Boehm and Richard Turner discuss this balance between agility and Taylorism by defining "home grounds" – where each of the approaches is most comfortable (for more information, we refer the reader to [1].

G. Melnik and H. Holz (Eds.): LSO 2004, LNCS 3096, pp. 122–130, 2004.
© Springer-Verlag Berlin Heidelberg 2004

There are reasons for formal rules. Some of them are legal, others are pragmatic/practical. For example, in traditional software engineering, the specification document is essential for both testing and maintenance. "Unless the specification document is precise, we cannot determine whether the specifications are correct, let alone whether the implementation satisfies the specifications." [7].

We would like to emphasize that the concept (object) of impreciseness is used in various ways by different people. Impreciseness could mean several things:

a) being abstract (by concealing low level details and focusing on high level views of the problem or the solution);
b) being incomplete (by telling one part of the story)[3];
c) being uncertain (by expressing probabilities for events, beliefs, estimates and so on);
d) using informal and vague expressions (i.e. expressions without clearly defined semantics).

Ordinarily, the first three types – abstract, incomplete, and uncertain – have merits in themselves and are adequate in many situations (last not least in the development of large-scale software). The last type (informal/vague) does not have common recognition and is often considered to be a flaw. However, conversations among team members and with the customer often include such informal, vague, and imprecise expressions. In the context of the present paper, we understand the term "impreciseness" as a quality of lacking precision and using vague or subjective expressions.

Our recommendation is that instead of attempting to eliminate impreciseness or at worse to tolerate it (if it cannot be eliminated), the teams should learn how to use impreciseness properly and to their advantage.

In the next sections, we discuss such potential advantages and also what it means to use impreciseness properly. We will also examine the relationship between impreciseness and organizational learning. For this purpose, we will have to look at the impreciseness-abstraction relationship and impreciseness-uncertainty relationship.

2 Scenarios

In order to illustrate our arguments and to motivate the use of impreciseness, abstraction and uncertainty, let us consider several hypothetical scenarios in the context of developing software for civil engineers and architects. Any other group of customers could have been taken. We emphasize here, however, that much of the need for being informal results from the fact that most customers are not computer scientists or software engineers and they deal with non-formalized problems.

Scenario A: Abstract Expressions

A requirement *"to connect to a certain database"* is abstract, but, nevertheless, has a clear meaning. A more detailed requirement would be *"to connect to a DB2 database via JDBC Level 3 application driver"*. Abstraction is useful because it allows us to focus on the problem at large and not on the particular, low-level details (the specific database driver in this case).

---

[3] Incompleteness can only be improved by getting more information from the customer. This is a problem of dialogs with which we will not deal here.

Scenario B: Uncertain Expressions

An instruction *"to budget for 3 to 5 person months"* to complete a task is clearly an uncertain expression. However, it still has a defined meaning. To make it more certain, one may use a phrase like *"budget for 3½ to 4½ person months"*. The reason for being uncertain is that we presently have only estimates for the budget. Closer investigation may lead to more accurate estimates.

Scenario C: Imprecise Expressions

Suppose we have to present features of the building construction to an architect. A non-functional aspect of this could be a requirement *"to make it user-friendly and understandable to architects"*. This is clearly vague and can be interpreted in a variety of ways. To interpret this phrase properly, it is necessary that one has background knowledge about the types of features architects like and consider user-friendly. A somewhat more precise requirement would be *"to use a graphical user interface like XYZ"*, where XYZ is some common package known to architects. It is not possible to make the statement *"user-friendly for architects"* precise in every respect. It is also not necessary because that would require a complete understanding of the architecture domain. To interpret such requirements one needs a developer who has some knowledge and experience in the area of usability and human-computer interaction. The advise to utilize an interface in a certain style makes it somewhat more precise but, still, does not have a well-defined, unambiguous meaning.

Through these three examples we observed various degrees (levels) of abstraction, uncertainty and impreciseness. These levels are not independent of each other, because impreciseness may only become expressible (visible) at a certain level of detail. For example, the term *"user-friendly"* makes sense only when you come to the level when the user is involved. At the highest level, in a conversation, such statement would not be considered as a useful contribution but rather as a distracter. Unnecessary statements in a conversation are often more confusing than helpful. A statement only makes sense and will be considered as constructive when one comes to such level of details of talking about the user.

On the other hand, not everything should be expressed in an imprecise way. There are cases when preciseness is necessary. An example of such requirement could be a due date or if the use of this particular XYZ interface is prescribed (because, for example, the company of the customer is required to use this interface by the contract). It is often difficult to say which level of impreciseness is the most useful one (and it is not even clear what *useful* means). We explain this first informally and will later relate this to cost functions.

If we consider *useful* as *valuable,* in our scenario it may be, that mentioning the phrase *"to use an interface like XYZ"*, in fact, provides no additional information (value) to an experienced developer.

3   Formal Aspects

Despite the fact that we are talking about abstract, uncertain or imprecise concepts, it is still necessary to introduce formal notions when discussing such concepts. We can draw a parallel with the theory of probabilities that deals with uncertainties but is, nevertheless, a formal mathematical discipline.

When considering all three types (abstractions, uncertainties and impreciseness), there exist partial orderings in the sense of *more* or *less*. Furthermore, with each abstract and each uncertain expression, there is a set of all possible interpretations associated with it. This set constitutes the meaning (the set theoretic semantics) of the expression. In particular, a set of all interpretations for an abstract concept is comprised of instances of all possible details. A set of all interpretations for an uncertain concept consists of all data points within the range specified by uncertainty (estimate). Similar well-established interpretations are given by probability distributions.

In contrast, one cannot associate a precise set of all possible interpretations for an imprecise concept, because a definition of such set is needed but unavailable.

In cognitive science this was well-realized several decades ago. Instead of defining a set of all possible interpretations, a notion of "category" was introduced (see [2, 5, 4, 6] for example). Bruner, Goodnow, and Austin, in their influential book "A Study of Thinking" [2] discuss ways in which people organize knowledge:

> *"We begin with what seems to be a paradox. The world of experience of any normal man is composed of a tremendous array of discriminably different objects, events, people, impressions. But were we to utilize fully our capacity for registering the differences in things and to respond to each event encountered as unique, we would soon be overwhelmed by the complexity of our environment. The resolution of this seeming paradox – the existence of discrimination capacities, which, if fully used, would make us slaves to the particular – is achieved by man's capacity to categorize. To categorize is to render discriminably different things equivalent, to group the objects and events around us into classes, and to respond to them in terms of their class membership rather than their uniqueness."* [2]

A category does not have a definition but it has prototypical and other members. What is regarded as prototypical depends upon the social conventions of the people involved in the communication. Other members of the category may exist and they are related to some prototype via certain links or patterns termed as "properties". The use of categories in human conversations requires certain flexibility and intelligence of the participants in order to interpret the category in their own contexts. E.g., the expression "*programmer who has experience with architects*" may have Bill as a prototype in the company. This category may have Mary as another non-prototypical member because she joined Bill during two such projects.

Categorization reduces the complexity of the environment. For example, when one uses a phrase "*we should do it in an object-oriented way*", the statement itself is imprecise. However, there are certain concepts associated with the category "*object-oriented programming*" (objects, classes, state, behaviors, encapsulation, inheritance, polymorphism, etc.), which, for an experienced software engineer is quite sufficient at a certain stage of the conversation. Any attempt to make this more precise (by considering all flavors and details of object-oriented languages/methodologies) will result in an endless endeavor, will still be incomplete, and will not be helpful.

In addition, categorization reduces the need for constant learning – we do not need to be taught about novel objects if we can categorize them. There are possibly hundreds of various implementations of relational databases. However, the category of relational databases allows us to understand the way a new database (which we never heard of) works because we associate it with the properties of relational databases (relations, tuples, keys, relationships, etc.)

This is closely connected to the problem of using common sense expressions, which occur in almost every human conversation. In the field of artificial intelligence, the attempts to formalize common sense have been less than successful, as can be seen, for instance, from the Cyc project[4]. In this project, started in 1984, the researchers set out to build a huge knowledge base system containing all concepts, facts, rules of thumb, and heuristics for reasoning about the objects and events of everyday human life. During the development of such knowledge base, it became clear that the killing factor was not the number of information units but the number of relationships among them. Therefore, the original ambitious goal was reduced significantly to more manageable but still useful tasks – the current implementation of the Cyc knowledge base consists of thousands of "microtheories", which are focused on a particular domain of knowledge, a particular interval in time, or a particular level of detail.

A possible consequence for formalizing common sense (concepts, facts etc.) in software engineering will be to develop similar such microtheories. Because software engineering is so complex that it spans all aspects of modern life, it would also require a vast number of such microtheories. Besides the sheer skepticism that this approach can ultimately work, we cannot even wait for this to be done[5]. Thus, success in such endeavor is simply impossible.

The next important question is whether we should use imprecise expressions at all. Instead of using an informal/imprecise expression associated with a category, the alternative is to use precise statements that describe one or more member of that category. In other words, we would have to select one of many possible interpretations of an expression. That would be justified if this interpretation (the selected one) is the only one that should be used for solving a specific task. This would require that we can foresee all of the future aspects in the context which we do not know yet. In addition, it would not require any use of human intelligence. This would result in difficulties in dealing with even small errors. In the earlier example of the qualification of the programmers Bill and Mary, a discussion about what abilities are precisely needed would be endless and useless.

There is a debate in IT industry on how many details should be planned ahead of time. The Cleanroom advocates not only encourage planning upfront but also performing a formal validation of that plan. The newly emerged fleet of agile methods does not share this view. In contrast, they emphasize that developing software in the real world involves gracefully and continuously adapting to change. Agile methods encourage teams to concentrate on clean code that works and the value delivered to the customer rather than the process itself. Having said that, agile methods do not reject the concept of planning. Agilists perform planning rigorously but only within a given iteration (which is normally short – 2-4 weeks).

The situation for imprecise concepts is even more challenging because, as can be seen from our previous discussion, it is easier to make a plan more detailed than it is to make an imprecise/subjective statement more precise.

---

[4] See http://www.cyc.com and http://www.opencyc.org.

[5] In case of the Cyc project, it has been going on in various incarnations for over 20 years now.

4 Learning

The last problem which remains open is to find out which level of impreciseness should be chosen. For this purpose we have to point out, what is considered as more or less useful. We have discussed this from the practical point of view earlier and will connect this question with quantifiable experiments now.

If a certain expression is too imprecise, then important issues (that can be made precise and are necessary to know) may be lost. If it is too precise, then certain possible interpretations (that are useful) may be missed.

If we are talking on a very high level, we need many expressions in order to come to the category that we want to describe. On the other hand, if we are communicating on the very detailed (low) level, we encounter a difficult task of synthesis in order to reach the concepts we are interested in. To illustrate this, let us consider a very simple example. Suppose the team leader is in the process of talking to the audience that knows graphics tools quite well and knows, in particular, about the valuable properties of the tool XYZ. Now the team leader wants to communicate the following message:

1) *"All components using graphics in the style of XYZ were very well received by the new customer"*.

Instead of using this statement she could also have said[6]:

2) *"All components using tools of the kind c_2, c_5, c_9 and c_{14} were very well received by the new customer"*;

3) *"All components that were implemented for architects and took care of aesthetic aspects were very well received by the new customer"*.

Description (2) is too detailed and description (3) uses terms which are too general. In addition, both descriptions do not deliver the same message if we want to emphasize the use of *"graphic tools for architects"*. At each level, we associate many concepts and instances with terms mentioned on this level. For example, in description (3), when one mentions *"for architects"*, this could also mean office tools, etc. Or, if we say *"aesthetic aspects"*, this could mean general principles, not necessarily related to architect's job. In description (2), with tool c_2, for example, we can associate its producer, the price or other things.

Description (1), though being imprecise, is the most appropriate one because it is the only one that generates the intended associations – the audience associates the useful graphics tools for architects with XYZ style. The common background here is the fact that all participants are aware of the fact that *"XYZ style is used for the architect tools"* and they know what is important about this style. This is related to the fact that statements which are equivalent but use different wordings, may generate very different cognitive associations. Indeed, much of the advantage of using certain imprecise expressions has just such motivation.

The possible cost of choosing the wrong level of communication is twofold: 1) the time consumed by the discussions, and 2) the number of errors due to misinterpretations. Both are common measures in software engineering.

Discovery of the right level that minimizes these costs is a learning process.

---

[6] Here we assume that they are logically equivalent; we also consider c_2, c_5, c_9 and c_{14} as a specific subset of the set of available tools $\{c_1, \ldots c_n\}$.

The problem here is that the level of impreciseness is not the only influence factor for these costs to occur. To investigate these factors, experiments are needed. Performing an experiment would require: 1) to name all the major influence factors for the cost; 2) to ensure that all other influence factors are invariant during the experiment.

It is further important to notice that this refers to all participants of the conversation – which eventually extrapolates to the entire organization as more and more people get involved in conversations. This clearly becomes a social process. Therefore, the expertise from sociology, social psychology and behavioral studies is required for designing, implementing and evaluating such experiments.

5 Common Background

In any conversation it is necessary that participants understand each other well – at least to some degree. When talking about precise statements, it often occurs that terms are being interpreted by people differently. This is even the case in such areas where it is least expected, like banking, for example. In converting currencies different stock exchanges refer to different points of time that are, however, not mentioned explicitly. Another example are recommendations of brokers. They evaluate shares by different methods, so *"strong buy"* can mean something different in London and New York [9]. In the context of our paper, we would rather consider *"strong buy"* as an imprecise statement.

For comparable reasons, in the database theory the concept of the mediator has being vigorously discussed for more than a decade. Originally, the task of the mediator was to provide syntactical translation. It turned out, however, that considering the semantics was even a more significant issue [10].

In order for people in a conversation to understand all notions in the same way, certain semantics must be used. This semantics can be regarded as a common background of the group. In particular, common terminology is a must.

In a conversation that uses imprecise statements, this requirement of the common background would be impossible to satisfy because the precise semantics is simply not available. Therefore, somewhat weaker requirement is wanted. Such a requirement cannot refer to the interpretations of possible semantics themselves. The only way to deal with this problem is to refer to the cost that arises when people use their subjective interpretations (which we call "personal semantics"). At the end of the previous section, we gave examples of possible costs measures.

The formation of the common background is again a social process that we correspondingly regard as a learning process of the organization. Therefore, our argumentation for the involvement of the interdisciplinary experts in experimentation stands here as well.

The problem of common background and common knowledge has attracted substantial attention in the past.

Unfortunately, many projects on designing and deploying experience and knowledge bases to create and sustain common background in organizations suffered from the lack of user involvement and initiativeness. This mistake of "build it and they will come" is common. If the organization recognizes informal conversations as a useful tool, than it is clear than the common background for this has to be formed using informal conversations.

In a more general perspective, the common background can be regarded as a special facet of organizational identity, spirit, traditions, and culture.

6 Summary

In this paper we have considered the notion of impreciseness and related it to abstraction and uncertainty. Our main concern was the use of such concepts in conversations in organizations that develop software. We argued that the lack of preciseness was not necessarily something that should be avoided, but, in fact, could be turned in an advantage. We have also related this discussion to the problem of formalizing common sense. An attempt to do so is utopian.

However, impreciseness has to be used properly. For that reason, we introduced a partial ordering which led to different levels of impreciseness. An ideal level would be the one that encompasses a set of interpretations precise enough for everybody in the conversation to utilize their own intelligence and abilities to solve the problem; and at the same time, high (imprecise) enough to be accepted by everybody.

Achieving such level is a social process. In the context of software engineering, it is regarded as a learning software organization process. The use of imprecise statements also requires a common background that can emerge through a learning process.

For evaluating the success of such learning processes we suggested the use of classic measures of software engineering – the time (effort) spent and the number of errors due to misinterpretations.

We pointed out that defining and implementing proper experiments cannot be done naively and will require participation of interdisciplinary experts (especially, sociologists and organizational psychologists).

7 Outlook of the Future Work

In the previous sections we have analyzed the role of imprecise statements in conversations among software developers. We have also pointed out situations where the use of such expressions may be to an advantage. This forms a necessary foundation for future experiments that will be conducted to substantiate our view. We hope that this ignites a discussion and leads to generation of new ideas.

The design and execution of such experiments is the next step of the current investigation. We are well conscious of the fact that the design of these experiments will not be trivial. The type of experimental work to be done can be outlined as follows:

1. Record a conversation between two randomly selected software developers without interfering.
2. Extract the imprecise statements from this conversation.
3. Collect initial set of metrics (elapsed time, the number of imprecise statements, the usage frequencies, the number of requests for clarification, etc.).
4. Independently confront both participants with these statements, asking the following 2 questions:
   a. What is your understanding of this particular imprecise expression?
   b. Why did not you use more precise statements in the current context?

5. Analyze participants' responses and get a qualitative insight how and why they used the terminology and expressions. It will be deduced whether the result was useful, or leading to errors, or needing additional sessions.
6. Repeat the experiment with two other people conducting a conversation about the same task (topic), during which participants are instructed not to use any imprecise statements.
7. Collect the same set of metrics as in step 3.
8. Perform comparative analysis.

Certainly, this experiment needs to be repeated with other participants. In addition, an advice of a professional psychologist is required, in order to ensure that there are no other influence factors and to enhance the external and internal validities of the study.

References

1. Boehm, B., Turner, R. Balancing *Agility and Discipline: A Guide for Perplexed*. Boston, MA: Addison-Wesley, 2003.
2. Bruner, J., Goodnow, J., Austin, G. *A Study of Thinking*, New York, NY: Wiley, 1956.
3. Hussmann, H. "Indirect Use of Formal methods in Software Engineering". Online http://www.inf.tu-dresden.de/ST2/ST/papers/icse17-ws.pdf. Last accessed March 1, 2004
4. Lakoff, G. *Women, Fire and Dangerous Things: What Categories Reveal about the Mind*. Chicago, IL: The University of Chicago Press, 1987.
5. Lakoff, G., Johnson, M. *Metaphors We Live By*. Chicago, IL: University of Chicago Press, 1980.
6. Mervis, C., Rosch, E. "Categorization of Natural Objects". *Annual Review in Psychology*, 32: 89-115, 1981.
7. Schach, S. Object-oriented and Classical Software Engineering, 5/e. New York, NY: McGraw-Hill, 2002, p.36.
8. Stroustrup, B. "Interview to Artima, Sep, 2003".
   Online http://www.artima.com/intv/abstreffi.html Last accessed March 1, 2004.
9. Wache, H. *Semantische Mediation für heterogene Informationsquellen*. Akademische Verlagsgesellschaft Aka GmbH, Dissertationen zur Künstlichen Intelligenz, Berlin (in German). Online http://www-agki.tzi.de/grp/ag-ki/download/2003/wache03.pdf. Last accessed March 1, 2004.
10. Wiederhold, G. "Mediators in the Architecture of Future Information Systems". *IEEE Computer*, 25(3): 38-49, 1992.

A Framework for Managing Concurrent Business and ICT Development

Frank G. Goethals, Jacques Vandenbulcke, Wilfried Lemahieu, and Monique Snoeck

SAP-leerstoel Extended Enterprise Infrastructures

F.E.T.E.W. – K.U.Leuven – Naamsestraat 69, B-3000 Leuven, Belgium
{Frank.Goethals,Jacques.Vandenbulcke,Wilfried.Lemahieu,
Monique.Snoeck}@econ.kuleuven.ac.be

Abstract. In this paper we propose a framework – the FADE(E) – for managing the concurrent development of the business and the ICT side of an enterprise. The framework is based on lessons learned from literature on Enterprise Architecture and management. It uses the concept of life cycle phases as a building block for setting up a roadmap (a planned life history) to the IT-enabled enterprise. By playing with the building blocks, organizations can manage and improve their software process.

1 Introduction

Nowadays, it is repeatedly stated that organizations should be agile, integrated and aligned. Organizations have to learn how to achieve these three goals. John Zachman, [1, 2] has been arguing for years that companies cannot expect to get alignment, integration, or flexibility, if they do not explicitly architect their enterprise (and their information systems) to have these characteristics. Just like Zachman, we believe that doing Enterprise Architecture is no longer an option; it is mandatory. Obviously, doing Enterprise Architecture is not really a lightweight way of working. Still, there is no magic, and there is no other way to achieve the goals of agility, integration, and alignment than through architecture [3].

The discipline called Enterprise Architecture (EA) has been around for more than a decade, and it is only now this discipline is gaining momentum. Many EA frameworks have been developed during the last 15 years (see e.g. [2] and [4]). Such frameworks show the 'deliverables' of the architecture process: the architecture descriptions. Unfortunately, in the past the focus has been too much on the deliverables, and less on the architecture process itself. This resulted in organizations with architecture descriptions sitting on a shelf, gathering dust. The paper at hand offers an EA framework (the FADE) that is not focused on the deliverables, but on the embedding of the architecture process in the normal way of working. As such, it is a management framework that can be used to develop a roadmap to the IT-enabled Enterprise. It shows the building blocks of a generic roadmap. By managing their roadmap, organizations can improve their software process, i.e., they can learn!

In what follows, we first discuss the concept of life cycle phases. This concept is used to link all the elements in the framework - presented in Section 3 - together.

G. Melnik and H. Holz (Eds.): LSO 2004, LNCS 3096, pp. 131–136, 2004.

2 The Enterprise Life Cycle

Enterprises are a living thing; they have a starting point and an endpoint (in time) and go through several phases throughout their life. The GERAM (Generalised Enterprise Reference Architecture and Methodology, [5]) presents a general model of the life cycle of an entity. Such a life cycle encompasses all activities from inception to decommissioning of the entity. These activities are categorized into "life cycle phases". A life cycle basically contains seven life cycle phases. These are shown in the left panel of Figure 1. The basic phases may be subdivided further. The design activities are for example often subdivided in two lower-level types of activities, resulting in a preliminary design phase and a detailed design phase.

It is important to note that life cycle phases do not imply a temporal aspect. Some of the processes may be performed repeatedly and in different succession and some may not occur at all during the existence of the entity. The concept of "life history" is used to take into account time and succession. The life history is seen as *the actual sequence of steps a system has gone (or will go) through during its lifetime*; the life cycle is defined as *the finite set of generic phases and steps a system may go through over its entire life history* [6, p9]. The concept of life history is illustrated in the right panel of Figure 1. Companies can be involved in several types of activities at the same time. For example, they may redesign processes while they are in the operational phase. It is clear that companies aim at being operational all of the time, but that change is inevitable. Companies that strive for continuous improvement are involved in multiple life cycle activities at any moment in time.

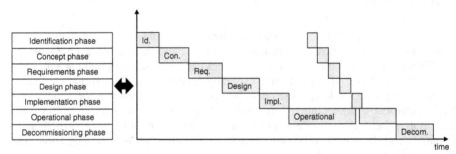

Fig. 1. The seven life cycle phases (*left panel*) and the life history of an enterprise (*right panel*)

3 Designing an IT-Enabled Enterprise

Throughout the life history of an enterprise business processes may be redesigned, new information systems may be implemented, etcetera. The life cycle activities may involve business related issues and ICT related issues. It is clear that a fit is desired between decisions made at the business side and those made at the ICT side.

For the purpose of our research we make a distinction between two groups within an organization: 1) Business people and 2) ICT people. Both groups are involved in designing the enterprise. Yet, they have a different point of view on the company. Therefore, we group the enterprise life cycle activities according to *who* is making decisions. Hence, we do not focus directly on decisions that relate to the business or decisions that relate to ICT. This is because we believe it does not make any sense to distinguish between these two types of decisions, as both types of decisions should be closely intertwined. Moreover, nowadays the electronic process often *is* the business process (see e.g. Amazon). A distinction between the people that make the decisions is, however, possible and relevant. In essence, this shows we believe the business-ICT alignment problem is a coordination problem between people. If Business people would know everything about ICT that ICT people know, they would - in our vision - be able to translate the business straightforwardly into ICT (and vice versa).

We do not only group people into an ICT-class and a Business-class. Orthogonally on this classification, we notice that people may be involved 1) in the *execution* of operations, or 2) in the *management* of operations. Furthermore, typically three levels of management are discerned, namely strategic, tactical and operational (see e.g. [7]). All of these activities are – of course – related to the enterprise life cycle phases. The so created framework is illustrated in Figure 2. We call this framework 'the FADE', the Framework for the Architectural Development of the Enterprise.

We believe that the life of an enterprise starts with the strategic identification phase, and ends with the strategic decommissioning phase. Therefore, if we speak about the enterprise life cycle, we mean the phases at the strategic level. At strategic level the desired future of the enterprise is puzzled out. Decisions made at strategic level typically cover a long time horizon of about five years. The mission, the vision, important principles, etcetera are defined. Clearly decisions at this level are not detailed at all, they are vague by nature.

A more detailed picture of the enterprise life cycle can be created by focusing on the implementation phase of the strategic level. This implementation phase actually involves the creation of more concrete plans at tactical level. At the tactical level a planning is made to structure the different projects that will be executed during the following one or two years. It is important to note that these projects are placed and fitted within the total enterprise architecture. Again, the implementation phase at this (tactical) level involves life cycle phases at a lower level, namely at operational level.

At operational level a detailed planning is made to execute the projects that were planned. Next the project is executed, i.e., the software is created, people are being trained, etcetera. Once the implementation phase (at operational level) has ended (e.g., the software has been programmed and installed) the operational phase is entered. By entering the operational phase at operational level the operational phase is also started at tactical level and at strategic level. At this moment the enterprise is up and running. After some time the created entity may be decommissioned. This may result in entering the decommissioning phase at tactical level and at strategic level.

We notice the presence of the strategic level, the tactical level, and the operational level both at the business side, and at the ICT side. Of course, the life cycle phases of business and ICT need to be intertwined if alignment is desired. Business and ICT should be co-evolving. By linking the management levels with the design of the enterprise (and its ICT systems) it is clear how alignment should be taken care of. In all of the life cycle phases, alignment should be kept in mind. This can be done by having information communicated across life cycle phases. For example, it is clear that the ICT strategy and the Business strategy should fit. If the Business strategy is to automate public processes (i.e. processes in which the company interacts with partners), the ICT vision should not be directed to the use of proprietary protocols, but to the use of open standards (e.g. SOAP). Also, concepts that are identified at the Strategic ICT level may be interesting as an input for the Business strategy, etcetera.

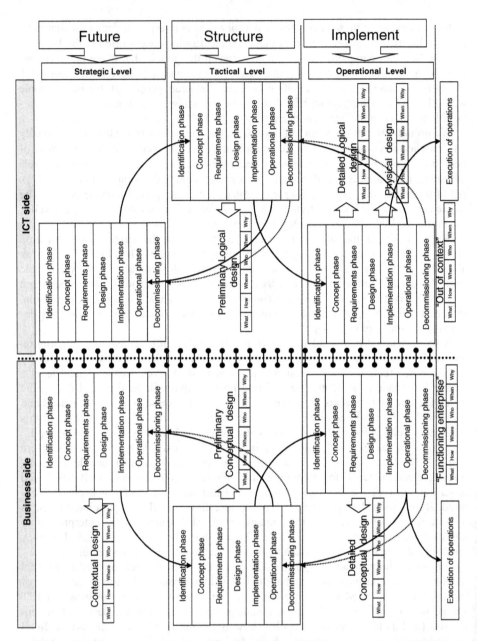

Fig. 2. Linking management levels, life cycle phases, and Zachman views in the FADE

It is important to note that the above ideas do not represent the life history of an enterprise. Rather, they show how the life cycle concept is applied recursively. By relating their current practices to Figure 2, companies can see their own life history. Managing this life history (i.e., setting up a roadmap) is important. It is for example clear that companies that are simply walking top-down through this figure are missing something: giving feedback to previous phases is important (and may result in restarting those phases).

Clearly, decisions made at one management level form restrictions that should be respected at another level. Programmers and the like may not like being restricted, but it does not make any sense to let them neglect hard constraints. It is illogical to let people work in a cocoon, without any coordination from outside (note that this is still true with the distributed computing paradigm, see [8]). Our way of working may not be very lightweight, but communicating existing restrictions is the only way to achieve integration and alignment. Architecture descriptions (related to the FADE, see below) should offer the users of the descriptions only and all the relevant information needed for them to make informed decisions.

Please note that our findings dovetail with the ideas of Maes [9] concerning the extension of the classic Strategic Alignment Model of Henderson and Venkatraman [10]. While Henderson and Venkatraman focused on the strategy and the operations, Maes stressed the importance of a 'structure' level (in addition to the strategic and operational levels), which is called "tactical" level in management terms.

Furthermore, the ideas presented here fit with the Zachman framework [2]. More specifically, the management processes go hand in hand with the creation of the models in the Zachman framework. Doing Enterprise Architecture should be part of the normal way of doing business; it should be embedded in the classic (management) processes organizations know. Without doing architecture, organizations cannot expect to get alignment, integration (things will only fit by chance if you don't engineer), and flexibility (what will you change if you do not know what you have got?). Organizations want their systems to be implemented fast, i.e., they focus on the short term. However, this causes employees to neglect doing architecture, what mortgages the long term. Companies have to balance the short and the long term by building this balance into their every day way of working. The relationship between the management levels and the Zachman design models is also shown in Figure 2.

4   Conclusions

In this paper we have proposed the FADE, the Framework for the Architectural Development of the Enterprise. This framework offers a collection of generic constructs that need to be taken in consideration when developing a roadmap to the IT-enabled Enterprise. The FADE is built on concepts borrowed from Enterprise Architecture, and as such recognizes the importance of this discipline. Doing Enterprise Architecture is a big job. Still, it is the only way to come to an agile, integrated and aligned enterprise. If organizations neglect doing Enterprise Architecture today, they will pay for it in the end. Also, when buying COTS it should be investigated whether the models that underlie the COTS fit the organization.

Developing classic software is one thing, developing software that is to be used for Extended Enterprise integration (EEi) another. In the past, many useless Web services have been developed [11], and many more will be developed if organizations do not learn how to develop software for this specific situation. In the context of the Extended Enterprise, the IT department of one company has to develop Web services that should be useful for users from other companies. Clearly, the developers first need to find out the requirements of these external users. Other parties should thus be involved in such a development project, and these parties may have a totally different software process installed. Another way of working is thus required in an Extended Enterprise context, and companies will need to learn how to proceed in such a case.

The assumption that IT people automatically know which Web services the counterparties need is naive (they may not even have a notion of what their business is). If no active coordination is happening, the right Web services will only be developed by chance. Enterprise Architecture is thus also needed at the level of the Extended Enterprise. Fortunately, the FADE is – by nature – extendable. This results in the FADEE, the Framework for the Architectural Development of the *Extended* Enterprise. The FADEE offers the building blocks to create a roadmap to the IT-enabled Extended Enterprise. Making the software process explicit and managing this software process is very important for the successful development of ICT within an Extended Enterprise. The FADE(E) thus far is a theoretical framework. The elaboration and testing of the FADEE is the topic of further research at the SAP-research chair at the K.U.Leuven.

References

1. Zachman, J.: Enterprise Architecture and Legacy Systems, Getting Beyond the "Legacy", Retrieved from http://members.ozemail.com.au/~visible/papers/ on April 6, 2004.
2. Zachman, J.: A framework for information systems architecture, IBM Systems Journal (1987), Vol. 26, No.3, 276-292.
3. Goethals, F., Vandenbulcke, J., Lemahieu, W., Snoeck, M., De Backer, M., and Haesen, R.: Communication and Enterprise Architecture in Extended Enterprise Integration, ICEIS 2004 conference proceedings (2004).
4. Kruchten, P.: The 4+1 View Model of Architecture, IEEE Software, November 1995, 42-50.
5. IFIP-IFAC Task Force: GERAM: Generalised Enterprise Reference Architecture and Methodology, Version 1.6.2. Retrieved from http://www.cit.gu.edu.au/~bernus/ims/gm21/tg4wp1/geram/1-6-2/v1.6.2.html on January 20, 2004; (June 1998) 29.
6. ISO/TC184/SC5/WG1: ISO/IS 15704: Industrial automation systems - Requirements for enterprise-reference architectures and methodologies (2000).
7. Proper, H., Bosma, H., Hoppenbrouwers, S., Janssen, R.: An Alignment Perspective on Architecture-driven Information Systems Engineering, in Proceedings of the Second National Architecture Congres, Amsterdam, The Netherlands, (2001) 11.
8. Cook, M.: Building Enterprise Information Architectures, Prentice-Hall (1996) 179.
9. Maes, R.: A Generic Framework for Information Management, PrimaVera Working Paper 99-03 (1999) 22.
10. Henderson, J., Venkatraman, N.: Strategic Alignment: Leveraging Information Technology for Transforming Organizations, IBM Systems Journal (1993) Vol 32, no 1, 4-16.
11. Frankel, D., Parodi, J.: Using Model-Driven Architecture to Develop Web Services, IONA Technologies white paper (2002).

Agile Knowledge Management in Practice

Hans Dermot Doran

Starscions,
Im Ahorn 22,
8125 Zollikerberg,
Switzerland
hans.doran@ibhdoran.com

Abstract. This paper describes some experiences with the implementation of knowledge management techniques in an agile development department. After placing the discussion in the context of the department tasks and resultant organisation, the experiences in managing the various, software engineering relevant, knowledge types are reviewed. Before drawing conclusions, KM relevant experiences using "agile-compatible" tools are discussed.

1 Introduction

The author took responsibility for a development department in a start-up environment of some 12 soft and hardware engineers in a phase where the team was under severe pressure to finally release its product, an Internet based home automation unit, consisting of some hardware units and PC-software written in Java and C++. The department was to be structured to provide fast response to new market conditions, in today's terminology to be agile, fast response being defined as the rapid prototyping and development of new products. This, combined with the fact that the company had entered into a technology transfer agreement with a respected university Artificial Intelligence laboratory, underlined the requirement for effective and efficient KM.

In the XP practices [1] the author saw an articulation of *a priori* knowledge that gave him the framework to structure, or at least begin to structure, the entire department including the software development [2], formulated in a fashion that was easy for the staff to relate to, understand and apply. Unlike organisations that are structured around their agile development teams, for instance as described by Mackinnon [3], this company was market orientated and commanded significant marketing and sales, production and customer-care resources meaning that the development department couldn't necessarily determine the working rhythm of the company.

The company's product was released on the retail market but the increasing interest from telecom companies led the author to initiate a development aimed at the telecom services market. This decision as well as the cooperation agreement with the AI lab widened the problem-domain knowledge required by the developers.

In the first instance there was a knowledge build-up required in interfacing with various technologies and their commercial instances, Voice over IP, Bluetooth, WAP, UTMS, home automation sensors and actuators etc. In the second instance, the new development and second-generation product, this shifted to the requirement for increased knowledge in the business models, and the technology behind them, used by the telecom industry. The third element, those interfacing with the AI lab, had to ac-

G. Melnik and H. Holz (Eds.): LSO 2004, LNCS 3096, pp. 137–143, 2004.

quire deeper technology knowledge that was then to be folded back into third generation products. Technology examples were genetic algorithms, adaptive neural networks and optical flow analysis.

Despite years of experience in knowledge intensive environments and the consultation of relevant literature, notably [4], the author surmised that there was no pattern available that could be followed to introduce KM initiatives for this particular situation (software orientated startup using agile practices), not that the situation was considered extraordinary. This left no option other than to assume the additional burden of conceiving and implementing KM initiatives in an already difficult situation.

2 Department Organisation

The KM requirement was tied to the department organisation which, as we have seen, was agile, XP to be specific. On assuming responsibility the situation was; none of the staff had significant project management or product development experience, although two of the senior programmers had completed post-graduate diplomas in project management; that the department worked under no development methodology; there was no requirements specification for the product; the code architecture had been glued together piecemeal; and the little code documentation there was, was of low quality.

The author determined that there were three tasks to be fulfilled in order of decreasing resource priority: Release Management, Development and Advanced Prototyping.

Release Management consisted of maintenance to the released product. Internal releases were produced every six weeks or so, the Product Manager being the customer and having the final say on if and when an iteration would become a public release, the release content being negotiated using the planning game. Development consisted of development projects proper, effectively everything that was market orientated and couldn't be fitted into a six-week iteration. Advanced Prototyping consisted of technology spikes made for third generation products. It also included the management of the technology transfer program.

There was no need to cooperate technically with, and it was not dependant on, other departments. The nature of the business was such that most specific engineering knowledge would have to be generated in house anyway, This meant that KM could be reduced to the management, of growth and maintenance of, process, problem domain and technology knowledge [5], thus having a reasonably limited scope, as compared to say, the KM structure required in a multinational pharmaceutical company.

3 Process Knowledge

The department had no previous experience of working under any kind of formal development methodology, the individual staff, whose experience levels were quite diverse, were obviously a different matter. A knowledge build-up with respect to process knowledge was a priority. It was thus decided to use a development project to trial development under classic XP practices under the auspices of a project manager, who later grew the team to five.

As previously stated the author saw *a priori* knowledge embedded in the methodology, in this case practices that would avoid issues experienced in previous situations. A problematic aspect of this was the difference between that what the author saw as *a priori* knowledge embedded in the practices and that as understood by the project manager which made discussions on the finer points difficult as first of all common understanding on the purpose and effect of a practice had to be negotiated. This difference also raises many, as yet unanswered, questions about the effectiveness and quality of conclusions made on the process implementation and of course, any subsequent mutations. These difficulties were accentuated by the fact that the author who, in contrast to the customer and project manager, was interested in not the end result but how it was achieved, and was left with little useable in the way of project documentation and thus was unable to fully assess the evolution of process knowledge gained. This despite the fact that the project proceeded satisfactorily and that it appeared to be consistent with other published experiences.

Finally, not prescribed by XP but often recommended, the post mortem [6,7] does have the effect of casting any conclusions made in stone leaving little room for re-interpretation at a later date. Re-interpretation may not be required from the project managers' perspective; his motivation is to get the project finished on time and in budget. But achieving conceptual consistency in leading the direction of an agile department can often require a reassessment of work done and knowledge possessed, canonical conclusions can only hinder this process.

4 Problem Domain Knowledge

Department meetings were held once a week where projects and their current status were presented and discussed. External visits, for example to industrial fairs or conferences, were not only discussed in these meetings but short reports written. The software developers preferred writing reports using the collaboration tool Wiki [8], the author and the hardware developers in Word files. This shall be discussed further in the tools section.

The initial product was placed on the market with little in the way of formal design documentation. This is the situation that one might expect from a typical XP project, although in this case development had proceeded without the aid of any methodology. At issue here is traceability, that is the ability to trace knowledge of design requirements and architecture through code and its documentation, this being considered a desirable prerequisite for maintenance [9]. The state of the inherited code has already been indicated however the author refused to allow unit tests, and resultant refactoring, to be created retrospectively [10] on the basis that the product life wouldn't sustain the extra investment, but in the course of normal maintenance various structural and code documentation improvements were made. The author accepted that the costs associated with any extra maintenance effort, with respect to a well-designed and documented solution, just had to be written off and since the developers were also the maintainers, the issue of knowledge transfer to a distinct maintenance team didn't arise.

As far as the product functionality was concerned, the articulation of the problem domain knowledge (rather than the implementation thereof) was embedded in the GUI. It soon became patently obvious that a few code comments would not enough to sustain consistency through maintenance. It was agreed that the product *concept* would be retrospectively specified. This documented especially the program look and feel, the reasons behind it and some of the design decisions. This then formed the knowledge base for the product maintenance, especially for the interface development-sales/product management.

Bugs and feature improvement from testers and customers were entered into a bug tracking system; the tasks to be completed were then negotiated between sales and development using the planning game. This will be returned to in the tools section.

5 Technology Knowledge

As discussed in the introduction, problem-domain related technology knowledge was generated in three areas. The first was; the interface with technologies of possible later interest, the second was; understanding the business behind specific technologies, the third was; the drip feed of advanced knowledge into the department. Once the product was released, the technological capabilities of the department were greater that what the market required or could absorb. This had several ramifications. Since technology work undertaken had to be considered speculative, it could not be assumed that the cost of knowledge acquisition would be reflected in gain at a later date, it was necessary to prevent the knowledge gain in any particular technology from being too deep. Secondly the work had to be framed in a way not natural to the mindset of young engineers, that is, knowledge was being generated for reuse at a later date, not to solve a particular problem or be articulated in a particular product. This required the setting of pseudo targets whose achievement, it was hoped, would encompass gaining the fundamental knowledge judged necessary by the author. Thirdly the knowledge gained would have to be stored. Storage was achieved on project completion, the signing off of a report which described the aims of the projects, often retrospectively as they were sometimes not clear at the project beginning, with salient conclusions being drawn, a list of caveats and other information that may have been considered useful. These reports, when written in Word documents, were collected on the file server in relevant project directories, otherwise written on a Wiki page.

Finally the requirement for maintaining working-technology knowledge required the establishment of a staff skills matrix; those thought deficient in a particular area being sent on formal training, for example, virtually all the staff received training in UML and in XP techniques. Successes were had with brown-bags, lunchtime talks given by partner companies, the technology transfer partners and others. In the evenings, once a week a group of interested developers got a study group together to discuss topics for relevant Java certification exams.

6 Tools

The recognition that a large portion of the knowledge base was implicit prompted the question as to what was to be gained by making it explicit. Furthermore, if knowledge were to be made explicit, how could one be sure that useful knowledge would be made explicit?

In a perfectly implicit system, one would only have to consider the interfaces to, for instance, customers, marketing & sales etc. As we have seen from the development project, a totally implicit KM system is organisationally unsustainable, so a certain quantity of knowledge would have to be made explicit as an intrinsic operational necessity.

Wiki was initially used as a collaboration tool. This web-based tool, allowing freely editable HTML pages to be generated and viewed using a browser, was actively used by all developers but, due to the forbidding URL's generated by the deep page structure and the lack of corporate identity on the generated pages, it proved impossible to spread its use to the rest of the company. From a KM point of view the tool was unsuitable because any changes made to a page were lost. The installation of Twiki [11] with RCS support solved this problem but the opportunity to find broader acceptance amongst the non-technical staff had been lost. In a subsequent employment, the author had Twiki installed with as flat a web-page structure as possible and the appropriate corporate identity embedded in the templates. The use of the tool spread quickly to other business units and was notably used in the sales and marketing environment to provide easy linking to the entire product-documentation scattered around various disk drives.

The tool was used extensively by the developers, every sub-project got it's own page; meetings, and occasionally reports were documented using this tool as well as knowledge nuggets concerning topics which were thought (by the developers) to have lasting value. With the judicious use of templates one could well imagine the simple and efficient entry of XP-project management relevant information that, due to the RCS support, could easily be placed in temporal perspective. Twiki pages are pure text files so that storage space requirements are negligible and maintenance requirements minimal.

BugRat [12] was used as a bug-tracking tool, but suffered from similar acceptance problems amongst the non-technical staff. Request Tracker (RT) [13] was later installed, also too late to make a significant difference. In addition to bugs, change requests, both functional and structural, were also documented using this tool.

Since this information was used in the planning game to negotiate the contents of the next release, the author could well imagine that by modifying the data entry page to accommodate all necessary information, including estimated completion times, actual implementation times, possibly formatted in such a way that the page could be pretty-printed, that such a tool could be used as a total planning and documentation tool for development iterations. This wouldn't really compromise the hard-line interpretation of XP, but would provide a valuable data source for project managers and their managers, as well as the maintenance team.

A large amount of day-to-day working know-how transfer occurred by email. It was only due to the lack of an intern to install suitable software, that this wasn't stored using a newsgroup framework.

Deliberately embedding as much tacit knowledge as possible in the staff and structure has the advantage of being cheap and relatively easy to maintain, providing the team remains small, communication is encouraged and the management keeps tabs on the skills accumulated by this staff. This does result in a game with the concept of company memory. When one of the staff leaves a part of this memory becomes defunct so as much as possible tacit knowledge has to be recovered from that person at the time of departure.

In this case, the solution was to use a commercial product called The Brain [14]. This tool allows the structuring of random information, including allowing freely definable links between embedded and stored elements, documents, pictures and the like, supported by a pretty nifty visualisation. In the case of those working on technology projects, as opposed to writing pure code, end of employment reports were written which highlighted the more unusual aspects of the projects worked on and stored in the relevant directories on the file server. The person then became an electronic node in the company "long-term memory" and all relevant documents, including those project documents stored on the file server, and code were linked to him as well as the project node, which eventually contained links to all those also working on the particular project. These initiatives were carried out over the space of a year. Since, during that period, all projects were still fresh in the collective memory and the staff turnover was low, there was little use for this tool but it appeared to provide the cheapest and simplest method for preserving the links between knowledge nuggets, projects, and people.

The author only appreciated much later that the self-identification of developers and the department rests in part on the articulation of unique knowledge. Since most of these initiatives ran unobtrusively with the day-to-day management of the department, it is unlikely that many of the staff recognised what was being achieved. In part this was due to the fact that the strategic reasoning behind many of the projects wasn't explained in a global context.

7 Conclusions

We have seen a practical application where KM had a high but secondary priority within an agile development environment. This environment pre-determined an implicit management model. The lack of a suitable implementation pattern forced the author to work his way through the fundamentals of software development relevant KM to be able to articulate which knowledge was being generated and determine the minimum amount of knowledge that had to be made explicit. The author would argue that this situation is far from unique and a suitable pattern would help managers in a similar position not only establish KM implementations but incidentally gain a deeper understanding of the finer points of agile based development.

We have seen several problems with the implicit model, mostly due to the lack of documentation created during an XP project hindering interpretation by those managing coherence over several projects but also on a departmental level where the lack of knowledge articulation prevented the developer's full appreciation of their own knowledge. The author would strongly recommend finding a way to illustrate the unique knowledge to developers on a regular basis if only to strengthen department cohesion. Several calls for a change in XP documentation philosophy have already been made, notably from those concerned with quality assurance aspects [15].

Finally we have examined some tools typically used in agile environments and their suitability to KM purposes. Noting that the use of these tools often precedes strategic initiatives such as KM and that these are tools chosen by developers, the author would argue that more research time be spent in the perfecting of plug-ins or adaptors for such tools to extend their scope to KM support rather than the creation of new KM tools.

References

1. Beck, K., Extreme Programming Explained. Addison-Wesley, Reading, Massachusetts. 2000.
2. Doran, H.D., XP: Good for Anything other Than Software Development? (Eds.) Marchesi, M., Succi, G., Proceedings 4th International Conference XP2003. Springer Verlag, Berlin Heidelberg 2003.
3. Mackinnon, T., XP: Call in the Social Workers. Ibid.
4. Leonard, D., Wellsprings of Knowledge. Harvard Business School Press, Boston, Massachusetts. 1998.
5. Lindvall, M., Rus, I., Knowledge Management for Software Organizations. In: Managing Software Engineering Knowledge. (Eds.) Arum A., Jeffry, R., Wohlin, C., Handzic, M., Springer Verlag, Berlin Heidelberg 2003.
6. Birk, A. Dingsoyr, T., Stalhane, T., Postmortem: Never Leave a Project without It IEEE Software 19:43-45 May/June 2002.
7. Dingsoyr, T., Hanssen, G.K. Extending Agile Methods: Postmortem Reviews as Extended Feedback. (Eds.) Henninger, S., Maurer, F. Advances in Learning Software Organizations. 4th international Workshop LSO 2002. Springer Verlag, Berlin Heidelberg 2003.
8. Wiki: http://www.wiki.org
9. Lindvall, M., Sandhal, K., Practical Implications of Traceability. Software Practice and Experience, 26:1161-1180. 1996.
10. Freeman, S., Simmons, P., Retrofitting Unit Tests. Proceedings 3rd International Conference XP2002. http://www.xp2003.org/xp2002/index.html.
11. Twiki: http://www.twiki.org
12. Bug Rat: http://www.gjt.org/pkg/bugrat
13. Request Tracker: http://www.bestpractical.com/rt/
14. The Brain: http://www.thebrain.com
15. Marchesi, M., Agile Methodologies and Quality Certification. Keynote Speech XP2003. Genoa. 2003. http://www.xp2003.org/keyspeeches/marchesi.pdf

Co-knowledge Acquisition
of Software Organizations and Academia

Dirk Draheim[1] and Gerald Weber[2]

[1] Freie Universität Berlin, Institute of Computer Science
Takustr. 9, 14195 Berlin, Germany
draheim@acm.org
[2] The University of Auckland, Department of Computer Science
38 Princes Street, Auckland 1020, New Zealand
g.weber@cs.auckland.ac.nz

Abstract. In this workshop contribution we discuss general conditions for a lightweight approach to collaborative learning of software engineering organizations and academia. Knowledge acquisition is a cornerstone in both professional and academic activities. However goals and driving forces are different in industry and academia. Therefore concepts can be perceived differently in professional and academic learning processes. Co-knowledge acquisition is capable to mitigate the gap that stems from different views. It is amenable to clarify misconceptions that are risk factors. We argue that it is sufficient to employ a lightweight cooperation between software organizations and academia in order to be beneficial for both. However, we argue that this cooperation should be targeted and between equals.

1 Introduction

We propose to employ a lightweight, question-driven, equal cooperation to foster mutual software engineering knowledge flow between industry and academia. Evidence for our claims is provided by the cooperation with a national railroad company [7][11].

Knowledge acquisition is a cornerstone in both professional and academic activities. However goals and driving forces are different in industry and academia. In industry productivity eventually targets return on investment. Product quality and product quantity are limited by productivity. Productivity is limited by the availability of resources. Knowledge acquisition is needed to improve productivity. Academic activity spans two areas that have to be integrated: research and education. While academic research has a subtle target, i.e., the construction of knowledge, higher education has the tangible responsibility to produce well-prepared professionals [9, 16]. Academic research is driven by the pressure to get contributions published in the scientific peer community. Higher education is driven by the demands of the yet uneducated. Altogether these differences result in the following: one and the same concept can be perceived totally different by individuals in a professional and in an academic learning process.

In software engineering we often observe that a justification for a concrete technology or method is plausible at first sight but is actually spurious. We provide the following examples:

G. Melnik and H. Holz (Eds.): LSO 2004, LNCS 3096, pp. 144–152, 2004.

- *Software technology example:* The plausible motivation, why the usage of Light-weight Directory Access Protocol (LDAP) should bring added value, is consolidation of business data, derived from the X.500 standard. But it is only a vision, and for this envisioned application LDAP has no unique selling points above other technologies, instead it has clear drawbacks, e.g. no relational query language. However, one important situation, in which the decision for LDAP is made, is to choose LDAP as an alternative to NIS+, because LDAP is compatible with SSL. The decision is made by technical staff, and the integrated data are account metadata. This decision is based on a hard reason, a technical feature missing by alternative technologies. LDAP is also used as naming service for configuration data. Even if there are projects, which use LDAP for the consolidation of business data, it is not clear whether in these cases the choice is good.
- *Software design example:* The model view controller pattern is an early design for event-based GUI's. Recently, the term MVC has been used for architectures of page-based presentation layers, which appeared superficially similar. However, these presentation layers are not event-based. The chosen architecture was however advocated as "proven" design pattern with reference to the original MVC pattern. This is a good example, in which the chosen architecture, also known as Model 2 architecture (its name within the Java community, but now generally used) may well be a very good architecture, but the justification is still wrong [10]. This reminds us about some classic demands for scientific conclusion, namely, that they should be true and based on sound argument, and not just true, or worse, true, but based on an invalid argument.
- *Software project management example:* Sect. 6 elaborates an example on software processes.

The origins of an exaggerated claim are not always as easy to detect. If the origin of a concept is industry, a claim sometimes stems from a marketing strategy. If the origin of a concept is academia, a claim sometimes stems from a silver bullet [6] vision.

Invalid claims lead to misconceptions. A misconception has its impact. In industry a misconception is rather immediately observable: *project delay*. In academia the misconception has rather longitudinal implications: job transition traumas with respect to education; starvation of scientific sub-communities with respect to research.

Given different industry and academic viewpoints an initial misconception can trigger further misconceptions. It seems that such a vicious circle can be broken by a peer-to-peer knowledge exchange between industry and academia. The discussion so far leads to the following main assumption: industry and academia can benefit from collaborative learning efforts. This main assumption led to the following recommendation [17] of the IFIP-SECIII working group on social issues and power shifts:

Provoke and facilitate frequent face to face exchanges and communications among top professionals in industry, top academic researchers and decision makers in education.

In this paper we discuss general conditions for a lightweight approach to collaborative learning of software engineering organizations and academia. In Sect. 2 we provide a reflection on learning in industry. A special risk for a good learning curve found in the domain of software engineering – the problematic use of metaphors – is identified in Sect. 3. In Sect. 4 we describe how the notion of co-knowledge acquisition evolved from the collaboration with an industry partner. In Sect. 5 we argue that it is sufficient to employ a lightweight cooperation between software organizations and academia in order to be beneficial for both. However, we argue that this cooperation must be targeted and between equals. Sect. 6 is a case study on how the refinement of a concept – the distinction between a descriptive and prescriptive reception of software engineering processes – can be exploited to mitigate risks. Related work is discussed in Sect. 7.

2 Knowledge Acquisition in Industry

The core asset of software engineering organizations is knowledge. This is true not only for software engineering organizations but for engineering organizations in general. The knowledge of an engineering organization is a body of distributed individual know-how. But organizational knowledge has another very important aspect, which is a *dynamic* aspect: organizational knowledge is a permanent process that is kept alive by social interaction. Knowledge is communicated between individuals, some individual are learning, others are teaching. This means engineering organizations are learning organizations, even without the need for adaptation to a changing environment. Traditional learning in engineering organizations has two main characteristics:

– Ad-hoc word-of-mouth.
– Hierarchical tendency.

A vast majority of knowledge is communicated ad-hoc word-of-mouth. Ad-hoc means that the knowledge is transferred on demand whenever it is needed to get a given task done in the midst of a running project. Modern knowledge management approaches make concrete proposals how to overcome this state of learning in action. Unfortunately, for some concepts a word-of-mouth knowledge transfer may be the significantly most efficient way. Consequentially, an ad-hoc word-of-mouth knowledge transfer is sometimes deliberately chosen, i.e., it is not in place just because of lack of maturity. It is more challenging to characterize the conceptual level needed to make knowledge permanent and communicable than to propose document file formats and process formats for such knowledge transfer. Despite of systematic knowledge offensives like the SWEBOK [1] guide to the software engineering body of knowledge or the Software Technology Review [13] it cannot be neglected that important areas of software engineering, like software/system-architecture or software/system-performance are still far from a systematic understanding and that existing know-how in these areas is still not amenable to a systematization.

The fact that in a word-of-mouth learning process there is necessarily a teacher and a learner has the risk to lead to hierarchies other than actually needed for rational management purposes. Some authors [14] consider this as a severe risk for enterprises and make it a main point of their discussion.

Learning in organizations has several orthogonal dimensions, each with its own risks and chances:

- Implicit learning vs. explicit learning.
- Project integrated learning vs. organizational support for learning.
- Education vs. development.
- Demand-driven vs. long-term strategic learning.
- Panic mode learning vs. continuous learning.

3   Metaphors Considered Harmful

In the discipline of software development metaphors are pervasive: engineering, architecture, objects, agents. The kind of metaphors used in software development is proportional analogy: the application of the name of one thing to another is based on proportion. A metaphor can be a brilliant learning device. However, sometimes metaphors are not used merely as cognitive devices. Sometimes a metaphor is used as the justification, driving force, and – last but not least – as the benchmark of a whole scientific sub-community. Metaphors are used in poetry and rhetoric. Using metaphors in both professional industry and systematic science is risky. Sometimes a metaphor is more invented than constructed. Sometimes a metaphor is much too plausible. Sometimes the proportion established by a metaphor is too weak: the two related things are only loosely coupled by the metaphor.

An example for a metaphor that is both rather invented and too weak is the rhapsodic reference of the design patterns community to the architecture pattern language of Christopher Alexander [2]. We quote from Alexander's keynote speech at the OOPSLA conference in 1996 [3]:

> "Now- my understanding of what you are doing with patterns...It is a kind of neat format and this is fine. The pattern language that we began did have other features, and I don't know whether those have translated into your discipline. I mean there was a root behind the whole thing – a continuous mode of preoccupation with under what circumstances is the environment good. In our field that means something."

Actually the design patterns approach has been partly misleading. Basically design patterns target software maintainability and reusability by fostering high cohesion and low coupling. The problem is that the allowed solution domain is narrowed to the world of mere software components. In practice, design activity is different. Design targets the solution of a lot of non-functional system requirements like performance, scalability, system maintainability, security and so on. Subject to design activity are systems consisting of hardware and deployed software.

4   Motivation from Experience

A collaboration with a national railroad company was a motivation for the systematic considerations presented in this paper. The co-knowledge acquisition evolved from a teaching and consulting project concerning the use of EJB in intranet application development. The project showed that in order to have an efficient transfer of knowledge it is important to have an adaptive approach to learning. The adaptive approach used in this project included the following kinds of sessions, which were scheduled according to demand: input-seminars, knowledge elicitation, technology chats. In a single input-seminar a body of knowledge was taught rather conventionally from the academic partners to the industry partners. Knowledge elicitation was achieved in sessions, in which knowledge transfer was performed the other way round, i.e. from the practitioner, which we call also the industrial participant in the following. In this part, the industrial participants were not supposed to give seminar-like presentations, but rather the academic participants did an interview with the industrial participants. This fulfilled a number of objectives.

- The industrial participants did not have to make heavyweight preparations, like presentations. Since the industrial participants are chosen due to their involvement at strategic positions within the development, the aim was to engage them as much as possible in interactive dialogue. It would have been for them quite a burden to prepare a seminar beside their ongoing workload.
- Limiting the alienation. For the industrial participants as well as for the academic participants, the interview sessions were a good opportunity to create a common understanding.
- Learning by teaching. The academic participants provoked reflection about practical knowledge by asking questions, which are of interest for themselves.

The latter issue in our view requires honest interest into the practitioners viewpoint on the side of academia. Not helpful are questions relating solely to personal research interests, like "I always wanted to know, whether you use the State pattern in your web application programming. If not, what are the deficiencies in your methods that prevent you from applying it?".

One of the collaborative learning effects addressed by the learning by teaching approach is overcoming one-sided views. This is a goal which can only be achieved by discussing the notions in the viewpoint of the other side. During our project this was addressed by informal plenary technology chats, where academic participants recommended new technologies, but tried to provoke critical questions, like they would be asked to a vendor's sales engineer.

Table 1. EJB topics discussed in the project during technology chats

question or topic	immediately answered	answered next meeting	research issue
JVM Configuration	no	yes	no
Caching of static data	yes	-	no
performance	no	no	yes
Application-level locking	no	yes	yes
wrapping of COBOL	yes	-	no
reuse of signatures	no	yes	yes

This led to quite a number of good questions, which partly could be answered, partly however initiated further research (and sometimes remained unanswered, see table 1). E.g., the demand for a flexible and generic approach to reuse signatures on the scale used in the project lead to interesting new research in the area of generative programming as well as modeling. Generally speaking, there is a readiness to use results from scientific research, if they are presented with a focus on the application in the project.

5 Co-knowledge Acquisition: A Heterogeneous Process

A cooperation between a software engineering organization and an academic research institute is initially a heterogeneous process: objectives and driving forces are different in the participating organizations. The proposed co-knowledge acquisition is oriented towards action learning principles [20, 21]. It has the following characteristics:

- Lightweight. The cooperation is organized as a sequence of meetings. Questions are posed. Answers are given. No overhead is imposed. That is, the cooperation is decoupled from running projects in that there is no pressure on any kind of measurable outcome. This does not mean that the posed questions are arbitrary. On the contrary they are demand-driven – targeted. It just means that the situation is relaxed – without cost pressure, without time pressure. This is the necessary precondition for a mutually open-minded atmosphere that fosters questioning and answering. In detail, there is no contract on outcome and no payment. Furthermore no formal process is defined.
- Peer-to-peer. The participants are on a par. There is no hierarchy among participants. There are no roles like teacher, consultant, trainer, or even expert in the cooperation. Otherwise it would contradict the target of mutual knowledge flow. Prejudices among participants do not pose a problem as long as they are communicated.
- Targeted. The cooperation is not about training skills. It is about finding answers and clarifying misconceptions. However, the questions are demand-driven; they stem from real-life industrial resp. scientific projects. The harder a question the better. Sometimes an answer can be found rather immediately just because of the other's participant's different viewpoint. Sometimes an answer can be constructed by a joined effort through the improved capabilities of joined different viewpoints.

6 Conceptual Case Study:
Learning about Software Engineering Process Models

As a starting point for this discussion, consider the following quote from Winston W. Royce, in the introduction of his seminal paper [23]:

I am going to describe my personal views about managing software development...I have become prejudiced by my experiences and I am going to relate some of these prejudices in this presentation.

A software process can be intended to be descriptive or prescriptive [12]. A software process can actually be used in a descriptive or prescriptive manner in a concrete software project. Consider a purely stage wise software process model. Such a stage wise software process model defines the software project as a sequence of phases, i.e., the process model does not encompass notions like iteration or preliminary program design. Applying this stage wise process model naively to a software project would mean: it is forbidden to do any design during the analysis phase; it is forbidden to do any coding during the design or analysis phase. Such a process can indeed be sensible, e.g., if the process captures special knowledge about a repeatable project in a concrete application domain. However, in general a project managed in such a strict stage wise way can hardly be successful, because in general there is a need for early design and early coding accompanying other activities. But the stage wise process model is not a hypothetical process, it is used successfully in everyday software projects. How is this possible? Because it is not used in a prescriptive manner. It is used rather as the project manager's viewpoint on the project in these cases; it is simply not understood as a device to narrow the developer's activities. However, it is used to control the activities: the ends of the phases are milestones that represent the important project estimation and planning efforts.

If a stage wise model is applied successfully it allows developers to do things different as long as the milestones are fulfilled: of course the developers are allowed to consider design and to code early on, if they feel that it is necessary to improve the quality of the product or to speed up the project. Now, the project management might want to take control of the observed proven activities in a project, in order to exploit best practices and to avoid common errors. For this reason the project management will confine the process model. Now not only the delivery of product portions at fixed dates is negotiated between the project management and the developers, but also the compliance to work patterns. The usage of a confined process model only makes sense if the practices contained are actually employed, i.e. if their accordance is controlled.

However, even with a confined process model it would be wrong to prevent developers doing things differently if necessary. The project management that might want to take control of all activities in a software project may end up in planning tasks with a granularity of an hour. In the resulting process there is no longer any space for using ones own initiative any more and the process has become prescriptive again.

A software process can be intended to be descriptive or prescriptive. A descriptive software process encapsulates observations about practices that worked. A truly descriptive software process is really a software process *model*. A prescriptive software process model is designed from scratch to be used as a normative reference in a software project. Both a descriptive and a prescriptive software process can be used in either a descriptive or prescriptive way. A descriptive model should not be used without need in a prescriptive manner.

Using a process model as a normative reference makes sense for such prescriptive processes that are accompanied by an assessment model and available assessment mechanism. This is true for the Capability Maturity Model CMM [18] and ISO 9001 [15]. It is possible to get a judgment from an external committee that states if a concrete process is in accordance with the defined practices. We call such process models *employable process models*. Without an assessment mechanism it is hard for project managers to decide if their project really follows a given process. Still, in our opinion a merely prescriptive process can be exploited as a knowledge base of good practices. But care should be taken as there is another source for learning about good practices: a competitor's successful project [22]. In opposition to verbose process models, *strategic benchmarking* is really used in practice. Furthermore the introduction of a new process model sometimes actually does not have the purpose to improve process quality but to take control of an otherwise rather chaotic process at all.

7 Related Work

Standard text books on learning organizations are [8] and [19]. Action learning [20] is a collaborative learning approach for empowering managers, which is used worldwide since about 50 years. A key to action learning is the learning equation L=P+Q for organizations. The learning equation states that learning outcome L consists of programmed knowledge P and questioning insight Q. Action learning is designed to foster questioning insight. A couple of proven action learning principles provide further evidence for the claims in this paper. Among the action learning principles there are [21]:

- Learning is cradled in the task.
- Formal instruction is not sufficient.
- Problems require insightful questions.
- Learning is voluntary.
- The contribution of peers.
- Fresh questions.
- Learning with and from each other.

The experience factory [4, 5] institutionalizes the collective learning of organizations in order to foster continual improvement and competitive advantage. A logical resp. physical organizational element is established separately form the development organization. Experience is packaged, developed and maintained.

8 Conclusion

It is questionable whether the so-called scientific method is the best practice in all circumstances. Candid scientists of the learning organization community reflect whether they are biased towards learning technologies against an apprenticeship approach. Candid computer scientists reflect whether they are biased in favor of computer tools in that they overemphasize the potential advantages of such tools. The proposed co-knowledge acquisition in this paper is a lightweight approach to foster targeted mutual knowledge flow on a par between industry and academia.

References

1. A. Abran, J.W. Moore, P. Bourue and R. Dupuis (editors). SWEBOK - Guide to the Software Engineering Body of Knowledge, Trial Version 1.00. IEEE Press, May 2001.
2. Christopher Alexander. A Pattern Language - Towns, Buildings, Construction. Oxford University Press, 1977.

3. Christopher Alexander. Patterns in Architecture. Keynote Speech, OOSPLA '96 - Object-Oriented Programming, Systems, Languages, and Applications. Conference Video, 1996.
4. Victor R. Basili, Gianluigi Caldiera and Dieter H. Rombach. The Experience Factory. In: Encyclopedia of Software Engineering - 2 Volume Set, pp. 469-476. John Wiley & Sons, 1994.
5. Victor R. Basili, Mikael Lindvall and Patricia Costa. Implementing the Experience Factory concepts as a set of Experience Bases. SEKE'03 Keynote Speech by Victor R. Basili. In: Proceedings of 13 th International Conference on Software Engineering & Knowledge Engineering, pp. 102-109, 2001.
6. Frederick P. Brooks. No Silver Bullet - Essence and Accidents of Software Engineering. IEEE Computer, vol.20, no.4. April 1987.
7. Ulrich Brugger. Huge Systems - A Deutsche Bahn Software Architects Viewpoint. Talk in the Computer Science Colloquium at Freie Universtität Berlin. June 2003.
8. Nancy Dixon. The Organizational Learning Cycle. McGraw-Hill, 1994.
9. Dirk Draheim. Learning Software Engineering with EASE. In (Tom J. van Weert and Robert K. Munro, Editors): Informatics and the Digital Society. Kluwer Academic Publishers, January 2003.
10. Dirk Draheim, Elfriede Fehr and Gerald Weber. Improving the Web Presentation Layer Architecture. In (X. Zhou, Y. Zhang, M.E. Orlowska, Editors): Web Technologies and Applications, LNCS 2642. Springer, 2003.
11. Dirk Draheim and Gerald Weber. Software Architecture for Enterprise Applications - Towards a Field Study Approach. Talk in the Software Systems Colloquium at DB Systems GmbH Frankfurt. February 2003.
12. Dirk Draheim and Gerald Weber. Form-Oriented Analysis - A New Methodology to Model Form-Based Applications. Springer, to appear.
13. J. Foreman, K. Brune, P. McMillan and R. Rosenstein. Software Technology Review. Software Engineering Institute, Carnegy Mellon University, July 1997.
14. Bob Garratt. The Learning Organisation: Developing Democracy at Work. Harper-Collins Business, 2000.
15. International Standard ISO 9000-3:1991(E). Quality management and quality assurance standards - Part 3 : Guidelines for the application of ISO 9001 to the developement, supply and maintenance of software. ISO, 1991.
16. Bertrand Meyer. Software Engineering in the Academia. IEEE Computer, vol.34, no.5. IEEE Press, May 2001.
17. Raymond Morel, Dirk Draheim, Marc Pilloud and Muddassar Farooq. Recommendations of the Working Group on Social Issues and Powershifts at SECIII. In (Tom J. van Weert and Robert K. Munro, Editors): Informatics and the Digital Society. Kluwer Academic Publishers, January 2003.
18. Mark C. Paulk, Charlie Weber, Suzanne Garcia, Mary Beth Chrissis, Marilyn Bush. Key Practices of the Capability Maturity Model Version 1.1. Carnegie Mellon Software Engineering Institute, Technical Report CMU/SEI-93-TR-025, February, 1993.
19. Mike Pedler, John Burgoyne and Tom Boydell. The Learning Company: a Strategy for Sustainable Development. McGraw-Hill, 1991.
20. Reg Revans. What is Action Learning ? In: The Journal of Management Development, vol. 1, no. 3., pp. 64-75. MCB Publications, 1982.
21. Reg Revans. The ABC of Action Learning. Lemos & Crane, 1998.
22. Gregory H. Watson: Strategic Benchmarking - How to Rate Your Company's Performance Against the World's Best. John Wiley, 1993.
23. Winston W. Royce. Managing the Development of Large Software Systems. Proceedings of the IEEE WESCON Conference, August 1970, pp. 1-9. IEEE, 1970.

Effects of Software Process
in Organization Development – A Case Study

Hogne Folkestad, Espen Pilskog, and Bjørnar Tessem

Department of Information Science and Media Studies, University of Bergen,
POBox 7800, N-5020 Bergen, Norway
Bjornar.Tessem@uib.no

Abstract. In this case study we present the approach, analytical framework, and results from a study of a software development enterprise using an activity theory perspective. The studied company chose to use Unified Process as their software development method at a stage where they were changing from mainframe technology into modern object-oriented technologies. The goal for them was to use a new development project as a tool for learning the technology and Unified Process, in addition to constructing the new software. In our study we have focused on the role of Unified Process in this process, and whether Unified Process had consequences for the development of the project team and the company. Our results indicate that the iterative approach of Unified Process ensures large effects in terms of learning, but Unified Process also improves on communication and work distribution in the company.

1 Introduction

During the last decade many so-called legacy applications running on mainframe computers have been scaled down to be running on Unix or MS Windows operating systems, and reengineered and rebuilt using object-oriented approaches. These changes have in many cases been forced, and are caused by the introduction of the Internet and with that, demand for new services. The effect of such changes on the organization or the users who are introduced to the new technology has been the subject of several inquiries [14,10]. However, there are not very many studies on how a software organization rooted in mainframe technology, is changed in order to be able to work with and be productive in the new technological framework. One example is Gallivan's study on how new software processes are adopted among software developers [5]. Still, this is an important issue for many software businesses who envision that their competence becomes obsolete and irrelevant in the near future.

The first option for these software organizations is of course to retrain the software engineers, and most companies indeed spend a lot of resources on this. Retraining has for example been studied by Nelson et al. [12], who describe some of the problematic issues in changing from procedural programming to object-oriented thinking, for example incorrectly mapping object-oriented concepts to central ideas in procedural programming and the costs implied from that. One possible avenue in addition to retraining, is to adopt procedures for organizational development, like the Capability Maturity Model (CMM) [13], which is designed for measuring and improving the

G. Melnik and H. Holz (Eds.): LSO 2004, LNCS 3096, pp. 153–164, 2004.
© Springer-Verlag Berlin Heidelberg 2004

software development organization. CMM focuses on processes for improving the software development methods used, including how to enhance domain knowledge and technical skills among software engineers. One third approach, focused in the work presented here, is when the software organization is willing to accept the extra cost of letting the software engineers learn the new technology and software process through participating in a real world software project. Learning by participation of course happens more or less consciously when introducing the new technology to the developers in all such organizations. However, there is a possibility for a software organization to be more conscious about this and hire new employees and consultants with the wanted competence to transfer their knowledge to the existing organization during a project, as well as accepting lower productivity for some time when the software engineers are building their competence.

In this context it must be relevant to investigate the approach which involves resource allocation for organizational development in a project where new technology is used and new work processes are adapted. Relevant research questions could be:

1. What are the effects of changing to a new process?
2. What are the causes for these changes?
3. What properties of the new work process are instrumental in the change?

The case study presented here involves a software organization that chose such an approach to handle the technological change, complemented with retraining through coursework. We gathered data regarding this process in the form of semi-structured depth interviews and also some of the business' documents regarding the development process and the project. To analyze the data we have chosen to use activity theory [4], which helps us focus on the different factors that may influence activities at all levels in a project organization focused on developing software. Through the use of this socio-cultural perspective we have been able to shed some light on the research questions posed above.

In the next section we describe the activity theory perspective and qualitative research in software engineering. We continue with a more elaborate description of the software organization and their choice of approach as well as the data we gathered. In section four we present our analysis and some findings as well as a discussion of the validity of the results, before we conclude with some suggestions for further studies.

2   Approach

2.1 Activity Theory

Activity theory is a socio-cultural approach to the study of work, learning, and other activities. It has its roots in philosophical work by Kant, Hegel, Marx, and Engels, focusing on the humans as active and constructive beings. Vygotsky, a Soviet psychologist, developed the theory having the perspective of socially meaningful activities as explaining factors for human consciousness and behavior. The theory was developed further and changed by Leont'ev and others as they emphasized practical or material activities. For a long time activity theory was mainly a Soviet perspective on psychology. However, during eighties and nineties the theory has been adopted by other European and American researchers interested in human activities. This interest was initiated by a collection of works in the field edited by Werthsch [18]. Approaches similar to activity theory are also found in the Anglo-American tradition, for instance Mead's symbolic interaction, and Dewey's pragmatism. Within computer science related areas, activity theory has been widely used in CSCW [2] and HCI [11].

According to Kuutti [8] activity theory is not a theory in the strict meaning. Instead it may be considered a framework for the understanding of human activity. The unit of analysis in studies using activity theory is activities. However, the activities must be seen in interplay between the individual and the collective. From this we get a basic model for activities consisting of subject, tools, an object, rules, community, and division of labor. In a sense the activity results in a transformation process that changes all the involved factors, as well as produces some outcome which may or may not satisfy the objects. The model is illustrated in Figure 1. The *subject* is the person or group of persons performing an activity. The *object* is the goal of the activity, something which is of use to all parts involved in the activity. The *tools* are any means we use in the activity, ranging from mechanical tools to software and natural languages. The *community* is the whole society that has interest in the object. *Division of labor* refers to the organization of community also in relation to other activities. The *rules* are explicit and implicit conventions and norms within the society. The relation between subjects, objects and community are not direct, but are mediated. We may say that the tools mediate the relation between the subject and the object in the sense that the object is fulfilled only through the use of these tools. In the same way is division of labor mediating the relation between the object and the community, and rules mediate the relation between community and subject.

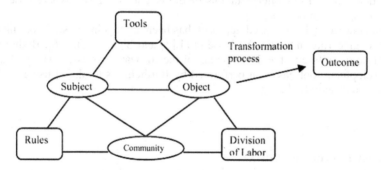

Fig. 1. Basic model for activity

Since activities are long-term formations, one may divide them into shorter processes. Leont'ev did this by dividing activities into actions and further into operations. Actions are considered to be conscious acts that need concentration, whereas operations are automatic acts done without reflection. It is important that activity theory makes it possible to study activities at different levels of complexity, considering activities at one level as actions at the next, etc.

Activities are not isolated, but are interacting in networks of activities. This interaction influence how the activity factors relate, and may lead to imbalance between them. Such circumstances are named contradictions in activity theory terms, and may lead to problems, ruptures, breakdowns, and conflicts in the practitioners' work. These contradictions are driving forces of development as they result in the innovations that change the activity theory factors.

2.2 Qualitative Research in Software Engineering

Empirical studies in software engineering are traditionally done in a quantitative manner. Qualitative studies have, however, gained more interest the last decade. As Seaman [15] points out, the qualitative research methods give us better tools to study the non-technical issues of the field, focusing on learning, work, human interaction, and other sociological and psychological aspects of software engineering activities. Of course this more explorative way of doing research has its issues. They are often considered uncertain and vague, and results are then often hard to summarize and simplify. However, uncertainty and vagueness is a characteristic of the software engineering domain, and thus the qualitative approaches fit well. The explorative qualitative studies also have their use in that they help to identify the relevant research questions for quantitative studies.

The case study [19] is one particular brand of qualitative studies where one or a few cases are studied with an exploratory purpose. The reason for doing such studies is normally that it is impossible to gather data from a large, representative set of subjects in a controlled way. From such studies, even though they do not have general validity, it is often possible to identify which factors that may influence the events we observe. The primary data source of qualitative case studies is normally interviews with participants and our interpretations of those, but may also involve observation and ethnographic approaches [17].

The qualitative and case based approach has been applied in the study of culture in software engineering in studies by Dubé et al [3] and Sharp et al. [16]. Both emphasize the role of culture in the development of the software process. A study of a software development tool has been performed by Barthelmess et al. [1] using a CSCW perspective and activity theory.

3   The Case

3.1   Timely Information Ltd

Timely Information Ltd (TI) is a government owned company with its main goal to keep and strengthen its position as a cost efficient company for management and distribution of information within a specific legal domain. The name is constructed as the company would like to remain anonymous. TI has been running updates and delivering reports mainly through batch applications running on mainframe computers. With the new technological options there has been a demand for more interactive services from public offices spread all over Norway regarding data updates, summaries, and reports.

As a consequence a new project named DOMINO was launched with the goal to transfer the services to a client-server based architecture running on Microsoft Windows™ servers. They have also chosen to use an object-oriented development practice including object-oriented programming languages. TI had since long considered it important for the company and the staff to upgrade the knowledge to be able to handle the new technological solutions. Some of the staff had on a voluntary basis and in smaller projects gathered some knowledge on object-oriented technology. However, TI saw this project as an opportunity to, in addition to building a modern information system, also to rebuild and enhance the competence in the staff. So they spent some resources on initial coursing of the old staff, employing some new staff, and also hiring some consultants specializing in the relevant technology. They chose to use a version of Unified Process [6], to some extent based on RUP [7], as their software development approach. In addition, they were willing to assume the extra cost of slower productivity involved in using a commercial project as a learning environment. The hope was that applying a well defined work process would result in a good system as well as high learning effects in the organization. The size of the project is about 30 man-years, and the project lasts three years to be finished in the beginning of 2005.

3.2 The Data

Data about the DOMINO project was gathered after the project had run one year. The main sources were seven one-to-two-hour semi-structured interviews with the members of the software developer group. Some of the interviewees were designers, some programmers on the client side, and some programmers on the server side. Included was also an interview with a project manager at the intermediate level with responsibility for software design and development.

In addition we had informal conversations with some of the project participants and also a more formal introduction to the project by the above-mentioned intermediate level manager. This, in addition to documents including requirement specifications, project plans, architecture specification, test plans, and overview of the first two iterations, etc., gave us a good understanding of the project and the existing software organization before we started the interview sessions. We have also maintained contact with TI after the data collection. Among others we presented our preliminary findings in a seminar six months after the interviews.

4   Analysis and Findings

The interviews we did were based on a macroscopic perspective, i.e., that we considered the whole software development process as the activity. However, there are also data at a more intermediate level that supports the analysis of Unified Process (UP) single workflows as activities in an activity theory perspective.

4.1 The Development Process as an Activity

Subject, Object, and Society
The **subject** in this perspective on the DOMINO project is the whole software development team. And this team's collective goal or **object** is without doubt the delivery of the final system in 2005. But since TI envisions DOMINO as an environment for learning, one other goal is to learn object-oriented development methodology and techniques. In fact, the adaptation of Unified Process was an important issue in the first iterations of the project.

> *"When we chose a method, documented and with templates, it was a definite goal to follow it. [...] So I felt that this was one of the most important things following from choosing UP and RUP templates."*
>
> (Intermediate manager on technology)

During the run of the project the object has been transformed more and more into software production, with less emphasis on the learning aspect. For example, did many of the interviewees mention that as the project went forward less emphasis was on UP in their work. We may say, in activity theory terms, that the subject, i.e., the development team, through the process had been transformed due to the learning effects.

One issue we had some input on is on how UP and the subject interactively supported work with the object. The interviewees seem to believe that the most important factor in producing high quality was the developers and the teams themselves, and that UP was only second order in this matter. However, UP helped them to constrain their activities so that they became more focused on their tasks at all times, and hence has influence on productivity and quality.

The **society** for this activity includes the rest of the staff within TI. Outside of TI we have typically end users in public offices, consultant companies, and government actors.

Tools

The **tools** used in the development process include all the concrete software and hardware used in the development. The business has had as a policy that they should use open source software as much as possible. There is, however, some dissatisfaction with this as some of the designers indicated that it would have been useful to buy licenses for professional modeling tools. Of more interest in a social setting are the abstract tools used like communication forms and interaction patterns. In TI they have a tradition for open and direct communication between the subjects. However, in this project they have tried to make communication more formal and also persistent by using a project web site where suggestions for change and other ideas have been published. This has only succeeded to some extent.

The iterative nature of Unified Process is considered to be very helpful for the project. In a sense, iterations have become a tool for learning and communication. Communication patterns has changed and improved, according to some of the interviewees, and the iterative approach with its repetitive practices has speeded up the project teams' convergence to a common language. On the other hand, several developers complained that iterations were too long (3-4 months), and this meant that they were not as productive as their potential. Long iterations lead to low intensity in work at times.

Rules

The **rules** of the organization include hierarchy, social relations, as well as Unified Process. TI is traditionally a flat organization, where people communicate openly and direct. However, it seems as if some of the developers would like more formal routines for communication and decision making. As one would expect, others complain that the new methodology introduces a cost in the form of more meetings:

"Much more unnecessary meetings, status meetings every day or several times a week. It irritates more than what is gained, to say it like that"

(Programmer)

It is not obvious that Unified Process is to be considered to be a rule, as it may also be viewed as a tool for the team. But in the first stages of using a development process, the process is mostly a convention for behavior, rather than a tool that is adapted for flexible use in concrete work situations. As the project develops, however, one would expect to see that at least some elements of Unified Process became internalized to become tools. This has in fact happened in TI, as they have been conscious about selecting parts of the complete methodology and these parts have in short time become a part of their tool box, whereas other components have not been considered even as part of the rule set. As mentioned above, the developers focused less and less on UP in itself, but were more focused on following the practices that they decided to adopt.

"I absolutely believe that we have had use of Unified Process, but see that Unified Process would be restraining if one was to literally follow all single detail of the process. Then you would have an absurd body of rules with no freedom of action."

(Designer)

Division of Labor
The **division of labor** we see within the project is based on teamwork, each team consisting of 3-6 persons. The assignment of tasks is mainly based on team members' preferences, and based on instructions from managers to little extent. This is of course related to the flat hierarchy found in TI. There are also occasions where developers shift from one team to one of the other.

The influence of Unified Process is evidential regarding roles and division of work. Even though the developers believe UP defines an overwhelming set of roles, they have identified a set of key roles which has been useful.

"There are maybe more roles than we have previously defined. So I believe that has helped us to distribute tasks in a sensible way."

(Intermediate manager on technology)

At the management level we see that the chosen division of labor has created problems. The requirements were defined before the project started, even before UP was chosen as development process. This has led to the feeling that requirements are not correct and that they are too static to be changed. This has lead to more discussion with users on the design and requirements through realization of the use cases. But this is not well managed and the initial requirements document and the derived use cases have not undergone changes. This is envisioned as a future problem, but the project team does not seem to have a strategy for handling this issue.

4.2 The Design and Programming Workflows as Single Activities

In this subsection we consider the activity of design and the activity of programming as single activities at an intermediate level within the organization.

Subject, Object, and Society

At this level the **subjects** of the activities are the different teams involved in the activity, and the **objects** are mainly to produce artifacts like design documents, code, or tests. Among the consultants, personal success is also a more noticeable goal, and this plays a role in how they continuously consider potential for future assignments.

When comparing the design and implementation teams, the design team seems to have a somewhat wider **society** to relate to. They have more contact with those who are responsible for requirements than implementers do, and maybe also the users. It is worth noting that the implementers are aware of the users' needs, but have less than wanted contact with them.

> *"I am sitting quite a distance away from the users, maybe longer than necessary, or should have been. ... The users should have been more involved."*
>
> (Programmer)

On the other hand, designers seem to have some contact with super users and are able to use this constructively in work.

> *"The ones we have very close contact to, are some super users. From this group we have picked a few to cooperate closely. They have definitely an influence, and we change the solution continuously as they have suggestions and comments."*
>
> (Designer)

The programmers lack the same contact with the users, even though the users' participation in the project has been considered important at the management level. The impression is that some of the reasons are that communication between programmers and users is asynchronous, and also that they do not have a good common language for communication.

Tools

The **tools** used in these two activities are of course software tools. If we look at the UML models as tools for communication, we notice that the design and implementation teams disagreed on how detailed these models should be. This is what we in activity theory would call a contradiction which the teams have solved through a transformation of their activities to something that are more in line with their needs. One other issue here is that the new designs were not as detailed as those the implementation team was used to get in previous projects. This has lead to more dialog among programmers than previously.

Rules and Division of Labor

When it comes to **rules**, these are mainly similar for the teams as those rules we see at the macro level. Of particular rules mentioned were daily builds and automatic testing, which are part of the Unified Process methodology and mostly relevant for the implementation team. **Division of labor** within the teams followed the pattern found in the organization in general. It is mainly based on preferences and skills. The implementation team also split into two teams, one for server code and one for client code. Division of labor is also relevant for the problems observed in communicating the designs to the implementation team. The programmers felt that the designers did not enough work on the design, and the designers did not feel they had the resources to fulfill these wishes. As mentioned, this has to a great extent been solved.

There is also a difference in the valuation of team work. Programmers tend to be working less in a team based manner, whereas designers seem to be on good terms and cooperate closely.

At last it is important to notice that the programmers in the DOMINO project had to do more of the low level design than they were used to. In mainframe systems projects they usually got a leaflet of pseudo-code and was asked to implement that. The consequence was that they were lacking on domain knowledge. The work division now implemented meant that the programmers had to take care of low level design themselves, which again had as a consequence that they learned more about the domain.

4.3 Research Questions

It is now time to use our data analysis to see if they have shed some light on the research questions posed earlier. As this is a case study we will make special versions of the questions to fit the investigated organization.

What Are the Learning Effects in TI Originating in the DOMINO Project?

There are several learning effects seen from the project. The fact that the object of learning of object-oriented technology gradually has been moved to the background, indicate that the participants are more confident in the use of this technology. The transformation of parts of UP from a rule set into a useful tool can be observed in how the design and implementation teams have worked to get a level of abstraction on the models which is suitable for both parts. So UP seems to be better understood and used in the project than it was from the start. In addition it is worth mentioning that the use of new roles and responsibilities for the teams has, as well as the direct contact with users, has lead to better understanding of the domain among designers and programmers. The DOMINO project has also lead to more formal ways of communication within the company, which is considered an improvement at least by some of the staff.

What Are the Causes behind These Effects?

It is tempting to attribute these effects to mainly one cause, which is the fact that the project follows an iterative and incremental approach. Answers from several of the interviewees indicate that the possibility to repeat activities had the effect that procedures and techniques were not as easily forgotten. Other studies verify that iterative approaches are more effective than others [9], and the learning effect is maybe the main cause for this. In DOMINO this has lead to increased understanding of object-orientation, Unified Process and probably also the domain. The iterations have given the designers and programmers an opportunity to trim their language for communicating models, and one must expect that this will have positive effects in later iterations. As humans, we handle problems in two ways, either avoiding it by finding roundabouts, or to attack the problem directly. The consensus developed between designers and programmers is a DOMINO example of the second, whereas the handling of the requirements problems is an example of the first. There is a risk that the lack of requirements management eventually will lead to problems for the project unless handled well. One more cause for learning effects is possibly the division of labor practiced, as programmers in particular has been forced to learn more about the domain.

What Properties of UP Are Instrumental in the Organizational Change in TI?
Some of the effects may be said to originate from the use of UP. For instance, is UP an iterative process, which is new to TI. The division of responsibilities also stems from UP's well defined roles and workflows. As seen both these has had effects on the organization. The organization also has changed its communication forms, involving some of the document types suggested in UP. Some of the new forms like regular meetings, 2-3 times a week and lately not as often, is not specified in UP, and are for some considered an improvement, whereas others are more reluctant. If we look at the one main visible problematic characteristic of this project, namely requirements management, it is not fair to attribute this to UP, as UP prescribes quite a different approach to this area. Of course on may discuss whether UP is fully implemented in this company, and that the effects we see are more effects of a collection of practices that are also found in UP, than UP itself. However, in addition to the three identified causes for change, iterations, roles, and formal communication, the DOMINO project team also uses higher level approaches found in general descriptions of UP, like use case modeling, four phases, etc. to the extent that I would say that UP contributes substantially to the effects we have seen.

4.4 Evaluation of the Approach

We believe that the use of activity theory in a case study like this has given us insights in how culture and work process may influence on each other and through this interaction change both. So as a scientific approach, activity theory is one of many socio-cultural perspectives that give the researcher possibility to explain what is happening in an organization, which may again stimulate new and more focused research.

In this case the introduction of UP mainly seems to a positive experience for the business, but this may not be the case in other companies. Factors like openness, flat hierarchy, and confident staff may be causes behind the results in TI, just as much as UP itself. The point is that such case studies are not easy to generalize beyond the single case, and may also not disclose the most important causes because we are not looking for them in the first place.

5 Conclusion

Through the use of activity theory in a qualitative approach we have in this study seen clear effects of Unified Process as a tool for organizational change, in this case to introduce the development staff to a new technology and methodology. The iterative approach of UP had obvious effects on organizational and individual learning. But also the communication patterns and division of labor imposed by Unified Process has had an effect on the studied company. As with all qualitative single case studies the results may not generalize. However, the study presents issues that should be taken into consideration in later investigation.

We believe that this study shows some of the potential in socio-cultural approaches, and in particular activity theory in the study of software development process. Activity theory has the potential to bring our understanding of the difficult social issues in software engineering one step further. We remove ourselves from the reductionism often found in quantitative approaches, and instead focus on the interaction between factors of an activity. Similar studies could be done of software organizations at all levels, but as of today the agile processes and their activities would be particularly interesting. Typical activities that could be studied are the more communicative activities of extreme programming, like pair programming, the planning game, design work, and customer involvement, and we have started efforts in this direction. At last we mention that we will try to repeat this study within TI in order to get an impression of status at the end of the project in the beginning of 2005. What has changed from the time when this study was undertaken and what are the causes for change?

References

1. P. Barthelmess and K.M. Anderson (2002), A View of Software Development Environments Based on Activity Theory, *Computer-Supported Cooperative Work: The Journal of Collaborative Computing*, 11(1-2), pp. 13-37.
2. F. Decortis, S. Noirfalise and B. Saudelli (1997). Activity Theory as a Framework for Cooperative Work. In F. Decortis, S. Noirfalise, & B. Saudelli (Eds.), *Activity Theory: COTCOS – T.M.R. programme*, pp. 8-21.
3. L. Dubé and D. Robey (1999), Software stories: three cultural perspectives on the organizational practices of software development, *Accounting, Management and Information Technologies*, pp. 223-259.
4. Y. Engeström (1999), Expansive visibilization of work: an activity theoretical perspective. *Computer Supported Cooperative Work: The Journal of Collaborative Computing* 8(1-2), pp. 63-93.
5. M.J. Gallivan (2003), The influence of software developers' creative style on their attitudes to and assimilation of a software process innovation, *Information & Management* 40, pp. 443-465.
6. I. Jacobson, G. Booch and J. Rumbaugh (1998). *The Unified Software Development Process*, Addison-Wesley, Reading, MA.
7. P. Kruchten (1999), *The Rational Unified Process: An Introduction* (2nd Edition). Addison-Wesley, Reading, MA.
8. Kuutti, K. (1996). Activity theory as a potential framework for human computer interaction research. In Nardi (1996) pp.17-44.
9. A. MacCormack, (2001). Product-Development Practices That Work: How Internet Companies Build Software. *MIT Sloan Management Review,* 42(2), pp. 75–84.
10. M.L. Markus (1983), Power, politics, and MIS implementation, *Communications of the ACM* 26(6), pp. 430-444.
11. B.A. Nardi (ed) (1996), *Context and Consciousness: Activity Theory and Human-Computer Interaction.* MIT Press, Cambridge, MA.
12. H.J. Nelson, D.J. Armstrong, and M. Ghods (2002), Old dogs and new tricks, *Communications of the ACM* 45(10), pp. 132-137.
13. M.C. Paulk, C.V. Weber, B. Curtis, and M.B. Chrissis (1995). *The Capability Maturity Model: Guidelines for Improving Software Process*, Addison-Wesley, Reading, MA.
14. D. Robey and M.-C. Boudreau (1998), Accounting for the contradictory organizational consequences of information technology: theoretical directions and methodological implications, *Information Systems Research* 10(2), 1998, pp. 167-185.
15. C.B. Seaman. Qualitative methods in empirical studies of software engineering. IEEE Transactions on Software Engineering, 25(4):557–572, 1999.

16. H. Sharp, M. Woodman, F. Hovenden, and H. Robinson (1999), The role of 'culture' in software process improvement. *25th Euromicro conference (EUROMICRO '99) – Vol. 2*, IEEE.
17. G. Walsham, (1995) Interpretive case studies in IS research: nature and method." *European Journal of Information Systems*, 4(2), pp. 74-81
18. J.V. Wertsch (1981), *The Concept of Activity in Soviet Psychology*. Sharpe.
19. R. Yin (1994). *Case study research: Design and methods* (2nd ed.). Beverly Hills, CA: Sage Publishing.

Knowledge Networks –
Managing Collaborative Knowledge Spaces

Michael John and Ronald Melster

Fraunhofer FIRST, Kekuléstr. 7, 12489 Berlin, Germany
{Michael.John,Ronald.Melster}@first.fraunhofer.de

Abstract. Based on our experience in several Knowledge Management projects, in this paper we are going to describe a peer-to-peer-based approach to constructing, mapping and managing collaborative knowledge spaces. The paper describes a shift of paradigms from more formalized approaches in knowledge management to task- and community-orientation. It gives some ideas of how an expert community can nevertheless engineer and contribute to a common knowledge structure, which is based on the integration of personal and peer-to-peer knowledge management approaches. The sketched approach outlines the usage of Wiki web technologies for bottom up knowledge engineering.

Knowledge Engineering for Expert Communities

The classical knowledge engineering process can be described as a sequence of different stages. The goal is to acquire, externalize and structure knowledge in order to represent it in a so called knowledge base. [1] The knowledge engineer extracts the implicit knowledge and proposes a common structure for the classification of knowledge items. He has built a knowledge model in which most of the important knowledge types (classes) and knowledge items (instances) had been specified, as only formalized knowledge can be processed by the computer. Therefore the knowledge engineer should find an accepted notation and later on a formalized representation in a computational data format.

Similar to the software engineering process, the modelling of knowledge can be seen as a process of several but often not clearly distinctive phases. In the requirements engineering phase will be defined, what the knowledge model serves for. The domain analysis will be done in order to extract the domain specific aspects and underlying logic. The first design of a knowledge model gives an overview and points out the general relations between different knowledge types before the model will be implemented in a data base. Last but not least the knowledge model, whether it has been a domain model or an ontology, has to be maintained and adapted to changing requirements [2].

The classical approach to knowledge engineering is appropriate for the design of a well elaborated and already implicitly defined domain. But some general problems arise concerning the methodology of designing and maintaining such a knowledge model. First of all, the different phases and stages of a knowledge engineering process are mixed up. In that case, the time consuming phase of knowledge acquisition and

G. Melnik and H. Holz (Eds.): LSO 2004, LNCS 3096, pp. 165–171, 2004.
© Springer-Verlag Berlin Heidelberg 2004

design will be skipped and will not lead to a confirmed knowledge model. The classical knowledge engineering approach was used for acquisition of specific and clearly divided domain knowledge in order to build a well defined and static model of a conceptual understanding of a shared domain. For that reason, the knowledge model should give an abstract high level structure to which the users should acclaim.

When this process will be applied to a more flexible domain like social networks and expert communities, it lacks the opportunity of changing and redefining the chosen knowledge structures. In the context of highly diversified, fluid or context sensitive structures, the knowledge model often has to be adapted at runtime. In many cases a knowledge model is released although the structure is not well elaborated or accepted by the users. Often the classical knowledge engineering process in social networks leads to the contra productive result that the built knowledge structures, their semantics and meaning are challenged. This leads to the fact that knowledge models already will be modified even if they have been released recently. The problem of maintaining and adapting knowledge models to flexible needs of the users takes a lot of effort.

In our case we used the classical approach for designing and defining the knowledge model of an expert community, not considering the flexible and social structure of a knowledge network. In the following sections we are going to describe our experience of the modelling of a knowledge community called "Virtual Competence Center for Software engineering". We will name the steps for building up this expert community. This will serve as an example for the classical approach of knowledge engineering. From the experience gathered within the constituting process the requirements and a conceptual framework for the support of knowledge networks will be developed. In this article there will be given some first ideas of how an expert community can nevertheless engineer and contribute to a common knowledge structure.

Virtual Competence Center of Software Engineering

The project "Virtuelles Software Engineering Kompetenzzentrum"[1] (Virtual Competence Center for Software engineering), funded by the Bundesministerium für Bildung und Forschung (bmbf), has as its goal to build up a knowledge network for know how transfer in systematic and experience based approaches in the area of software engineering. The aim is to support small and medium-sized enterprises to produce software as part of their products in order to improve the quality of software products and reduce the costs. VSEK aims at establishing a Germany-wide network of academic institutions, system vendors and software users. The organizations involved are institutes of the Fraunhofer Gesellschaft and universities with an explicit focus on software engineering. In VSEK the future trends in professional software development are to be linked with best practices. In the first phase of the project, the knowledge base was set up and filled with an initial set of knowledge. This methodological support of software production and the interrelated experience were then applied to two industrial sectors (safety critical systems, eBusiness).

---

[1] Further in the text the German abbreviation VSEK for "Virtuelles Software Engineering Kompetenzzentrum" will be used.

Repository Scheme and Software Engineering Body of Knowledge (SWEBOK)

The expert network was built with the classical knowledge management tools and methods. In order to provide a context-specific navigation in the knowledge base, an expert group was established to build a knowledge model in which most of the important knowledge types (classes) and their relationships were specified. Knowledge elements are chunks of text describing the knowledge and relations to other knowledge elements. The elements are then rendered into HTML by the portal software. The knowledge model was implemented as a repository structure in a three level hierarchy. A detailed description of the structure can be seen in the technical report [3]. The initial repository scheme served several purposes:

- building a common understanding of the project focus
- creation of a common structure for content generation
- identification of similar working areas among partners

Depending on the selected types, several views, like a process-oriented view, a problem view etc., could be implemented into the knowledge base. In figure 1 the repository structure is shown.

In our case, the model was first implemented into a system and used for knowledge acquisition. Based on this repository structure, the first phase of content creation was started. A distributed content generation took place. The authors entered content according to the repository structure with its predefined knowledge types and relations between the types. This approach of planning and controlling the knowledge structures did not fully succeed because the experts did not accept a fixed structure for their personal knowledge acquisition. The restriction of the repository scheme was perceived as a regimentation and required extra effort at conciliation towards the authors. The experts used the structure in their own ways for content creation, some authors preferring certain types of knowledge elements and relationships. These individual interpretations led to a certain degree of heterogeneity in the knowledge base with a rather heterogeneous body of knowledge elements, different styles and structures of the thematic knowledge areas as a result. The non-existent opportunity of communicating and adapting the structure to the needs of the authors prohibited a common understanding of the semantic net. A common understanding and use of the repository model had yet to be accomplished. The quality of the texts within one knowledge element and the number and kind of relations between elements had to be restructured, provided and reengineered by the numerous authors and a dedicated quality group [4].

Another goal of the project was the creation of a knowledge map for software engineering knowledge, a so called ontology.[2] The repository scheme did not specify any topical classification for the content, but only for the type. Initially, the following steps were taken: The software engineering topics which the project partners worked on were accumulated and (re-)structured. In parallel, existing ontologies were researched and assessed as for their appropriateness in the project. In this process, the software engineering ontology developed by SWEBOK was found and evaluated. The

---

[2] An ontology "is a formal, explicit specification of a shared conceptualization", see: TR Gruber „A Translation Approach to Portable Ontology Specifications", Knowledge Acquisition 5 (1993) 199–220.

project partners decided to use the SWEBOK classification up to the second level, as the focus of the project was not the creation of a new software engineering ontology, but imparting of methodological knowledge to the small and medium-sized companies. For the classification into the SWEBOK ontology, a team of specialists was established. This team decided for every knowledge item produced which category this element belongs to. The SWEBOK ontology was also used for navigation at the user interface and helps accomplishing the following goals:

– creation of a precise vocabulary of concepts for communication between experts
– identification of missing parts in the competency presentation
– to enable communication with the target group

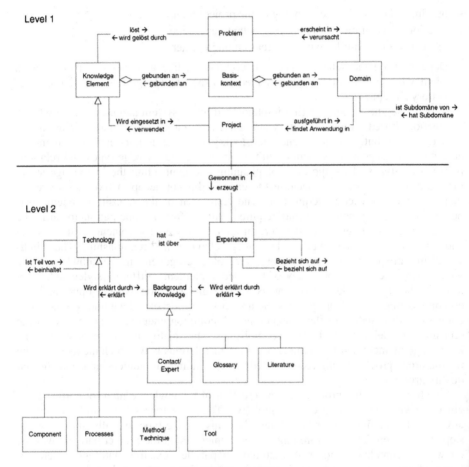

Fig. 1. The VSEK repository structure

In the course of the project and the collection of knowledge elements, the SWEBOK classification proved not to be sufficient and flexible enough, though. First, SWEBOK is very much oriented towards the phases in the software development process. All knowledge elements had to be assigned to a certain phase, which was not always possible or useful with elements occurring across several phases. As a consequence, we had knowledge elements of technologies that could not be assigned directly to one SWEBOK class, and knowledge elements of methods relevant to *all* categories. As a further problem there occurred the fact that current themes and technologies (Enterprise Application Integration, UML, to name just two examples) were not contained in SWEBOK. To include different viewpoints among the partners the revised SWEBOK also contained the topics project management and usability engineering at the first level entry into the ontology. As a positive aspect of the SWEBOK classification can be stated that with the SWEBOK ontology inside the community a neutral navigation structure for research topics was given. In addition the standardized topics motivated the experts for a new phase of content generation in order to claim their research fields. Meanwhile, nevertheless, the missing SWEBOK topics and neologisms of the experts let a new thematic net growing. For that reason, a further VSEK-specific ontology has been built up for current and technology-oriented knowledge elements and themes named "Themenzuordnung" ("Thematic assignment"). Under one "topic", there may be subsumed any new topics: An option "Enter by topics" gives an overview of the topic and recommends a sequence of the knowledge elements. For maintenance, the ontology development was carried out as an initial process but had to be continued permanently and iteratively in order to define and classify new concepts as well as to review topicality and consistency of already existing associations and semantic relationships between different topics. So the questions to be answered for the modelling of knowledge networks are: What does a common structure serve for, if everybody treats it for his own use an in his own manner? What are the lifecycle models for ontologies that allow adapting them to the changing requirements of knowledge networks? Some conceptual ideas of how to answer these questions are given in the next section.

Bottom up Knowledge Engineering for Community Knowledge and Expert Networks

One of the most evident challenges is how to bring the centralized and unidirectional knowledge engineering process into line with the changing needs in a highly flexible knowledge network. The classical knowledge engineering process does not cover social aspects of human interaction. It proved not flexible enough for building a knowledge expert community. Knowledge often appears in a spontaneous, immediate and ad hoc process of notifying, remembering, connecting and associating different knowledge items. The question is what processes can be established in order to support these agile modelling methods. A possible solution is the approach described beneath and the gradual and uncomplicated integration of personal knowledge into organizational knowledge using peer-to-peer knowledge integration. Besides the mechanisms for distributing knowledge between knowledge islands and across organizational borders, this approach will change the way ontologies are developed and built. This process of bottom-up and top-down ontology engineering will be described as peer-to-peer knowledge integration. The goal is to enable the knowledge flow between central and individual spaces and to allow the sharing of knowledge items within a defined user group.

Personal Knowledge Process: "Personal knowledge process" means the transfer of personal, even private, aspects into an individual knowledge repository and further (re-)structuring for personal use. Often a knowledge item was created for a specific context. With the context sensitive description of the knowledge item, the end of the knowledge chain is reached: knowledge items were acquired, structured, used and stored for individual specific needs. The items can not be reused in other contexts. Only user feedback on the personal knowledge space will change the individual and isolated chain into a closed and evolutionary knowledge cycle. In the next steps, the personal ontologies are discussed and integrated into global ontologies.

Peer-to-Peer Knowledge Integration: Knowledge networks can be seen as the junction-point of organizational and individual knowledge – producing valuable organizational knowledge which is independent of individuals and contexts – since the knowledge has been used and approved several times. In order to exchange knowledge effectively, the actors have to create a common understanding and to speak the same language. This common understanding is not given from the beginning, but is the result of a time consuming discussion process. The same language is both precondition for and result of knowledge management and effective and efficient communication. The different actors in a knowledge network perform and change their established knowledge structures continually depending on the view they have. Additionally, they give feedback to the knowledge of other community members – an evaluation process of the personal knowledge will take place in the knowledge communities by peer-to-peer integration of personal ontologies. The resulting consensual knowledge structure is created by a process of moderation of formalized and unformalized knowledge.

Wiki Web Technologies for Community Knowledge Management: The concepts and ideas presented in this paper require extensive tool and technology support. At the Fraunhofer Institute for Computer Architecture and Software technology FIRST, the focus is on integrative collaboration between several business partners with the aim of developing a technology that allows partners with highly diversified technical orientations – and spread over a wide geographical area – to participate in a joint knowledge process as described above. The knowledge management tool SnipSnap developed by Fraunhofer FIRST accomplishes easy content creation using Wiki and Weblog technologies and so lowers the obstacle to actually do knowledge management by making expert knowledge explicit. [5] The web-based collaboration tool SnipSnap allows easy, distributed content generation for collaborative knowledge management. A Wiki enables documents to be authored collectively in a simple markup language using a web browser. Weblogs are frequently updated sites that point to on-site-articles as well as articles elsewhere on the web, usually with comments. SnipSnap is first of all a tool for personal knowledge management. All registered users are given their own personal home page and access to an unlimited number of topic pages. By using the basic editing rules, users manage their skills and experiences, store ideas and maintain annotated bookmarks. For a better accessibility, the user once registered is automatically logged in, and with a simple mouse click he can edit existing or create new content. Recently, the tool has been enriched by means to categorize Wiki pages and to connect pages semantically. Virtual labels mark and evaluate the content. The next task to be performed is the implementation of peer-to-peer functionality and integration into the existing tools. In addition, the drafts are to be validated in different contexts and should be object to further studies. A validation of the ontology moderation process will be carried out in the ongoing KOGITO project.

Acknowledgements

This work was partially supported by the German Bundesministerium für Bildung und Forschung and the Virtual Software Engineering Competence Center (VSEK [6]).

References

1. Nonaka I./Takeuchi, H., The Knowledge-Creating Company, Oxford University Press, 1995.
2. Fernández, M. Overview of Methodologies for Building Ontologies. Workshop on Ontologies and Problem-Solving Methods: Lessons Learned and Future Trends. (IJCAI99). August. 1999. Paper available at http://sunsite.informatik.rwth-aachen.de/Publications/CEUR-WS/Vol-18/4-fernandez.pdf. Last visited 12.04.2004.
3. Feldmann, R.; John, I.: Pizka, M.: VSEK Repository Schema. Initial Version - V.1, 11.12.2001, http://www.visek.de, 51 S.
4. Bügel, U.; Hofmann, B.; John, I.; John, M.; Schneickert, S.; Willrich, T.; Qualitätssicherung der Wissensbausteine. Version 03, 06.06.2002, http://www.visek.de/servlet/is/8025/, 21 S.
5. http://snipsnap.org. Last visited 12.04.2004.
6. VSEK – Virtuelles Software Engineering Kompetenzzentrum). www.software-kompetenz.de. Last visited 12.04.2004.

Author Index